WOMEN
OF THE
AFGHAN WAR

Old woman at Accora Hattack refugee camp.

WOMEN
OF THE
AFGHAN WAR

Deborah Ellis

 Praeger

Westport, Connecticut
London

Library of Congress Cataloging-in-Publication Data

Ellis, Deborah, 1960–
    Women of the Afghan War / Deborah Ellis.
      p.   cm.
    Includes bibliographical references and index.
    ISBN 0–275–96617–8 (alk. paper)
    1. Women—Afghanistan—Social conditions. 2. Afghanistan—History—Soviet
occupation, 1979–1989—Personal narratives. 3. Afghanistan—History—1989– 4. Taliban.
5. Oral history. I. Title.
HQ1735.6.E45 2000
305.42'09581—dc21   99–053424

British Library Cataloguing in Publication Data is available.

Library of Congress Catalog Card Number: 99–053424
ISBN: 0–275–96617–8

First published in 2000

Praeger Publishers, 88 Post Road West, Westport, CT 06881
An imprint of Greenwood Publishing Group, Inc.
www.praeger.com

Printed in the United States of America

The paper used in this book complies with the
Permanent Paper Standard issued by the National
Information Standards Organization (Z39.48–1984).

10 9 8 7 6 5 4 3 2 1

Copyright Acknowledgments

Every reasonable effort has been made to trace the owners of copyright materials in this book, but
in some instances this has proven impossible. The author and publisher will be glad to receive
information leading to more complete acknowledgments in subsequent printings of the book and in
the meantime extend their apologies for any omissions.

All photographs are courtesy of Deborah Ellis. Photograph #2 was given to Deborah Ellis—pho-
tographer unknown.

"Men are using religion as an excuse to dominate us. We should not submit quietly to such oppression in the name of religion."

Royeka Sakhawat Hossain, an eighteenth century
Bengal woman activist and writer

"Grant us grace fearlessly to contend against evil, and to make no peace with oppression."

Book of Common Prayer, The Koran

CONTENTS

LIST OF PHOTOGRAPHS

ACKNOWLEDGMENTS

First and foremost, I want to thank those women in Russia, Pakistan, and North America who were so generous with their time and their stories. Their lives are the purpose of this book.

I am also grateful to Marianna Vronskaya for her friendship in Moscow; to Adeena Niazi's family in Pakistan who very kindly allowed me to stay with them for several nights; to my good friend and translator Benazir Hotaki, who permitted me to drag her around Peshawar; to Hadi Kolam for his help at the refugee settlement in Zelenogradskaya; to Homa Zafar and Annemie, who gave me much to think about; to Nancy and Brad Friesen who let me stay in their house and read to their children; to Sajida of RAWA for friendship and inspiration; to Brenda at the Dunnville Market Place for typing this thing; to the Collective at Margaret Frazer House for their tolerance, to Dad for his letters from home, and to Ken Hancock for his extreme patience when my papers threatened to take over our house.

It has been a privilege to work on this project, to meet so many remarkable women whose character and courage have reminded me that there is a reason to hope.

All royalties are being donated to Help The Afghan Children, 4105 N. Fairfax Dr., Suite 204, Arlington, VA 22203.

INTRODUCTION

Women telling each other stories of their lives is at the core of feminist consciousness-raising. It underlines the reality that the world is made up of many lives, and all of them matter.

This book is about women telling how decisions made by two super-power governments twenty years ago are still affecting them today. Some of the speakers were selected because of their work and experience. Most were random—whoever would talk to me. They were recorded by me in several trips to Moscow and Pakistan. I used interpreters for those women who could not speak English.

I am not a social scientist, a sociologist or an historian. I am a social justice activist, and I believe that what we let our governments get away with today affects what happens to people tomorrow.

That is why I present this book.

CHRONOLOGY OF MOMENTS FROM AFGHAN WOMEN'S HISTORY

Tenth Century	Mahasty, an outspoken woman, is twice put in jail for voicing her views on women's ability to take a more active role in women's society.
	Rabi'a Balkhi was the first woman known to write Persian and Arabic poetry. Against the plans and wishes of her family, she fell in love with a Turkish slave. She wrote several love poems to him. When these were discovered by her brother, he threw her into a steam bath and cut open her veins. According to legend, she wrote one final poem, about love, on the wall of the steam bath, using her own blood for ink.[1]
1400s	Queen Gowhar Shad of Herat ruled her empire and her husband, Shah Rukh, a weak, ineffectual, and incompetent man. In power for fifty years, she was an enthusiastic supporter of the arts, and her court was a magnet for architects, poets, musicians, and philosophers. She founded colleges and wrote laws. When her husband finally died in 1447, she continued to rule for another ten years. She was still going strong at age eighty when she was murdered by a rival family member.[2]

1700s	Three women were part of a council advising on the affairs of state. Their names were Nazo, Zainab, and Zarghoona, and they were well respected for their wisdom. Zainab also worked to provide educational opportunities for women in harems.
1747	King Ahmad Shah, also called Durr-e-Durran (Pearl of Pearls), ended the inequitable practice of divorce that hurt women. He encouraged the remarriage of widows, if possible. If that was not possible, they were permitted to keep living in their late husband's house, and also they had the right to keep any income from that property.[3]
1880	Malalai, a Pushtun woman, took off her veil and waved it like a flag over her head, leading male warriors into battle with the British during the Second Anglo-Afghan War. Malalai is still admired today, and many girls' schools have been named after her.[4]
1919–1929	King Amanullah wanted to modernize the country and emancipate women. He announced that religion does not require women to cover their faces or wear any special type of veil. Queen Saroya and other women in the Royal Family appear in public without the veil. Importance is given to the education of women.[5]
1923	The constitution guarantees equal rights for women and men.[6]
1953	Daoud becomes prime minister, and encourages women to play an active part in government and the workforce.[7]
1957	For the first time, Afghan women attend a conference of Asian women in Ceylon.
	Women whose husbands are with the diplomatic corps wear modern dress at their overseas posts.
	Afghan radio begins broadcasting female singers and announcers. There are initial protests, but they die down.

1958	The Afghan government sends a female delegate to the United Nations.
1959	Women begin to work as flight attendants and receptionists for Ariana Airlines, without the veil. They also begin to work at the telephone company, a ceramics factory, and other occupations.[8]
	Policies are enacted to allow greater roles for women in education and the workforce, to voluntarily remove the veil, and to be able to consider a future for themselves beyond the walls of their homes.[9]
	Women are allowed to go to University.[10]
1964	Women are officially enfranchised in the 1964 Constitution, which states that all Afghans are guaranteed the right to dignity, education, and the freedom to work.[11]
1968	On July 22, some members of the governing board of Kabul University propose that Afghan women not be allowed to study abroad. Hundreds of women demonstrate in protest.[12]
1977	Article 27 of the 1977 Constitution gives all Afghan women and men equal rights before the law.[13]
	Meena Keshwar Kamal founds the Revolutionary Association of Afghan Women, an organization dedicated to struggling for women's rights. She is assassinated in Quetta, Pakistan, on February 4, 1987, by Islamic fundamentalists.[14]
1978	Civil war begins. The Communist government's aggressive literacy programs for women is one of the main reasons for the fighting.[15]

1979

The Soviet Union invades Afghanistan. The emancipation of Afghan women moves quickly. There are greater opportunities for education, employment, and professional training, especially for women in the cities. Many women make use of these opportunities, and many others fight against the Russians with the Mujahideen.[16]

Women students outnumber men at the Universities.[17]

1980s

The Communists legally guarantee the equal rights of women and men. More and more women hold positions in business, government, the diplomatic corps, the police, the army, and in Parliament. Women are teachers, nurses, entertainers, doctors, and lawyers. Education and employment for women becomes more acceptable through much of Afghan society.[18]

On April 21, 1980, high school girls in Kabul hold a demonstration against the Soviet occupation of Afghanistan. Named the "children's revolt," the demonstrations went on for many days. Thousands were arrested, mostly teenage girls. Fifty students were killed, thirty of them female.[19]

1990s

Afghan women are frequent victims of land mines. The lucky ones receive treatment at Red Cross hospitals. The unlucky ones have to undergo amputations without any pain medications and without receiving prostheses afterwards. Many husbands do not see the need for their wives to have false legs because they don't need to leave the house.[20]

1992

The Communist regime of Najibullah falls, and the Islamic State of Afghanistan takes over the country. The constitution is thrown out. Although women continue to work and go to school, they are urged to dress modestly.[21] The government declares that women should cover their hair, refrain from wearing make-up, and should not laugh in public.[22]

1992–1996   Amnesty International reports that thousands of
                         unarmed civilian women are killed by unexpected
                         and deliberate rocket attacks on their homes,
                         mostly in Kabul and other cities.[23]

                         Women are killed for being related to men wanted
                         by the various Mujahideen groups. Others are
                         killed for resisting rape or abduction. Many young
                         women are abducted to be wives of Mujahideen
                         commanders. Some are sold into prostitution.
                         Some are stoned to death. Some just disappear.[24]

                         Women who are working in professions, or in
                         government jobs, are assassinated because some
                         Mujahideen groups consider their minds to have
                         been poisoned. Many educated women are as-
                         saulted in their homes or offices.[25]

1993   The Supreme Court of the Islamic State of Af-
                         ghanistan declares that women should be com-
                         pletely covered by the veil when they leave their
                         homes.[26]

1994   The Taliban Militia captures Kandahar in Novem-
                         ber, 1994. They immediately close all schools for
                         girls and forbid women to work outside the
                         house.[27]

1995   September 5, the Taliban capture the city of
                         Herat.[28]

1996   The Taliban capture Kabul on September 27,
                         1996.

                         In December at least twenty women are arrested
                         in Herat for protesting the restrictions imposed on
                         them by the Taliban. They are sent to prison.[29]

1997   In Bamiyan Province, militia groups made up of
                         Hazara women came together to fight religious
                         fundamentalists. They also set up a university for
                         women, in spite of the region's extreme poverty
                         and remoteness.[30]

1998   September 12, the Taliban captures Bamiyan.

NOTES

1. Louis Dupree, *Afghanistan* (Princeton, N.J.: Princeton University Press, 1973), 77.

2. Edward Girardet and Jonathan Walter, editors, *Essential Field Guide to Afghanistan* (Geneva; Crosslines, 1998), 54.

3. N. D. Ahmad, *The Survival of Afghanistan* (Lahore: Institute of Islamic Culture, n.d.).

4. Dupree, *Afghanistan*, 411.

5. Giradet and Walter, *Field Guide*, 55.

6. Physicians for Human Rights (PHR), *The Taliban's War on Women* (Boston: Physicians for Human Rights, 1998), 29.

7. Giradet and Walter, *Field Guide*, 55.

8. Dupree, *Afghanistan*, 425.

9. PHR, *The Taliban's War on Women*, 30.

10. Giradet and Walter, *Field Guide*, 55.

11. PHR, *The Taliban's War on Women*, 29.

12. Dupree, *Afghanistan*, 651.

13. Ibid., 29.

14. "The Burst of the Islamic Government Bubble in Afghanistan," *Revolutionary Association of Women of Afghanistan* no. 2 (1997): 5.

15. Giradet and Walter, *Field Guide*, 55.

16. Ibid., 55.

17. PHR, *The Taliban's War on Women*, 30.

18. Ibid., 30.

19. Giradet and Walter, *Field Guide*, 268.

20. Ibid., 58.

21. PHR, *The Taliban's War on Women*, 30.

22. Giradet and Walter, *Field Guide*, 57.

23. Ibid., 57.

24. Ibid., 58.

25. Ibid., 58.

26. Department of Legal Ruling and Studies of the Supreme Court of the Islamic State of Afghanistan, August 27, 1993.

27. PHR, *The Taliban's War on Women*, 24.

28. Ibid., 24.

29. *The News* (Islamabad) Dec. 26, 1996.

30. Giradet and Walter, *Field Guide*, 59.

CHRONOLOGY OF EVENTS LEADING UP TO THE SOVIET INVASION

1893	The Durand Line is created, an artificial border drawn by the British between Afghanistan and what was then India.[1] It was cut through the middle of Pushtun Territory, and the Pushtun tribes have never recognized it.
1919	King Amanullah comes to power.
	The Third Anglo-Afghan War, lasting only one month, ousted the British after nearly one hundred years of influence.[2]
1919–1929	King Amanullah, interested in reforming Afghanistan's social life, begins modernization, including a major emphasis on education. He sends students, including women, out of the country for higher education and encourages women to take part in public life. The women of the royal family appear in public without the veil.
	The King signs a Treaty of Friendship with the USSR in 1921 and is impressed with Lenin's anti-imperialism stance. Afghanistan receives aid from the Soviets, including the beginnings of an air force.
	Social reforms anger tribal and religious leaders, who lay siege to Kabul and force him to resign.[3]

1929   Habibulla Ghazi takes power for nine months, until he is imprisoned and executed by Nadir Shah.[4]

A branch of Amanullah's family takes power, with Nadir Shah at the helm. He prefers the British to the Russians, and restores friendly relations with England. With money from England and practical aid from Germany, the family builds up Afghanistan's security forces, enabling them to strengthen their hold on the country. The country grows economically, with trade and industry increasing. Social reforms, however, go backwards. Girls are again kept out of school, and women are forced to wear the *burqa*.[5]

1933   King Zahir Shah takes over after his father, Nadir Shah, is murdered in a family blood feud. Only nineteen at the time, his uncles reign behind the throne for the next twenty years.[6]

1934   Afghanistan joins the League of Nations.[7]

1947   The British leave India, which is divided into India and Pakistan. The issue of the Duran Line is not resolved in the process. There is movement among the Pushtun Tribes to create an independent nation of Pushtunistan.[8] In the meantime, the Cold War puts India into the Soviet camp and Pakistan into the American camp. The United States provides Pakistan with modern weapons and assistance to build up its army.[9]

Free elections are held for Afghanistan's seventh parliament. This parliament, dominated by reformist ideas, lasts until 1953.[10]

1951   A bill is passed in Parliament to permit freedom of the press.[11] For a year, Afghans enjoy an uncensored press, although, with such a high rate of illiteracy in the country, this did not affect many people. Editors used this forum to call for much greater reforms.[12]

Students at the University of Kabul join in the call for a more liberal, advanced society by forming a student union. Although it contained only thirty students, the union began to make the government uncomfortable by exercising its right of free speech. The government ordered the union broken up, and several of the student leaders had to flee the country.

1952

The government further cracks down on liberal movements, shutting down the free press and jailing many activists.[13]

1953

On September 20, Daoud Khan, cousin to the King, carries out a coup inside the royal family. With the cooperation of King Zahir Shah, he becomes prime minister.[14] He continues the modernization of Afghanistan. With American aid to Pakistan growing, and the issue of Pushtunistan far from resolved, Daoud encourages further investment from the USSR. Requests to the United States for military aid are refused.

1955

On December 15, Khruschev visits Kabul with Soviet Premier Bulganin. They announce their support for Afghanistan's demands for a referendum on Pushtunistan.[15]

On December 18, the USSR loans Afghanistan $100 million for joint Soviet Afghan development projects. Most of these projects are aimed at improving Afghanistan's infrastructure.[16]

1956

Afghanistan signs a $25 million arms contract with the USSR, which quickly grows to $120 million by 1960. In exchange, the Soviets get $70 million worth of raw materials.[17]

1959

Greater freedoms are enjoyed by women, including employment opportunities and declarations by the government that the *burqa* is not required by the Koran angers the Mullahs, who begin to agitate against the regime. Fifty of them are arrested by the secret police.[18] They are released a week later, after assurances that the removal of the veil is voluntary, not mandatory.

1961   Afghans begin training in the Soviet Union and in Czechoslovakia; there are seven thousand by 1970. Only a few hundred students are trained in the United States, Turkey, Britain, and India.[19]

1963   Daoud resigns and King Zahir Shah becomes stronger, traveling the country widely, attracting the support of many people. Dr. Mohammed Yousef becomes the new prime minister.

1964   A new constitution is written.

1965   Censorship of the press is lifted, and dissent flourishes.

On October 24, demonstrations shut down the parliament.

October 25—Demonstrations continue. Demonstrators are shot at by the army. Three people die.[20]

A magazine called *Khalq* ("The Masses") appears on news stands. It is published by Nur Mohammad Taraki. Six issues appear before the government shuts it down.[21]

The People's Democratic Party of Afghanistan is created. The *Khalq* and Parcham parties also come into existence.

1969   Student demonstrations spread. Between five and fifteen are killed by police.[22] Political unrest grows.

1972   Two years of drought creates widespread famine, during which some one hundred thousand people die.[23] Many feel that a substantial number of deaths could have been avoided with better government management.

1973   Daoud overthrows King Zahir Shah, who flees to Europe. Daoud pronounces an end to the monarchy and sets himself up as president. He is supported, in part, by the parties of Parcham and Khalq.

1975   Daoud shuts down all nongovernment newspapers.[24]

1976

The first *shab-namah* (evening news or night letters) begin appearing, full of messages of opposition.[25] Fundamentalist Muslims grow in strength.

1977

Gulbuddin Hekmatyr and Burhanuddin Rabbani, Islamic fundamentalists, launch attacks from Pakistan into Afghanistan. Training, money, and weapons come, in part, from the Pakistan government.[26]

Khalq and Parcham, rival parties, kiss and make-up under the auspices of the People's Democratic Party of Afghanistan (PDPA).

1978

April 27—The PDPA takes power in a military coup. It is known as the Saur Revolution, Saur meaning April. Nur Mohammad Taraki becomes Prime Minister.

April 30—The USSR recognizes the new government.

Summer—Decrees to reform land distribution, the education system, and the rights of women draw great anger from Mullahs and conservative elements in the society.

June—Islamic resistance groups attack police and army posts in the countryside. Fundamentalists see the new government as a threat to their religion and way of life. The Mujahideen parties in Peshawar recruit followers, including deserters from the army.[27]

Tensions break out again between Parcham and Khalq. Taraki throws Parcham members out of his cabinet.[28]

October 17—A decree reforming the bride price is announced, and a new, red flag is unfurled. Both events fuel the Islamic resistance.[29]

1979
February 14—U.S. Ambassador Dubs is kidnapped by guerrillas who want to exchange him for members of their own group who are in jail. Afghan police storm the place where he is being held, and both Dubs and the guerrillas die.[30]

The situation goes from bad to worse, as guerrillas gather funding, arms, and strength, and infighting within the government grows.

September—Taraki is killed. Hafizullah Amin takes power.

December 27—The Soviet Union crosses the border, claiming an invitation. Amin is ousted and killed. Barbrak Karmal takes his place.

NOTES

1. Louis Dupree, *Afghanistan* (Princeton, N.J.: Princeton University Press, 1980), 425.
2. Anthony Hyman, *Afghanistan Under Soviet Domination* (London; Macmillan Press, 1982), 40.
3. Ibid., 41.
4. Dupree, *Afghanistan*, 120.
5. Nancy Peabody Newell, *The Struggle for Afghanistan* (Ithaca, N.Y.: Cornell University Press, 1981), 38–39.
6. Hyman, *Afghanistan Under Soviet Domination*, 44.
7. Ibid., 45.
8. Ibid.
9. Ibid., 29.
10. Dupree, *Afghanistan*, 494.
11. Ibid., 495.
12. Ibid., 496–497.
13. Hyman, *Afghanistan Under Soviet Domination*, 26–27.
14. Ibid., 27.
15. Dupree, *Afghanistan*, 509.
16. Hyman, *Afghanistan Under Soviet Domination*, 16.
17. Ibid., 29.
18. Dupree, *Afghanistan*, 533.
19. Hyman, *Afghanistan Under Soviet Domination*, 29.
20. Dupree, *Afghanistan*, 592.
21. Ibid., 601.

22. Ibid., 621.
23. Hyman, *Afghanistan Under Soviet Domination*, 63.
24. Dupree, *Afghanistan*, 653.
25. Ibid.
26. Hyman, *Afghanistan Under Soviet Domination*, 67.
27. Mark Urban, *War in Afghanistan* (New York: St. Martin's, 1988).
28. Ibid.
29. Ibid.
30. Hyman, *Afghanistan Under Soviet Domination*, 99–100.

THE RESPONSE

The strongest voice of opposition to the Soviet invasion came, not surprisingly, from the United States. President Jimmy Carter, trying to shore up support for his presidency from an increasingly right-wing public, instituted a variety of sanctions early in 1980.

He announced an embargo of U.S. grain for cattle feed. At the time, the U.S. was the largest single supplier of this grain to the Soviet Union, a position Argentina quickly filled.[1] He canceled the right of Soviet trawlers to fish in U.S. territorial waters. He forbade the opening of any new Soviet consular offices in the U.S., and pledged to not open any more American ones in the USSR. He declared an embargo on American companies selling high-tech goods to the Soviets, and suspended cultural exchanges.[2] He also asked the Senate to delay discussion on the SALT II agreements, effectively ending détente. He reinstated registration for the draft, and set the stage for increased military spending.

On January 20, 1980, Carter told the Soviets that he would give them one month to leave Afghanistan, or the U.S. would boycott the Moscow Olympics. When they did not leave, he formally announced the boycott.[3]

The Olympic boycott was joined by Japan, China, West Germany, several smaller countries, and Canada.

Sue Holloway

In 1980, I was competing in Kayaking. I was twenty-five years old, and had competed in the 1976 Olympics.

I went to Europe anyway, with the rest of the team, to participate in the pre-Olympic regattas.

It was kind of funny. At all events, there was a split between the boycotting nations and the nonboycotting nations. We athletes of the boycotting nations were all drinking ourselves silly, while the nonboycotting nations were on their usual good behavior.

We would just get hammered all the time because there was absolutely no point to anything. There was nothing at the end of the day. Usually, you'd go through all these preparations as a build-up for the Olympics. You had a purpose. Not having a purpose, there was just no point to what we were doing.

The rest of my teammates were going through the same emotions I was. There weren't too many who didn't think it really stunk. There were very few people who thought this was the right thing to do. We all felt very used, like pawns. The athletes were never consulted. The government decided, and that was that.

The 1984 Olympics were held in Los Angeles, and this time the Russians boycotted.

I decided to go anyway. I won the silver and the bronze medals. My winning is always still qualified by people who bring up the Soviet non-attendance.

I definitely thought the boycott was totally useless. I thought so at the time, that it wouldn't make any difference, that it was wrong, because they were using people who had no power. And then, of course, as the years went by and the Russians still weren't out of Afghanistan, I felt proven right. If it had done any good, we could have looked back and said, "at least something good came out of it," but nothing did.

NOTES

1. Anthony Hyman, *Afghanistan Under Soviet Domination* (New York: St. Martin's, 1984), 172.

2. Nancy Peabody Newell, *The Struggle for Afghanistan* (Ithaca, N.Y.: Cornell University Press, 1981), 192.

3. Ibid., 193.

FRIENDS

Somewhere under the ground in Kabul is a photograph of two small girls, best friends, best buddies. They are looking boldly at the camera, giggling the way small girls everywhere do. The little girls are now sixty, and living far from home. The photo has been buried to save it from the Taliban, who tear up any photograph they find.

Benazir Hotaki is my translator and guide for much of my time in Pakistan. She and Alkolajan have been best friends for fifty years. They were both high school principals in Kabul before the Taliban arrived. Now they are refugees. Alkola lives with her husband and other family members in a house in the Hyatabad section of Peshawar. Benazir lives with her grown son, Abdullah, a Tae Kwon Do expert, in a single room in another part of Hyatabad.

We spent an evening drinking tea and chatting in Alkolajan's house.

Benazir

Alkolajan and I have been best friends for fifty years. We began sitting beside each other in the fourth grade, and kept doing so all through school. We liked each other as soon as we met. Although we liked other classmates as well, we were happiest when we were just with each other.

We used to pass notes back and forth to each other in class, and I'm proud to say that we were so good at it, we never got caught! We were very happy with each other, never argued, never called each other bad names the way some friends do. We took all the same subjects all through school, except for foreign languages. I studied English, and Alkola studied German.

Benazir Hotaki, left, and Alkolajan, friends for over 50 years.

We liked the same things. We played basketball, and we liked to read stories and poetry. On nice days we would take our cameras to the parks in Kabul and photograph flowers. Nature was something we loved to study and write about. When we became teenagers, we would read fashion magazines and try out new hairstyles on each other.

We both became teachers at Zargona High School in Kabul, both teaching Persian literature.

Our weddings took place very close in time to each other. Alkolajan was a beautiful bride, and her husband, the groom, was very handsome. Her husband is like a brother to me. Her wedding took place in a big hotel, and it was very beautiful.

My husband, Abdul Gahafoor Hotaki, graduated from the Police Academy in Kabul, and also got a degree in fire-fighting from London. He was a police officer in Kabul's criminal division until the Communists came, when he lost his job. For many years, he didn't work. When the Taliban came, he disappeared. I have not heard from him since. He does not know I'm in Peshawar. I don't know how we will find each other again, if he is still alive.

Alkola was the first one of the two of us to go to another country. After I became head teacher at Zargona High School, Alkola went to Germany to get more education. We wrote to each other while we were separated, and she brought me back many gifts. She had only been in Kabul a short while when the opportunity came up for me to go to Australia.

My children were very small. Dina, the oldest, who is now in the U.S., was thirteen months, and Nasef, my second child, was only three months. I had to leave them with relatives. Even now, they don't call me mother. They call me Benazir. I gave up a lot to get an education. My children didn't know me when I came back to Afghanistan and didn't want to be with me.

I got my master's in education at Queensland University in Brisbane. I was very busy when I was in Australia. I belonged to the Business and Professional Women's Association, the Soroptimist Club, the YWCA, the United Nations Association, and I spoke about Afghan women in many places, like the St. Lucia Garden Club and the Girl Guides. I would go to the Cathedral there with friends. We Muslims respect Jesus as a great teacher.

Benazir shows me a copy of the English-language *Kabul Times*, January 5, 1970, with an article about her time in Australia. The newspaper also has an article about Spiro Agnew's visit to Kabul with his wife. The photos of the women in the newspaper show the same silly beehive hair-dos that women in the West were so fond of.

Back in Kabul, Alkola had been made the principal of Malali High School, and I took over as principal of the Afghan Women's Society Vocational High School, a very large school for women. Three thousand students went to that school.

I began to go abroad for conferences and seminars, representing Afghan women. I went to Ulan Batar in Mongolia, to Indonesia, Moscow, Manila, Bangkok, and other places. I loved meeting new people and having new experiences. I ate horse cheese in Mongolia. Did you know that in Azerbijan there are twenty-five different kinds of apples, and peaches the size of soccer balls?

I have been selected three times as the best mother of the year, and three times as the best teacher of the year. I have been awarded several medals and certificates of merit. I have devoted my life to training and educating the young generation of my country, especially girls and women. I feel very happy that many of my previous students are doctors, teachers, and engineers. I still love to read, but unfortunately I had to leave all my books behind when I left Afghanistan.

Now, I am jobless. I have no way to survive economically. I live in Peshawar with lots of difficulties.

Having an education and not being able to use it is like having money and not being able to buy food.

Afghanistan is now worse than Nepal. Nepal is a developing country, every day it gets bigger and better. Every day, Afghanistan gets worse and worse.

Alkola

As soon as I saw Benazir in the school yard, I knew we would be friends. I am a little quieter than Benazir, but still, we are best friends.

When the Taliban came, I was principal at Malali High School. The Taliban do not like educated people, so I came to Peshawar.

Every Friday, at the stadium in Kabul, they cut someone's hands off, and show them to people. Both women and men are forced to go and watch. If a woman, even in a *burqa*, goes outside without her husband or brother, she can be arrested, held in jail, and brought to the stadium on Friday. She is tied to a pole, still in her *burqa*, and is beaten until she faints or dies. People are also executed by having their throats cut. For amputations, the doctor's face is covered. He sometimes gives the victim an injection to cut the pain, then he cuts the person's hand off. The people in the stadium are silent when this happens. They do not cheer.

The Taliban follow educated people. Many are in prison. Most have left the country.

My mother was a dentist, an educated woman. [*She shows me two small photographs of her mother that she keeps in an envelope, tucked away in a closet.*] She is now dead, and I miss her, even though soon I will be an old woman.

Benazir

Alkolajan and I have seen many horrible things in Afghanistan over the course of our fifty years of friendship, much bombing, many rockets, much death and sadness.

Alkola was the first one to come to Peshawar, and for two years, we had no news of each other. After the Taliban took over, I also came to Peshawar, and we saw each other again.

Alkolajan is exactly the same at sixty as she was at nine years old. She hasn't changed at all. But our friendship has become even closer. War has punished us very much. Our lives are full of sadness and disappointment, and our minds no longer work correctly, but we still have our friendship.

THE RUSSIANS IN AFGHANISTAN

The Soviets did not find Afghanistan a cake-walk. Very little was broadcast at home about the war, so soldiers were not prepared for what they would face. They were told they were protecting their southern borders, that they were protecting Afghanistan from the Americans. Having heard for years about the schools, roads, and hospitals the Soviets had built in Afghanistan, the soldiers did not expect the hostile reception they received.

Although arms and money began being secretly funneled to the Mujahideen months before the Soviet invasion, the election of Ronald Reagan stepped up the pace and brought it out in the open. The Soviets were faced with sophisticated modern weaponry, much of it made in the USSR and ending up in Mujahideen hands after detours through Egypt and elsewhere. One of the very sad ironies for the Soviet soldiers in Afghanistan is that they found themselves being killed and wounded with weapons from their own country.

Much of the grass-roots opposition to the Soviet presence came from women. They were the first to organize huge demonstrations in the streets. They were the first to gather at the gates of Pul-e-charki Prison in Kabul, demanding the release of political prisoners.[1]

In January of 1983, four hundred women were in the Salon of the Mourning Woman in Shahrinau Park in Kabul. Many of the women had lost husbands and sons to the war. During their prayers, women started to speak about their loss. The volume and emotion of the event rose. They demanded the bodies of their dead, and the release of people from jails. Government forces surrounded the pavilion and fired tear gas at the women to disperse them.[2]

Many students, from high-school and up, were involved in anti-government protests. In 1980 high school girls led anti-government protests all over Kabul, with many killed by police, and thousands more arrested.

Tajwar Kakar, whose resistance name was Tajwar Sultan, was a teacher and headmaster at a school in Kunduz. The authorities declared that the May 1 holiday would be observed in the city. In protest against the Soviet occupation, she had her teachers tell their younger students to gather wasps and keep them in small boxes. On the day of the parade, the children, running as though they were randomly out of control, darted through the parade, opening their boxes at the feet of the marchers. Wasps went inside trousers and skirts and started stinging. Marchers scattered, leaving banners and posters of leaders' portraits on the ground. The women quickly gathered up twenty-five light arms and pistols. They sent the machine guns to Mujahideen groups in the countryside, and handed the pistols over to women in the urban underground.

The women's underground was organized in three sections. One group investigated people suspected of collaborating with the enemy. Another group followed the suspects and discovered their connections. The third group was the Operations Group, who carried out assassinations. One woman named Fadia was very effective in luring Russian men away from their platoon and assassinating them. She is said to have killed at least fifteen men before she was captured.[3]

In the countryside, women sometimes carried and used weapons. When the Soviets would come to search a village, they would be fired upon by women from windows. In a village in Ghazni, one woman killed ten Russians before being shot herself.

Village women cooked for the Mujahideen fighters and carried food out to them in the hills. They did the men's laundry. Because their men were fighting, women took over the field work as well, usually working at night because of bombing runs during the day.[4]

In Herat, a woman who lost both her brother and her father in the fighting formed an independent group of women guerrillas. They were given weapons and carried out missions in the countryside. Women had been involved in the armed resistance in Kandahar since 1981. They hid weapons under their *burqas* as they walked from place to place. Some would lure a Soviet or government soldier to a house where men would be waiting to kill him.[5]

Women paid a heavy price for these activities. Hundreds of women and girls were arrested and tortured. Many were executed. Tajwar Kakar spent a year in prison for her resistance activities.[6]

Fahima Nasery, a math and physics teacher, wrote and distributed resistance messages. She was arrested at a demonstration in May, 1981, and taken to Sadarat Prison for women at the Prime Ministry. She was crowded into a cell with fourteen other women. There was no space to move in the cell. It was filthy, hot, and crawling with insects. A hole in the middle of the room served as a toilet. Some of the women had lost their minds from the torture. One, a sixty-five-year-old woman, wet herself every time her name was called by the guards. Several women had children with them. One woman had a six-month old baby when its mother was taken out to be tortured.[7]

Amnesty International documented the types of torture practiced in Afghanistan while the Soviets were occupying it. They found evidence of beatings with sticks, wire cables, and rubber lashes; people being made to stand for long periods of time in the burning sun, or in a tank of water in the winter; electric shocks; having a bottle or a hot wire inserted in the rectum; and being burned with cigarettes. Women were regularly sexually assaulted, and were often left alone in a room for days with a dead body.

Formal announcements of deaths in custody were rarely made. Instead, prison guards would stop accepting clothes or personal articles from family members. Many people, women and men, simply disappeared.[8]

Until 1983 very little information about the war got back to the Soviet public. As casualty numbers grew, and as the politburo realized that they were in for a long stay in Afghanistan, they felt a need to begin to prepare the public for a long war.

In the early part of the war, bodies came back without ceremony. In order to claim the bodies of their sons, mothers would have to agree not to mention Afghanistan on their son's tombstone. The dead soldiers were brought back in zinc-coated coffins because of the high heat in parts of Afghanistan much of the time. The coffins were sealed shut, although it is the Russian Orthodox tradition to have the body on display at the funeral. The bodies that were not mangled were placed in coffins with small windows above the face. Those that had been badly damaged in the war were placed in windowless coffins. With no way to open the coffin, and being forbidden to do so anyway, parents had no way of knowing if it was really their son they were burying.[9]

The Ministry of Defense, in a then-secret report, gave casualty figures as of September, 1980, as 8,492 killed, and 15,000 wounded. In September of 1985, Procurator V. I. Chistakov made a statement to the House of Political Education that roughly fifteen thousand had died in the first few years of the war.[10] With a government eager to contain public opinion and avoid the type of antiwar movements that grew in the United States during the Vietnam War, accurate, reliable figures are still difficult to come by. Word got out through witnesses such as airport workers, who would see a special military plane land at the freight terminal at Moscow's Sheremetevo airport and everyday disgorge a hundred or more coffins from Afghanistan.[11]

Funerals for the dead began to turn into antiwar demonstrations, so the government stepped in to try to manage them. They staged official military funerals, making speeches about the bravery of those doing their international duty, handing out posthumous medals, and comforting the grieving mothers and widows.

They were not able to contain all outbursts of anger and grief. In 1984, after trying unsuccessfully to obtain the body of her son from Afghanistan, a woman set herself on fire in front of the Party Headquarters in Kharkov, in the Ukraine.[12] A woman in Kalinin became hysterical after learning about her son's death, and drew a large crowd, which turned into a protest against the war.[13]

Other antiwar demonstrations were held in Georgia and Armenia outside recruitment offices. These were organized and carried out by women who feared their husbands and sons would be sent to Afghanistan. Hundreds of women were arrested.[14]

In Leningrad, a feminist group called Maria called on men to go to prison rather than allow themselves to be shipped to Afghanistan. They sent a letter to the committee for Afghanistan. They sent a letter to the Committee for Afghan Women, expressing solidarity with them in their struggle for justice. They continued to speak out publicly against the war until they were arrested and sent into exile in Siberia. Slava Denisov, from Dushanbe, near the Afghan border, was confined to a psychiatric hospital after she collected signatures on a petition against the war.[15] Antiwar work also sent the Sakharovs into exile. Posters against the war began appearing on lampposts and walls.[16] Underground literature, or Samizdat, tried to keep track of antiwar activities, but as it was quickly suppressed, we have information about only a few of the events that must have taken place.

As the body count increased, opposition grew. Glasnost arriving in 1986 meant there was more news about the war being released to the public, but it was still controlled news. The reports didn't mention the suffering of the troops or the harsh conditions in Afghanistan. They didn't even release casualty figures until after they announced the troop withdrawal.[17] Instead they gave glowing accounts of the soldiers' bravery, generosity, and kindness toward the Afghan people.

Parents began to go to great lengths to avoid sending their sons to Afghanistan. Those who could, paid huge bribes to officials. Others feigned illness or madness, and some cut off one of their fingers.[18] As much as possible, orphans were sent to the front, to reduce anger from parents.[19]

As time wore on, the problems facing the soldiers in Afghanistan grew. The regular tour of duty was two years, and the soldiers who had been there awhile, the "Old Soldiers," as they called themselves, bullied and tyrannized the new men, taking the best food, and treating the new recruits abominably. Soldiers also contracted illnesses such as heat stroke, dysentery, typhoid, hepatitis, and pneumonia.[20] Alcohol and drug abuse grew, with soldiers selling their belongings and food rations to buy drugs.[21] In a 1987 government poll, one out of every six people blamed the war for the growing problem of drug addiction in the Soviet Union.[22] When they returned home, Afghan vets were met with more problems. They were greeted with indifference by a public that had no real idea of what they'd been through.

Some veterans, disgusted by what they saw as frivolous attitudes emerging in Russia's young people and in the society in general, formed vigilante squads called "Afghantsi." They carried out their own brand of justice on those they considered antisocial, such as corrupt officials, drug pushers, and black marketeers. They felt betrayed that what Russia had fought and suffered for was being dragged down into Western-style degradation by these undesirable elements.[23]

Many veterans thought badly about the war in which they had been forced to serve. Georgy Getman, the leader of the Moscow branch of Shchit, an organization for Afghan war veterans, called the war, "A political force and a criminal affair."[24] Viktor Nazarov, one of the few Soviet prisoners of war (*the Mujahideen generally executed prisoners*) said on his return to the Ukraine after eight years in Afghanistan, "Everyone was drafted, whether you liked it or not. It was a war, no one asked if it was good or not. War is fought over power."[25]

Retired General Lev Serebrou, Deputy Chief of the Union of Afghan Veterans in Moscow, who saw one thousand of the thirteen thousand men he commanded killed over three years, summed up Soviet attitudes toward the war when he said, "It's a pity for the people who became toys of the politicians. . . . There was no reason for so many to die. It could have all been avoided, and it should have been."[26]

NOTES

1. Afghan Information Center Bulletin no. 57, Dec. 1985, p. 10.
2. Afghan Information Center Bulletin no. 23, Feb. 1983, p. 9.
3. Afghan Information Center Bulletin no. 57, Dec. 1985, p. 10.
4. Ibid.
5. Ibid.
6. Ibid., p. 11.
7. Afghan Information Center Bulletin no. 54, Sept. 1985, p. 11.
8. Amnesty International, *Torture Under Soviet Occupation*, November, 1986.
9. Taras Kuzio, "Opposition in the USSR to the Occupation of Afghanistan," *Central Asian Survey*, 6, no. 1 (1977): 99–117.
10. Ibid.
11. Ibid.
12. Ibid.
13. Ibid.
14. Ibid.
15. Ibid.
16. Ibid.
17. T. H. Rigby, "The Afghan Conflict and Soviet Domestic Policies," in *The Soviet Withdrawal from Afghanistan*, edited by Amin Saikal and William Maley (Cambridge: Cambridge University Press, 1985).
18. Taras Kuzio, "A War About Which Soviet People Do Not Boast," *Arabia: The Islamic World Review* (January 1986).
19. Kuzio, *Opposition in the USSR to the Occupation of Afghanistan*.
20. Mark Urban, *War in Afghanistan* (New York: St. Martin's, 1988), p 123.
21. Ibid.
22. Diego Cordovez and Selig S. Harrison, *Out of Afghanistan* (New York: Oxford University Press, 1995).
23. Kuzio, *Opposition in the USSR to the Occupation of Afghanistan*.
24. *Moscow Times*, October 3, 1996.
25. *Moscow Times*, March 11, 1993.
26. A.P., April 20, 1992.

RUSSIAN WOMEN IN AFGHANISTAN

Like any other group of men, the Soviet Army in Afghanistan needed women to look after them. The role of the military in Afghanistan was kept mostly a secret from the general population, and the role of women supporting the military was an even deeper secret. Many who went did not tell their friends where they were going, and when they returned, did not tell anyone where they had been.

Although women served in a wide range of capacities, from geology to engineering, to the more traditional occupations of medical and clerical support, most people assumed that the women were there to serve the sexual needs of the Russian troops. Many of the Russian troops had the same idea, and women who were harassed and attacked had no recourse to justice; the Russian officers had other things to think about, even if they were inclined to take women's complaints seriously. The women were not part of the military, and therefore, the military was not responsible for them.

The women were under military discipline, however, and there was no civilian authority in Afghanistan to which to appeal. They had to go where they were sent, do the tasks they were told to do, and could not go home without military approval and transport.

They lived under the same conditions as the soldiers, took the same risks, and were killed by bullets and grenades. The Soviet military could not have functioned without the sweat, labor, and cooperation of the women who were essentially drafted into the service. Yet their contribution has never been acknowledged.

Anika is an organization of women who served in Afghanistan alongside the Russian army. It was formed to provide a way for these women to get support from one another, to publicize the difficulties they and their sisters have gone through since their time in Afghanistan, and to campaign for their rights. "Nika" is a Russian word for "Victory." They call their organization Anika because there was no victory, for anyone, in Afghanistan. Over the course of two trips to Moscow, I met with several members of Anika.

Lyubov Yakovleva is the founder of Anika. I met with her and her colleague, Tanya Shetpa, in a noisy coffee bar near the Prospect Mira subway station in Moscow. The background noises fade away as they tell their stories.

Lyubov Yakovleva

We feel we have been used.

When Tanya talks, she will cry, and you will cry. But being roughly treated by bureaucrats, I have become rougher myself.

All of the women who were sent to Afghanistan had rich, full lives. They only sent the best of the best to Afghanistan. We had to be cleared by the regional Party Committee, then the city Committee, then the district, and, finally, by the Ministry of Defense itself.

They did not send married women to Afghanistan, without their husbands. It did not matter to them that a woman had to leave children behind without her care, but they would not let her leave a man behind without her care.

My ex-husband gave the government permission to send me to Afghanistan. I arranged a certificate so that my mother could be the guardian of my daughter.

I decided that nobody should know where I was because of fairy tales we were fed in the mass media that there was peace in Afghanistan, and everything was OK, and I knew the situation was quite different. I knew that they would be terribly worried and upset if they knew the truth.

I worked at first as a chief lab assistant at this unit in Kabul. I was sexually harassed in there. I wrote a letter to the Ministry of Defense, and was sent to Pul-e-Khumri.

Pul-e-Khumri was called the Valley of Death. When there was an Afghan war against a British invasion, forty thousand English soldiers died in Pul-e-Khumri. They died of various diseases, typhus, hepatitis, cholera, malaria, amoebic disintery, and so on. That is why they call it the Valley of Death.

Later on, I was sent to assist on the Road of Life. This was the road out of Afghanistan, the only road that connected Afghanistan with the USSR. It went through the mountains. We had to protect this road. All cargo—food and supplies—had to go this way. When trucks went by, there was always lots of shooting from the locals.

Once, we were in a deep valley, and we were attacked from both sides. It was five A.M., and we had just started moving, when the shooting started from both sides. The shooters cut the Afghan truck-train from the Russian truck train. They separated us. Very big trucks full of fuel started exploding. The truck I was in had a collision with a mountain.

There was an explosion. I was thrown away from the truck. I could feel something wrong with my legs. That was how I got my injury.

I went to Afghanistan when I was thirty-nine, but looked younger. Now I am fifty-three, and look older.

It was a very, very difficult life. The living conditions were extreme. Everyday someone would die. The relationship becomes more emphasized. A good person becomes transparent, so does a bad person. It was very interesting, because in regular life, all these differences and discrepancies are leveled out.

Everything was like running on razor blades. If it's love, then it's very emotional. If it's hatred, then it's hatred.

You had real friends there, but you also had real enemies.

I had some Afghan friends, but Afghans were also shooting at me.

In Kabul, if we met the Afghan people in daytime, we were friends. However, in the evening, at night, we had to close the windows and shut the doors. There was a saying, "You enter my house, you are a friend, but when you leave my house, you are an enemy."

In Kabul, I was not as free in my movements. There was shooting, explosions, killings. In Pul-e-Khumri, we were more open, and closer, with Afghan people, especially women. We didn't know the word "enemy." We had very good, friendly relationships with them.

We were not aware of the Afghan women's problems. But, when I came back to Moscow, when their revolution started, I thought about them strongly, because I recalled them saying, "We are progressive women of Afghanistan, and we are going to have problems."

I think that these women are now dead. They were wives of famous, progressive military leaders, and also they were our friends. So, I don't think they are alive. I wish I could get a glance of their lives now, or of the situation for women there now.

When I was thirty-five, I had to pass examinations to enter the physical culture institute. I ran one hundred meters and five hundred meters in the same speed as sixteen-year-old girls, and did the swimming, the weight-lifting.

I cannot run anymore. I walk only with the aid of a cane. I had amoebic dysentery, malaria, and four operations on my colon. I have this psychological trauma. It's called "Afghan syndrome." I spent forty-five days in neurological hospital, restoring my sleep cycle, relieving my stress, but nevertheless, when I talk about it, I start crying. At night, in my sleep, I still fight. For three years,

Lyubov entertaining Soviet troops in Afghanistan.

I cried every time the word "Afghanistan" was mentioned to me, so did Tanya. And when I hear the songs of the Afghan soldiers, then we just cannot help crying. . . .

For us, it is like ointment to our souls that at least somebody is interested in our problems.

Tatiana

I was thirty-two when I went to Afghanistan.

I did not apply to go there. I don't know of any women who applied to go to Afghanistan. They were chosen. It wasn't an order, exactly, but it was pretty close.

This was in 1987. I was a member of the Communist Party, but I still had to undergo many, many check-ups before going to Afghanistan. They searched my life thoroughly for political loyalty. I had to be approved by all levels of the Party committees and military committees.

We had no special training when we went over. The City Party committee gave us some little instruction in how to behave, and once we were in Afghanistan, we were taught to fire a gun. That is all.

We were flown into Kabul. For the first two weeks, I stayed in a transit camp there, with other women, while the military decided where it would send me.

The camp was very terrible. Everyone immediately wanted to go home. It was like a concentration camp.

Forty people shared one tent. We slept in bunk beds. There were two tents for women, the rest were for men. The food was terrible. There was no good water to drink—it had a lot of chlorine in it. The water tank was five hundred meters from our tent. It wasn't long before people began to come down with many diseases. And we women had a difficult time with our monthly period—no one had even considered that.

I was sent to Shendan, the furthest location there. Shendan is south of Herat, not far from the Afghan border with Iran. It is in the desert.

We traveled there in a truck convoy, the kind that Lyubov had also been on.

Such a delicate issue, if you wanted to use the bathroom! You couldn't step one meter from the road because of land mines. They had to put two trucks close together. The women would hide between the wheels of the trucks and do their business that way, while men stood guard. The water for washing and drinking was always in the last truck in the truck-train. When there was a stop, we'd have to quickly jump out of our truck and run to the end, get some water, then run back again.

Everyone told me I was lucky to be going to Shendan, that the war was quiet there. It didn't seem quiet to me. The airbase, where I worked, was shelled every day. There was shooting, explosions, people died.

I wasn't injured by the fighting, but I worked in very difficult conditions. The days reached sixty degrees Celsius. There was no air conditioning where we worked. We were sweating all the time, our clothes were always drenched in sweat. The flies were terrible. Whole crowds of them would cover us, biting, looking for damp spots—our eyes, our lips, everywhere.

We never saw any Afghans on the base. It was too heavily guarded. Two-thirds of a kilometer away, there was a fence, and we were not allowed to go beyond that.

I was a year in Afghanistan before I got sick. I got sick from the heat, and our nutrition was very improper. We had no fruit, no vegetables except for canned cabbage. I lost weight, my strength left me. When I finally got permission to go to a medical unit, they told me I had pneumonia. I had lost eighteen kilos.

I was treated in Shendan for two months, then sent back to work again. I kept working for sometime, but it became clear to me that if I stayed there any longer, I'd die. I asked to be sent back to the USSR. Permission was denied.

My boss said it was not medically necessary for me to leave. Not medically necessary! Other women had died there, for the same reasons!

Only thanks to a very assertive girlfriend was I able to get a release. I did not have the strength to break through the wall of bureaucracy.

Finally, I was sent back to Moscow. It was an awful hell for me. I had no health left at all. I weighed thirty-eight kilos [approximately eighty-three pounds]. I would stagger from a gust of wind.

I was sent to a regular clinic. There are no special places for women like us to go to, even though the health problems we suffered are irreversible. I am not able to work. All that was written on my record was that it was medically not advisable for me to stay in hot climate. My illness was never associated with Afghanistan.

I was given only the smallest of pensions. It is not enough to live on. When I went to the local military committee for assistance, they told me that they wouldn't help me, because I had never been part of the military. They hadn't sent me to Afghanistan—I had chosen to go. Their explanation was "You went there yourself—you volunteered. We have no responsibility for you."

I have a friend who was injured in Afghanistan by an explosion. She is now completely handicapped and has been bedridden for the past eight years. For all that, the government will not admit that her injury comes from the war. She is classified as having only a general illness, and gets only the smallest pension. She worked in Afghanistan as a medical sister, assisting on the operations of wounded soldiers.

The war in Afghanistan drastically changed my life and my fate. I will never get back what I lost there, and I still don't know what we gained. Did we gain anything?

A few months later, I meet with Lyubov and Tanya again, and this time they bring Galina with them.

Galina

When we were chosen to go to Afghanistan, we had to pass through medical examinations. We had to be extremely healthy, but everyone who came back has some medical problems. Ten years after the war, the government did a study, and found that those who were involved in the war have massive health problems. Women were not a part of that study, but we were affected in the same way.

I came to Afghanistan with my husband in August, 1979, as contract workers, not linked to the military. My husband was a builder and went to Afghanistan to build roads. That's a peaceful profession. We decided to move there. I was forty.

I first came to Kabul in a time of peace. At that time, Afghan people were very good and comfortable. When the war started, the situation changed. Before the war started, a Russian lady was very well respected, in the shops, everywhere. After the war started, some people would throw things at Russian ladies, tomatoes, things like that.

We had no information about the war at the beginning. There was no publicity at all. We did not expect the war to be started. It completely surprised us.

We continued to mix with Afghans after the war started. They were living in the Middle Ages. The people were very poor and dependent on the Russian people to give them civilization. Generally speaking, though, relations between Afghans and Russians changed.

I accepted a position as a cook for the air force battalion stationed in Kabul. Although my husband was a civilian, because of the war, he came under the authority of the military.

We lived in the military camp, in a tent. The kitchen was outside. There was a gigantic tent, which we used as a dining room. There was a big stove in the kitchen that used diesel fuel to make the fire. There was a soldier whose duty it was just to take care of the fire.

I felt very sorry for the boys who had to serve in Afghanistan. It has a horrible climate, an unhealthy climate, and the war was a horrible situation. We tried to help them as much as possible. The money we were paid was almost nothing, but we worked as hard as we could to help the men and the officers. There was no one who could say some warm words to them, and they needed that. I tried to help with that.

In the beginning, the soldiers who came to Afghanistan were not allowed to write letters home about where they were serving. Every letter from Afghanistan was censored. People back home were not allowed to know anything about what was happening in Afghanistan.

I had responsibility for food, for provisions, and I was given a submachine gun, a kalashnikov, to prevent theft. There was a special building where provisions were kept. Only once, in the darkness, some people, I don't know if they were Afghans or soldiers, they tried to get into the building for something. I didn't shoot, but I did make noise. I used my machine gun to beat against the iron bars on the windows, and I shouted, "Go away immediately, or I will start shooting, even though I don't know who you are!" Whoever it was, they went away.

The pilots never discussed their missions, because that was a state secret. It was also forbidden to ask questions, so to avoid trouble, for me and the pilots, I did not ask questions.

Every soldier, from time to time, worked in the kitchen, doing chores there under my direction. I knew all of them, and I visited their tents from time to time. When they had some free time, they would sing. They would organize concerts. Sometimes very famous Russian singers and actors visited Kabul to entertain the troops.

More experienced soldiers who had served sometime already in Afghanistan forced new soldiers to work for them as slaves. It is a horrible problem in the army that still goes on.

When people back in Russia began learning about the war, parents would do everything they could think of to keep their sons out of Afghanistan. That's why some of the soldiers who came to Afghanistan were unfit for duty. They had parents with no pull, or perhaps they had no parents at all, and came into the army from the orphanages.

Soldiers dying received no publicity. They just disappeared. We never knew what happened to them. Had they finished serving in the army? Were they transported to another unit? Did they die? We were never told. There was a special army unit who transported the dead back to Russia, without any publicity.

My husband and I returned to Russia at the same time. It was the Soviet time, and Soviet propaganda was very strong. There was no publicity about the war in Afghanistan. People were not interested in what was going on there.

When I started working again, and came to my office, my colleagues didn't want to listen to me tell them how soldiers, boys the same age as their children, felt in Afghanistan, lived in Afghanistan. It insulted me very much.

Afghanistan now has a permanent war, which started twenty years ago, and is still going on, but now everything that could be destroyed has been destroyed. The war with Russia initiated the permanent war they have now.

Lyubov and Marina are twin sisters who served together in Afghanistan. They live together in a suburb of Moscow. Galina, Tanya, Lyubov and I visit them at their apartment.

Lyubov Koromyoslova

I am thirty-seven now. I was twenty-one when I went to Afghanistan with my sister. We volunteered. We wanted to work in another country, but for other countries, we would have to be split up. Afghanistan would take us both together.

We went to Afghanistan in 1983, to Shendan. We served in a medical battalion, taking care of patients after they came out of surgery. In the beginning, we stayed in tents, but later on, we stayed in block houses.

We had no information on Afghanistan before we went there. We knew very little about the war, almost nothing. Actually, the Soviet government didn't call it a war. They called it a "limited contingent of troops answering the request of foreign government."

Our compound was quite far from the town of Shendan. We never went into town. It was not allowed. The compound was often shelled, so living there was dangerous. We were in Afghanistan for two years. I was homesick for Russia all the time. I missed the trees and the natural environment of Russia. I missed my friends and relatives. We ate Russian food on the airbase. All of our food came from Russia, so at least that was familiar.

The airbase used to have very good concrete roads, but after many attacks, those roads were torn up and replaced with gravel roads, to make it easier to hear if the enemy was coming.

My legs began to give me pain a year or so into my time in Afghanistan. I tried wearing different shoes, but that didn't help. The pain became worse and worse. It got so bad that I could barely walk.

The doctors examined my legs, and gave me some tablets, but they didn't help. The pain just got worse. They wouldn't send me home, though. I had to stay in Afghanistan and complete my contract.

When I finally did get back to Russia, the pain in my legs continued to get worse. I tried to help myself for awhile, but eventually I had to go to the hospital. The problem turned out to be some bone fragments in my legs that were decomposing.

The doctors didn't know what caused this problem. I was healthy before I went to Afghanistan. I've had three operations on my legs, but they are still bad. In the hospital I met a man who had the same problems as me. He had also been in Afghanistan.

My sister and I came home from Afghanistan at the same time. We didn't talk very much about where we had been, not even to relatives. People were just not interested.

Now I am officially handicapped. Although I came home in 1985, I had to work, with the pain, until 1988, when they finally declared me handicapped. I get a small pension, the regular pension for handicapped people. I get nothing special for having been in Afghanistan. I almost never leave the apartment. My legs are too bad.

Marina

My sister and I did the same kind of work in Afghanistan. We shared a room there with two other women, from the Ukraine. We exchange letters now and then. Both of them are still working as nurses. I have some health problems from that time, but not as bad as my sister's. At least I am able to work.

Life was much simpler in Afghanistan than it is now in Russia. Back then, friends were friends and enemies were enemies. Of course, since we lived in the compound, we didn't have any contact with the enemy, except when they shelled us. The Afghans we came in contact with were on our side. There was real friendship between these Afghans and the Russians.

I don't know whether the Afghan War was right or wrong. Mostly, it was a civil war, and we were just there to help. The Russian Army brought food and medicine to the Afghan people. Many Afghans dreamed of going to the USSR for a free education.

The Soviet soldiers we met were mostly just boys, eighteen and nineteen years old. My sister and I looked after those with heavy wounds, so they didn't talk much, except to cry for their mothers.

The strangest thing about going back home again was that nothing was different here. Everything was the same as we had left it, only we were different. One night, soon after we got back there was a bad thunderstorm, and I thought we were being shelled!

I don't think Russia is to blame for the problems that Afghanistan is having now. So many years have passed since the Russians left, and the Afghans are still fighting each other.

The interview ends and the party begins. A table is set with bread, cheese, and homemade cakes. Lyubov produces a bottle of wine. They present me with gifts: two record albums of songs sung by Russian soldiers in Afghanistan, photographs of Kabul before it was destroyed, and a painting done by Galina's grandson. We drink our wine, and they tell me stories of a cat named Grafchik, or Little Count, who lived in the compound where the sisters worked, and of a dog Lyubov knew that fell in love with the commandant of her division. They talk of parties in Afghanistan with lots of booze, food, and party dresses. We drink toasts to the success of this project, and to friendship among women. We laugh and talk until the shadows lengthen and it is time to go.

Helen Womack is a British journalist living and working in Moscow. She covered the Soviet withdrawal from Afghanistan.

Helen Womack

I was with one of the first groups of international journalists to go into Afghanistan with the Soviets rather than with the Mujahideen.

In May, we went first to Kabul, and then a group of us were given access to the first tank convoy that was pulling out of Jalalabad. We rode in the tank convoy from Jalalabad up to Kabul, then left the soldiers as they continued up the road to the Soviet border. We took planes and met them as they crossed the border, so we saw the first group to leave.

The withdrawal took from May 1988 to February of 1989 before it was completed.

It was the first time we journalists had ever been so close to the Soviet army since the end of the Second World War. We weren't allowed to mix with the soldiers very much. Our press conferences were with the officers.

We got to talk with the soldiers a little bit, but in the presence of the officers. They just kept repeating that they'd been doing their international duty.

You could, however, in a way sense their private feelings. They were utterly knackered and fed up. They were sick of all these endless farewell parades that were organized along the road. You could read it in their faces that they just wanted to get out.

All along the way, the tanks would stop and there'd be boring speeches about how they'd done their international duty, and you could see on the soldiers' faces that they were just bored to death with it all. They just wanted to get home as quickly as possible.

There were Russian women around. There is a section of Kabul called Microeon, which just means "suburb" in Russian. That's where the officers and their wives lived. The ordinary soldiers lived in barracks, of course, but the officers and their wives lived in these chicken-box flats. They led quite isolated lives. They were advised not to go to the bazaar, and certainly not to speak Russian in the streets.

There was a case before we arrived where a couple of Russian women had gotten very frustrated sitting in their flats, leading these sterile lives. They actually dressed up as Afghans and went to the market, and they were lynched because they'd outraged local tradition. They were killed. The crowd tore them apart.

We were warned not to speak Russian in the market, to make it very obvious that we were English. Even though, of course, a century earlier the English had also tried to conquer Afghanistan!

The incredible beauty of the landscape really sticks in my memory. It was stunning. And I remember the terrible destruction. I remember a hillside which was absolutely covered with black flags. The Afghans used black flags as temporary markers for graves. Maybe they would later put tombstones there, I don't know, but at the time it was just a sea of black flags. That was very moving.

I remember seeing also the Russian barracks, seeing the neatly made beds with black ribbons across them and photographs of the soldiers who died. And the overwhelming feeling that these were poor boys from the Soviet provinces. I didn't meet any privileged kids from Moscow or St. Petersburg. These were all working-class lads from villages in the Ukraine and so on. Kids who never really had a chance, you know, cannon-fodder. Very much like the make-up of the American army in Vietnam, a lot of blacks and poor kids who couldn't pay their way out, who just had to do their military service there.

Three other women rode on the tank convoy from Jalalabad with me. It was quite rare for a woman to be there. I had quite a battle to persuade the general to take women on the convoy.

I went up to the general on the tarmac and I shouted at him, "Look, you're preventing us from doing our jobs!" I remember screaming at him, "If a woman can give birth, she can go to war!" And he said, "Right, if that's you're attitude, then get on the plane!"

So we all got on the plane and went down to Jalalabad.

We were given the option of sitting inside the tank or sitting on top. If we were inside the tank and the tank ran over a mine, we'd be dead. On the other hand, if we sat on top of the tank, we were vulnerable to snipers. We all chose to sit on top, really because it was so hot, and also we were dressed in civilian clothes, and we hoped that the Afghans would see that and not shoot at us.

The worst thing that happened to me, as the tank-convoy pulled out, was that I got hit in the mouth with a piece of camel dung. The crowd at Jalalabad threw all sorts of things at us as we moved out. They were there with these flags and flowers, but among the flowers they had nails and stones and God knows what.

It took all day to get to Kabul. The worst thing, in fact, in the end was that I couldn't go to the toilet. You see, the convoy wasn't allowed to stop anywhere along the road because of the Mujahideen holding the territory through which we were passing. It was OK for the men because they could just piss off the sides of the tanks, but the women couldn't do that. That actually was the worst thing about the trip. It was very dusty. I wanted to drink but I was controlling what I drank because I knew it would make me need to piss. So for the whole journey, we couldn't go to the toilet, and in the end that just took your mind off everything else.

After we got to Kabul, the Soviets continued in the convoy, and we flew up to the border. We were put in a military transport plane. It was one of those planes where people sit down the aisle facing each other, hanging onto a rope. The center aisle was piled with red paper flags for the waving-good-bye ceremony in Uzbekistan. Then somebody lit a cigarette, and I just about went ballistic! I yelled, "Put that cigarette out!" Everyone looked at me as if I was bonkers, but we were literally in a flying waste-paper basket. Everybody obeyed me. Not a single man dared smoke for the entire flight after that.

I found in myself reserves of strength I didn't know I had. Basically, I'm a coward, but I found reserves of physical resilience and also authority that I didn't realize I had. And as soon as I was away from the war, of course, those strengths were gone again.

The experience was very, very frightening, and I went through it once, but it isn't anything I want to repeat. I was frightened for my life most of the time. I wouldn't want to go to a war zone again.

Russians have moved on. The whole Chechnya disaster has overtaken Afghanistan as an issue. And, to be honest, most Russians don't even think about Chechnya now, unless they happen to have a loved one there.

You can see the consequences of both of these wars when you're driving around Moscow. You see invalids in wheelchairs or on crutches, begging at crossroads and on the sidewalks. You can tell from the age of the beggar whether he was disabled in Chechnya or Afghanistan.

Apart from that, unless you were there, you don't really think about it. The Russians have got their own economic problems now to worry about. Only at the very end of the war in Afghanistan did the Russian media talk about it at all. For years, even if you had a loved one there, you didn't really know it was going on. The coffins started coming home, and whispers went around, but no talk. Eventually people began to realize what was happening, but not immediately. If you didn't have anybody there, it didn't affect you very much.

It was very much, again, like Vietnam for the Americans. It was a war for those who were involved, but most of society wasn't really touched by it.

Therefore, you have the resentment of the veterans, who think, "My God, we did all that and no body cares about us." Add to that the fact that Afghanistan was a shameful war, a war that the Soviet Union lost.

There were a few dissidents around at the time, and I'm sure they all opposed it. I can't remember now, but there certainly wasn't the mass Mothers' Movement that there is now against the war in Chechnya. And that, of course, is because there was a completely free media, and night after night coverage of the war in Chechnya. There was nothing like that during the Afghan war. There were only government lies, or silence.

Shekeba (thirty-two years old)

I have been in Pakistan for five years. We left Kabul and came directly to Islamabad, where we are still living.

The Mujahideen did not allow us to bring anything out of Afghanistan.

When the Russians came to our country, they were in Mazar-e-Sharif. I was in the second class in Mazar at the time. All the people in my family were very sad because the Russians had an idea to take over our country.

I was afraid of the Russian soldiers. I saw Russian women, too many of them, when they came to search my house. I felt very sad and afraid.

The Russians put land mines in my grandfather's house. Two of our nephews died from that. The meat from their bodies was on the walls, and ceiling. There was blood and small pieces of child flesh everywhere.

After the Russians left, the Mujahideen started fighting each other for power. I was very happy that the Russians left our country, and I thought there would be peace, but there was no peace.

I remember a very bad fight. Rockets fell. I saw a lot of people murdered in the street. I helped the women as best as I could. Our house was turned into a hospital for people too injured to be moved. That rocket attack killed almost one hundred and fifty people. Lots more were injured.

I was very sad to leave Afghanistan, but we had no future there. We learn to live with broken hearts.

Sameema-Bibi's house in Jalozai Camp is very poor. She has been waiting for us to come before she lights her fire of small sticks. She greets me warmly, clasping my hand between two of hers, and smiling her welcome. She insists that, as a guest, I sit in the place of honor, on a cushion beside the little metal-box stove.

Sameema-Bibi

I am seventy-six years old. I come from Laghman province. I came to Pakistan ten years ago. I live here with my son.

When I lived in Kabul, I had several sons. Khalk and Parcham arrested two of them, and I never heard from them again. I came here with the rest of my sons, four others, because I was afraid for their lives.

One of the four was taken by police. I don't know why. There's been no news for a long time, so he's probably dead, too.

I've never been to school, but I taught myself to read.

We had a good life in Afghanistan until the Russians were there. They came to my house, grabbed the keys, opened all the boxes, looked in everything. There was a lot of fighting. Sometimes there was bombing.

When I was a girl, life was comfortable. There was peace, no trouble. The trouble started when the Russians occupied our country. They took my sons, and I had to leave Afghanistan.

It was a difficult trip. We traveled in the very dark of night. The driver of the car couldn't turn the lights on, because if the Russians saw the lights, they would drop bombs on us.

We always had a lot of guests in our house, or we went to other people's houses. There was a lot of food. Everything was cheap.

There were lots of Russians in Kabul. I saw Russians all the time. They kept coming into my house, looking for things.

I met lots of Russian women, too, in Jalalabad and in Kabul. A doctor in Afghanistan had a Russian wife. He was killed by his wife. She strangled him with his own necktie. Could be she was a Russian agent. We heard lots of stories of Russian women who killed their Afghan husbands if the husbands were against Russia.

Shabona (twenty-six years old)

I have one son. His name is Aliedada. We are from Ghazni, in Central Afghanistan. I am a Hazara [one of the tribes of Afghanistan].

I came to Pakistan four years ago, because of the crimes of the Jihadis. There were parties like Gulbuddin Hekmatyar's party, lots of parties. All these parties were fighting. They forced my husband to join or die. That's why we fled. He didn't join. We came here instead.

It was difficult journey. We came by car. The roads were very bad. We went from Ghazni, to Kandahar, Kandahar to Quetta, and Quetta to here.

My husband was a teacher in Afghanistan. He taught third grade. I attended school only up to grade three. It was a very small school. It was twenty years ago. I go now to classes for adult women in the camp. I study Dari, and some books from the Red Cross.

My mother and brothers are still in Afghanistan.

My father was taken to prison in 1978 when the Russians came. We never heard from him again. The Russians attacked our province, and took my father to a prison in Kabul, Pul-I-Charki prison. Most of the intellectuals who were against Russia were taken there. I was seven years old. I remember a little bit about the day that it happened.

It was during the day. Father was in school, teaching. The government sent him a message at school that he should go to the mosque to meet some government people. When he went to that mosque, they arrested him, and sent him to prison nearby. After a few days, they sent him to the prison near Kabul. I remember that seventy or eighty people were taken to prison that day. All were against Russia.

Until I came to Quetta, four years ago, I thought he was alive. All those years, I was thinking of him as alive. In Quetta, I came to know that he is dead. Someone told us that all those prisoners were killed, and buried somewhere in a huge grave.

My father's name was Gulam Haida.

My mother and brothers are still in Afghanistan. Sometimes, I get news. When people come out, they bring news. The Taliban is now in power in my province.

I hope I will go back someday, when the fighting is over. We had a big house in Afghanistan. It was surrounded by lots of trees, lots of fruit trees—apple, almond, apricot, mulberry. I would like to see it again. I will continue to study and hope.

Aliman (forty-eight years old)

We lived in Kabul. I was a teacher of Afghan history, teaching both boys and girls.

We came to Pakistan two years ago.

We had a good life in Kabul, but the Russians changed all that. They forced girls and women to be part of demonstrations against the Mujahideen. They forced women and youth to join organizations. They took the youth to Russia to educate them to be pro-Russia.

We did not take part in any demonstrations. Whenever we saw one, we went the other way, to escape taking part. Nothing happened to us for not taking part.

My husband is an engineer. He is also in this camp.

I saw lots of Russians, both women and men. They were often at seminars given for teachers, not just Russians, but from eastern Europe also.

Lots of Afghan women married Russian men. Most of these marriages were successful. They are now back in Russia.

I was never personally mistreated by the Russians. The Russian language teachers at my school were women. They were kind people and treated the students well.

We opposed the Russians because they occupied our country, imposed their culture on Afghan people, and were anti-Islam. Russia is the main cause of today's disaster, because when Russia invaded Afghanistan, the foreign countries came in and trained and armed the Mujahideen. Those monsters of Afghanistan were worse than the Russians, and now there's the Taliban.

People were happy when the Russians left. They celebrated, just to express their happiness. At that time, though everything was expensive. I blame Russia for that. They wanted everyone to be busy with economic problems. It was hard to find flour. There was a lot of difficulty when the cold weather came.

The Russian troops left in 1989, and the Mujahideen took power in 1992. Until 1992, people were happy, life seemed easier. When the Mujahideen took power, they committed such crimes, it made people forget about the Russians.

AFGHANS IN RUSSIA

The Moscow office of the United Nations High Commission for Refugees (UNHCR) estimates that there are over twenty-three thousand Afghan refugees in Moscow, of which fifteen thousand have been in contact with their office. Only three hundred of these receive direct aid from UNHCR. Most manage somehow on their own, in rooms and apartments all over the city. A small percentage are housed in Laggas, refugee settlements a short distance outside of Moscow.

It is a struggle for Afghan refugees to get officially recognized as refugees. Their lack of documents makes them particularly vulnerable to harassment from police.

There is virtually no mixing between Russian women and Afghan women. Russian women are facing tremendous difficulties of their own, such as being 70 percent of the newly unemployed, enduring drastic drops in incomes for those who are working, and rampant sexism in the workplace, with few enforceable mechanisms available to ensure justice.[1] These difficulties, coupled with a society-wide desired amnesia around the Afghan War, means that Afghans move like ghosts through Russian society. Unfortunately, they are still visible to the police and to neofascists, who regularly harass Afghans and others who do not look Russian.

The Afghan government sent many Afghan students to Russia for higher education. When the system changed, many of these young women and men were still in Moscow. They were asked to pay for their education. Those who had no money had to leave school. They were not able to afford to go home, and their connections, however tenuous, to the former regime would put them at risk back in Afghanistan.

Some of the Afghans living in Russia supported the Soviets during the occupation. The more recent arrivals, however, fled to Moscow because they saw it as a gateway to Europe and North America. For most, the gateway has become a brick wall, a dead end that has left them stuck in Moscow, unable to work without documents, and unable to go anywhere else without money.

(Hanifa and her husband, a medical doctor, and their twelve-year-old son are my guides to the Afghan community in Moscow. I talk with Hanifa and her family in the single room they share with other Afghan families. The room is furnished like many Afghan homes, with mattresses, or toshaks, along the walls, and a tall cupboard standing in one corner to hold their belongings. Their apartment building is in a forest of identical, eyesore buildings built during the Soviet era.)

Hanifa

I was a journalist in Afghanistan, specializing in reports on women, families, and education. I was also a high school teacher. I taught literature.

Before 1979, Kabul was an ordinary city, quiet, very nice to live in. Women could walk about with their heads and faces uncovered, like in most other cities in the world.

My husband is a doctor, and for awhile, after the Soviet invasion, we lived outside Afghanistan, in Paris, where my husband got further training. We went back to Kabul in 1986, because we were worried about our families, and because we wanted to be of service to our own people. My husband began work with Doctors Without Borders, and I divided my time between teaching, journalism, and volunteering with Afghan Women's Association.

The people of Kabul were having a lot of problems at that time. The religious parties poisoned food and drinking water. They killed lots of teachers, or poured acid on them. Also there were many explosions of land mines and rockets.

When the Mujahideen came into power, everything got worse. They were fighting each other, and the battles for Kabul were terrible. There were many rockets and there was much death.

We changed our address nine times during that time, trying to find a place that was safe from the bombing. Once we went to a place in the north of the city, where my husband was one of only four doctors for half a million people. There was no running water, hardly any food.

I kept up my work with the Afghan Women's Association. We had eight hundred members, and we tried to make things easier for Afghan women and children. It was difficult, because people kept moving around during the bombing, and Kabul was often in chaos.

Under the Taliban, things got even worse. It became impossible for women to go out. The Taliban were watching everywhere, hitting women who went out, hitting men who didn't have beards. One thousand people disappeared, just in one section of Kabul, soon after the Taliban took over.

One night, the Taliban came into our home, and demanded proof that my husband and I were married! They spent three hours yelling at us that we were lying, even though my son was right there with us! They were also angry with us because we had lived abroad, and we were both educated.

Four times they came and wanted to kill us. I don't know why they didn't. They accused us of drinking alcohol and eating pork. They said, "Doctors can't believe in God."

We left Kabul soon after. We left behind all the nice furniture and things we had bought in Paris, all our books, everything I wrote, all my articles, everything.

The night we left Kabul, there was a battle between the Taliban and the Mujahideen. It was taking place right where we were. We were on the front lines! We drove through the streets with our car lights off, so we wouldn't draw attention to ourselves.

We went to Mazar-e-Sharif. A trip that would generally take less than a day took us almost three days. We spent the first night in a cave. There were six dead bodies right in front of us, at the opening of the cave.

We paid some smugglers to take us to Dushambe, then we paid more smugglers to get us to Moscow. And so here we sit. We live in one room, and share the bathroom and kitchen with another family. We have no visa, no permission to be here, no papers. Whenever we go out, we have to watch out for the police. The Moscow police go after foreign people. They know we have no papers, and they take us to jail until our families can pay them money to get us out.

Once, my husband was taken to jail for having no papers. I was teaching at the time, in a small school we have set up for Afghan refugee children. My son went down to the police station to get my husband out. We didn't have money, so my son talked the police into letting my husband out! He kept saying, "My father is a good man, he is a doctor, he is not a criminal!" My son is only twelve. I guess the police were impressed with him, because they let my husband go.

THE WOMEN IN THE STAIRWELL

The Afghan Refugee Center in Moscow is near the Sevastoposkaya Metro Station. Also known as the Afghan Business Center, and the Sevastoposkaya Guest House, the center is made up of three tall buildings in a concrete yard. The yard is fenced in, and a turnstile moderates the flow of people in and out. A few temporary shops have been set up outside the yard, selling Russian bread and groceries. Inside the fence, a couple of Afghan men cook kebabs on an open grill.

Afghans coming to the Center from the metro station keep their eyes open for the police, often taking a circular route to avoid a police car. This area is like shooting fish in a barrel for Russian police, who are eager for a few shake-down roubles from vulnerable Afghans.

I meet Hanifa and her husband outside, and we go into the main building together. A Russian guard stops us and asks our business. Luckily, Hanifa's husband has called ahead and made an appointment for us. Once the guard has called up to confirm, we are waved through. We take the elevator up to the tenth floor.

We wait in a sitting room with heavy furniture and deep red carpets and drapes. In a short while, we are invited into the office of Mr. Gulam Mohammad.

Mr. Mohammad, a Pushtun and a former General in the Afghan Army, is the general director of the Afghan Refugee Center. His office is full of more heavy furniture, including a long table that extends out from his desk to form the shape of a T. The television set is on. "Smokey and the Bandit" provides a strange background of sounds to our discussion.

Gulam Mohammad

The Russian people respond badly to Afghans. They give us nothing. This Center is totally Afghan funded. We get no government money, no UN money. Physically, the Russians accept us as human, but under the law, they do not accept us. Afghans have no right of immigration to Russia.

Afghans are here on Russian government graces. Afghan women in childbirth are not allowed into Russian hospitals, unless they can pay, of course, but Afghan women have no money to pay. When our people die, we have no place to bury them. The government charges three thousand American dollars to bury them. Without the money, the body is cremated. Under Islam, this is very bad.

He is called to other business, and we do a quick tour of the tenth floor. There is a big kitchen where a group of men are busy dishing up platters of rice and meat for another group of men who have taken a break in their meeting. One of the rooms is used as a mosque, but we are not able to go in, as there are prayers going on inside. Around another dark corner is the office of the first Afghan newspaper in Russia. Farooq Fardah is the Editor.

Farooq Fardah

The biggest problem faced by Afghans in Russia is the lack of documents. With no papers, it is difficult for Afghans to get money. Certainly they can get no official jobs. There is no way for them to claim any human rights. The police harass Afghans and other foreigners regularly. They arrest them and hold them for money. Afghans have no way to complain about this.

The tour of the center continues. Hanifa's husband opens a stairwell door, and motions for me to go through. I oblige, thinking we are going up or down to the next floor. I stop cold on the landing. The stairwell is full of women and children.

"These are newcomers from Afghanistan," Hanifa says. "They live in the mosque, but whenever there are prayers, or men want to use the space for a meeting, the women and children must come into the stairwell."

Aziza

I am from Herat. My three children, my husband, and myself left there fifty days ago. First we went to Turkmenistan, then we came to Moscow. We left Afghanistan because of the Taliban. My husband was found in Ismail Khan's army of Herat, and the Taliban consider him an enemy.

We have been living in the mosque for forty days now. The guest house give us rice and bread three times a day, but we have no money for anything else. My husband goes out everyday to try to find work as a porter. He is not often successful.

Malali

We arrived here twenty days ago. We are from Mazar-e-Sharif. We left Mazar just before the Taliban attacked the city a second time. Now they have taken Mazar, and we are lucky to be out.

I am an engineer. I graduated from the University of Kabul. I have two daughters.

We have no visas, no official permission to be in Moscow. We were brought here by smugglers from Tajikistan. It cost $250 each.

We spend many hours everyday in this stairwell. It is not a good place for children.

There are four other families living in the mosque, and new people arrive almost everyday. The children are all ill, and there is no medical care. It is cold

Women in the stairwell.

in this stairwell and it is cold in the mosque at night. There are not enough blankets. It will be very difficult when the winter comes.

I go back to the Guest House a few times during my stay in Moscow, bringing bags of food and a few other things they need. Each time I go, there are more families in the mosque, and more desperation.

THE REST HOUSE ZELENOGRADSKAYA

Mr. Gulam Mohammad has arranged for me to visit a Lagga, an Afghan refugee settlement. I wait with Hanifa and her family inside the subway station for our guide. When he arrives, we go outside to the train station and stand in the chilly sunshine waiting for the right train.

People stand at the front of the train car, holding up items for sale and giving a sales pitch to the travelers. Each salesperson waits her turn. The stream of sellers is endless, but orderly. Two small girls sing a song, then move down the aisle, collecting roubles and kopeks for their efforts.

Zelenogradskaya is a tiny station in the midst of a thick evergreen and white-birch forest an hour outside of Moscow. We get out of the train and cross the tracks to a small clearing, where a few shops have set up business.

A rusty sign over a footpath points the way to the Rest House Zelenogradskaya. The path leads through a beautiful wooded area. Several buildings are in ruins among the trees. Among the ruins, two Kurdish women have set up a nan bakery, and some Afghan men have set up a kebab grill. A few make-shift tables out front turn the ruins into a cafe in the woods. This used to be a Soviet holiday camp, where groups of workers and their families would come for their annual vacation from the factory and the city. A huge sign in the side of the building harkens back to those days.

A Russian guard sits behind a glassed-in booth, just inside the Rest House, and accepts my passport without a smile. We head up the winding, uneven, cement steps. The inside of the building is in an appalling state of disrepair. The hallways are dark, with floorboards ripped and pushed up. There are holes in the walls, and the smell of rot is heavy.

Thirty-five Afghan families and twenty Kurdish families live in this Lagga. The UNHCR helps some of the families with rent and food, but not many families, and the help is not enough. Still, there is a waiting list to move here, and to other Laggas. There are few novelties at the holiday camp, and we soon have an entourage of children and parents who follow us around.

Wazhma (nineteen years old)

I have been in Russia for six years. I have not been to school since I have been here.

I miss Afghanistan. I miss my friends there, I miss everything.

For fun, the only thing to do here is go to someone else's room, or have someone visit you in your room. There's nothing else to do. There are no facilities for sport. Some of the families are fanatics, and they wouldn't allow their daughters to do sports, anyway.

Hakemah (thirty-nine years old)

[Interviewed by Hadi Kolam, Kurdish representative at the Lagga]

I am from Herat Province. Seven years ago, I was forced to abandon my fatherland, Afghanistan. It is so hard to live in foreign lands. We did what we had to do. My husband was an army colonel, therefore we had to leave.

Where else would we go but to Moscow? Afghanistan and Russia are ancient neighbors and friends. I had to save the life of my seven children.

Unfortunately, the Russians do not appreciate the value of friendship. When they arrived in our country, we gave them flowers, bread, and smiles. In contrast, they drank our blood.

This camp is full of hardship and pain. We are living in a small room without a kitchen, a shower, or hot water. It is like a jail. Our daily life is not more than housework, and sitting with our hands around our knees, thinking about our children's fate, and the fate of our homeland.

Much I have suffered from the Russian winter. It's really tiresome and horrible.

Meeting or talking with Russians seldom happens, only when we go to the market. The vagrants, thieves, and Mafia threaten our lives. In addition, the Russian police harm us. I am afraid when I have to go out from my home to buy things.

When the Mujahideen took the reins of government, my husband was in hiding. By many ways they tried to arrest him. Some Mujahideen watched our home all the time, and searched our home regularly, hoping to catch him. They made our friends afraid to help us with some of our basic needs, such as drinking water. It is my last bitter memory of my ruined country.

Some of the women have set up a library in one of the vacant rooms. They received some help from the wife of Gulam Mohammad, of the Afghan Refugee Center. It provides a place for people to go. The walls are lined with bookshelves. There are a few books in Dari and Pushtun, and some children's books in Russian. Lots of people use it everyday, and the women who organized it show it off with pride.

Nooria

We came here through Iran. We have been here for ten months. We have four small children.

My husband was working in the Ministry of the Interior in Afghanistan. When the Taliban came to power, they arrested him, put him in prison, and beat him. After they released him, we sold our house for very little money, and went to Iran.

Things were not good in Iran, so we went to Turkmenistan. We paid a smuggler to get us to Moscow. We spent ten days in the Mosque at the Sevastoposkaya Guest House, then we came here.

The drinking water is two kilometers from the Lagga. People haul it back here in jugs. It still has to be boiled to make it fit to drink. There is no hot water, and no place to bathe, except at the sink. Many people here have arthritis and rheumatism.

Adela

I am a chemist. My husband and I left Afghanistan in 1997, six months after the Taliban took over Kabul. My husband is a graduate of the School of Journalism in Kabul. Here he sells things in the market, does any kind of work he can find that will pay him something.

The Taliban took everything from us, liberty, work, everything. As an educated woman, to be covered by the *burqa* was horrible. I felt ashamed, like a criminal. I did not like to have my face covered up.

It was a very difficult journey to get here. We had three children with us. We had to cross a desert, and the car we were in often broke down. We went from Afghanistan to Pakistan, then to Iran, then to Russia.

We decided to come to Russia because Russia is more like a European country than Pakistan or Iran, where women have no liberty.

We came to Moscow in the hopes of educating our children, but the schools here refuse to let them in. When we came here, I had a lot of hopes, but all my hopes have been dashed.

Fezia (forty-three years old)

[Interviewed by Hadi Kolam]

I had to leave Kabul in August of 1992 when the Mujahideen came to rule and scare the Afghan people. My husband was an active journalist who intensively fought against ignorance and illegal drugs. I also worked as a journalist, preparing religious broadcasts.

Women meant nothing to the Mujahideen, especially those who had worked with the Communist regime. We felt no safety when they came to power.

We came to Russia because we thought the Russians would be sympathetic to our suffering, because they are our friends and must understand what happened to us.

But you see this very small room where we are living with our five children! We cannot move freely. This one room is our bedroom, bathroom, water-closet, kitchen, children's play area, and place for reading. Russia contributes nothing to our aid, which comes to us from UNHCR and a French charity organization.

One of our daily duties is carrying water from the well almost a mile away. We spend our time just taking care of this tiny room, sweeping, washing, and taking care of the children. Sometimes if we find an old newspaper or book to read, it helps us forget our pains.

Please don't ask me to remember the winter. I feel fear and unrest during the long Russian winter. It is a time of death for us, living in such conditions. When the winter comes, we cannot even go to the balcony. Most of the people here do not have proper winter clothes, so must stay inside.

Afghanistan was our home. I often think of my job, the way I was out working everyday. I could never imagine my life being hopeless like today. Up until the last minute before the Mujahideen took power, I was preparing my radio program.

Before the Russians came, we had a quiet life. Afghanistan is beautiful. People were living comfortably. We owned a house and lived without problems.

After the Russians arrived unending fighting covered Afghanistan from the south to the north. People didn't like Russian culture. A lot of people went into the mountains and became Mujahid, and waged war against the Russians and against Afghans, too.

Many people in Afghanistan have lost members of their families. My sister's daughter was killed in Jalalabad, and another one of our relatives was killed by the Mujahideen.

I forgot to say farewell to my mother. She was standing by the door, watching me leave, and she asked me to return to her as soon as peace came to Afghanistan. She died before I could get back to her.

Nazaneen (twenty-seven years old)

[Interviewed by Hadi Kolam]

My husband was educated in the Soviet Union, and the Mujahideen considered him to be a foe. The Mujahideen acted savagely with their opponents and killed the intellectuals, especially anyone they suspected of any kind of contact with the Soviets.

When we decided to leave Afghanistan, we thought it would be best to go directly to Moscow and apply to the Russian authorities for shelter and security. Alas, it was a dream!

We cannot exist without rights. My life is a gradual death. I spend all my time trying to bring up my two small children, washing clothes, sweeping and cleaning the room, cooking in the bathroom.

We have freezing weather in Russia every winter, very different from our winter in Afghanistan. We have no hot water to wash in, and no safe water to drink. The rooms here are cold and damp, with mice and bugs.

We try to have good relations with Russian people, but unfortunately, they don't like people with black hair and dark skin. It is a corrupt culture.

The Russian police treat us unjustly and inhumanely. They arrested our thirteen-year-old child just for being on the street without papers. They impose high penalties on us, and hit us and other refugees whenever they like.

We are invited to an engagement party taking place in the Lagga that evening, but Hanifa is beginning to feel ill, so we decide to head back to the city.

It is dusk as we walk back through the woods along the footpath. There is a smell of woodsmoke in the chilly air. It feels like northern Ontario.

Some people from the Lagga are walking with us out to the train tracks. I watch through the back windows of the train as they wave good-bye long after the train has pulled out of the station.

NOTE

1. UNHCR Moscow Office.

HOLY WARRIORS

The Soviet invasion of Afghanistan prompted contradictory changes in the life of Afghan women. For some, it advanced their emancipation in the shape of greater opportunities for education, training, and employment. For others, it meant the destruction of their homes from bombs and rockets, and the death of family members from land mines. For those who were fighting with the Mujahideen, it meant enhanced standing in the community and the opportunity to learn new skills, such as the organizing of rallies and the use of firearms. For some it meant torture and imprisonment in Soviet prisons and private Mujahideen jails. For many, it meant exile to the stifling existence of a refugee camp.

After the Soviets pulled out of Afghanistan, the changes became more uniform. Heavily armed and funded Mujahideen groups battled each other for control of the country and imposed fundamentalist restrictions on women as an extension of their control. Security for women became nonexistent, as their homes were invaded and their bodies were used as rewards for victorious soldiers.

Mujahideen groups were fighting the Kabul government as early as 1975.[1] They attacked People's Democratic Party of Afghanistan (PDPA) symbols such as police stations, army posts, and anyone considered to be associated with the government, including teachers. They bombed schools, offices, and development projects.

Mujahideen groups were receiving U.S. aid even before the Soviet invasion. As soon as the Russians entered, aid increased. On September 22, 1981, Egyptian President Anwar Sadat said in a television interview with NBC that as soon as the Soviets crossed the border, the Americans contacted him to arrange transport of weapons from Egypt to the rebels, on U.S. planes.[2]

Egypt, Pakistan, and China supplied the rebels with bazookas, mortars, grenade launchers, land mines, rifles, and shoulder-fired anti-aircraft missiles. These were largely Russian-made weapons supplied through Egypt. The Soviet origin of the weapons was useful to the Americans, who did not want U.S. technology falling into the hands of the Communists in the event of capture. It also allowed them to perpetrate the myth that the guerrillas were arming themselves with weapons taken from dead Communist soldiers.[3]

The image of the brave mountain men, fighting the mighty "Godless Communists" with only a rifle slung around their shoulders and a blanket draped across their backs made good television. Media flocked to Peshawar, and the various Mujahideen groups competed against each other for attention. Some employed English-speaking spokesmen to increase their chances of getting on television.[4]

Refugees began pouring into Pakistan and Iran to escape the Soviet bombing of villages. Many of the families in the camps were headed by women, whose husbands were either dead or off fighting in the *jihad*. Humanitarian aid agencies swarmed into the area. Peshawar came to resemble a Wild West town, with all the major Mujahideen parties having their headquarters there.

Anti-Afghan feelings did not take long to surface in Pakistan, as the massive influx of people and their grazing animals created environmental and economic problems.[5] Many Pakistanis resented that the Afghan refugees were being given food, shelter, and an allowance without having to work for them.[6]

Not everything was on the up and up. In 1980, a UN representative, after touring the camps, told the London *Guardian* he was appalled at how much aid went into the black market.[7] Afghan guerrillas also padded their pockets with money from heroin trafficking. Although the U.S. government knew of this, and knew it was being done, in part, by Gulbuddin Hekmatyr, the largest recipient of U.S. aid, it chose to do nothing.[8]

Women alone in the camps often found themselves at the mercy of the camp commander and his officials. Humanitarian aid was always given to the camp commander to distribute. Some went out the back door to the black market, some got to where it was supposed to go, and some was withheld from women who withheld sexual favors.[9]

The women who fought the Russians alongside the male members of the Mujahideen had the right to expect that a just society of some sort would emerge when the Soviets had finally gone. Women in the Nuristan Province, for example, engaged the Communists in battle just as the men did. The newspaper, the *Nuristan Front*, said, with pride, that its women "offered their blood for the Islamic revolution like red tulips at springtime."[10] However, the promised paradise was not to be.

The Communist government fell in 1992, and the country plunged into the horror of many different factions battling for control. The rights and dignity of women went out the window. As part of the war, women were abducted, raped, threatened with death and even murdered in front of their families.[11]

The constitution was thrown out and was replaced by the Islamic State of Afghanistan.

On August 27, 1993, the Supreme Court of the Islamic State of Afghanistan issued a ruling on the veil and other matters concerning women's behavior. Using as its justification the argument that men are too excited by women and therefore tempted away from the Islamic way of life, the ruling listed a number of restrictions on women's freedom and mobility. It declared that women should be completely covered. They should not be perfumed, wear clothes similar to men's, wear makeup, or have Western-styled hair. They should be educated only at home by fathers, brothers, or other close relatives, and they should only learn the basics of Islam, not worldly subjects. It ruled that girls should not be taught to write, because they would only use that skill to write love letters to strange men.[12]

The incidents of grave human rights abuses grew. Many people were arrested and held in order to get money from their relatives.[13] There were private jails all over Afghanistan and Pakistan, some inside the refugee camps, where people were held without due process. Thousands of civilians disappeared into the jails. Torture was routinely practiced. Women in custody would be raped and sexually assaulted.[14] Amnesty International has documented the case of a woman who was arrested on the street in Kabul by two armed Mujahideen guards who took her to a private detention center where twenty-two "Freedom Fighters" raped her for three days. When she was finally allowed to go home, she found her three small children dead from hypothermia.[15]

All of the warring parties were involved in torturing their prisoners. Sometimes guards would perpetrate torture in the victims' homes, sometimes even on the street, to show off their brutality.[16] Ethnic and religious minorities were often a focus for their hatred.[17]

Women were being killed for being out after curfew on the way to the hospital to give birth. Women and children were shot by snipers when they went to get water from one of the few water taps that was still working. Parents were assassinated for allowing their daughters to go to school.[18]

Everyday, in every way, women were betrayed.

THE MONSTER: GULBUDDIN HEKMATYR

There are many eligible for the title "Most Vicious Warlord." All have blood on their hands. Most of the Mujahideen parties can claim ownership of atrocities, massacres, and gross violations of human rights, but for sheer consistency of destruction the title must go to the Hezb-e Islami party of Gulbuddin Hekmatyr.

Sibghatullah Mujaddedi, one of the more moderate of the resistance leaders, has called Hekmatyr a monster who has killed more innocent Afghans than the Soviets did.[19] Hekmatyr, born in 1947, studied engineering at the University of Kabul, where one of his favorite recreational activities was throwing acid in the faces of female students who did not wear the veil.[20] (At that time, especially in Kabul, a veil was not legally necessary, nor was it customary.) Sadly, his propensity for vile behavior and his proven track record of hatred for women did not prevent him from becoming a prime candidate for receiving U.S. aid.

Gulbuddin fled Afghanistan for Pakistan after Daoud took over in 1973, and by 1975, at age twenty-eight, he had become a leader in a Mujahideen group. With the help of the Bhutto government of Pakistan, he led attacks into Afghanistan to try to destabilize the government.[21]

During the Soviet occupation, the United States sent $6 billion worth of military aid to the guerrilla groups. More than half of this went to Hekmatyr's organization.[22] Not only did he fight the Communists, he also fought against the Mujahideen groups, sometimes in the same battle! With so many resources at his disposal, he expanded his "empire" to become Afghanistan's main drug lord of the day.[23]

The U.S. government knew exactly where their money was going, and continued giving Gulbuddin money and military aid even after the Soviets pulled out.[24] In addition to being a rabid anti-Communist, he was a rabid anti-Shi'a. The United States hoped he would keep Iran on edge, thereby furthering U.S. policy in the region. His human rights record was not a deterrent. One CIA official said that the United States supported Hekmatyr because "fanatics fight better."[25]

Like some of the other Mujahideen groups, Gulbuddin had private jails and torture chambers in Afghanistan and Pakistan. Shamshatu Refugee Camp, fifteen kilometers north of Peshawar, was home to one of his prisons. Another was found as far away as Karachi.

In addition to terrorizing the civilian population, Gulbuddin is in large part responsible for the destruction of Kabul. After the fall of the Communists in 1992, the leaders of the warring factions formed themselves into a sort of government. Hekmatyr was prime minister until late 1994. Most of Kabul was controlled by an alliance led by the Jamiat-e Islami. Hekmatyr's party led an alliance which controlled the rest. Out of concern for his security, Hekmatyr lived outside the capital. Wanting complete control, he sent a carpet of rockets and bombs into Kabul, terrorizing civilians and almost completely destroying the city.[26]

He became prime minister in 1996, in alliance with Rabbani, in order to try to keep the Taliban at bay[27] after the Taliban captured his headquarters south of Kabul in 1995.[28] He is now in exile in Iran, but a man with such a hunger for destruction is not likely to be idle for long.[29]

On February 20, 1995, a group of women and children, relatives of those who had been victimized by Hekmatyr inside Pakistan, demonstrated outside of the Ministry of the Interior in Islamabad.[30] The Mujahideen fundamentalists, especially but not exclusively Hekmatyr and his party, are responsible for abducting and killing thousands of Afghan intellectuals and people of skill, as well as murdering many, many thousands in rocket attacks. It will be a long time before Afghanistan can recover from such a tremendous loss.

Georg, Shelter Now International

I have been in Peshawar since 1984. Until 1992, the camps held mostly rural Pushtuns. The camps were controlled by the Mujahideen. There was a *jihad* atmosphere in Peshawar, a very conservative atmosphere.

In 1992, the Kabul government fell, and Peshawar had a large influx of Kabuli people. For awhile there were ten thousand Kabulis living in the desert outside Jalalabad. Thirty-five thousand of them settled in Nasir Bagh. This is one of the older camps where the conservative refugees lived. This caused a lot of descension. The older refugees called the Kabulis infidels and communists.

Peshawar was just flooded with refugees. Anyone with a relative outside the camps would squeeze in with them. Only those with no choice went into Nasir

Bagh and the other camps. Until May of that year, the UN registered the refugees, but stopped in June because the influx was too great.

Most of the new refugees in Nasir Bagh lived in tents. These people were teachers, doctors, army officers, civil servants, people with Ph.D.s. One man with a Ph.D. from a French university wandered around the camp for years, his Western suit and briefcase becoming shabbier and shabbier. He went quite mad.

In 1990, our projects in Nasir Bagh were completely destroyed. We had worked in Nasir Bagh for seven years at that point. We worked with five hundred camp residents and built one thousand houses. We had a milk distribution center which gave milk to ten thousand children a day.

At the request of the social welfare division of UNHCR, we built a compound in the widows' section of the camp. This women's center had walls all around it and a door in the wall that was guarded. No men were allowed in there. Inside was a sewing project, a vegetable garden, a children's playground, a big kitchen where the women could cook food together, a place for courses to be held, a place for women to do things together without men looking at them and judging them.

Problems started very soon. Men threw stones and rocks over the walls. Gulbuddin's party operated a school and threatened to expel any student whose mother went to the women's center. Someone claimed to see women on a swing, and said it was a sin for women to do that. We had to tell the women to stay off the swings. The men accused us of taking pictures of the women. They accused us of all kinds of things.

During Ramadan, Gulbuddin's party started to stir up more problems. They made a plan against us.

On the first day of Eid, they preached in the mosque, and said if the men did not destroy the women's center, none of the prayers they said during Ramadan would be answered.

The men ran from the mosque to the camp and completely destroyed the center. They tore down beams, ripped up the gardens, looted, smashed everything until there was nothing left. Then they attacked the girls' school and destroyed that, including the chairs.

SNI had a factory in Nasir Bagh for making building supplies. The crowd of men destroyed that next. The car-repair place, six trucks that were inside it, 175 tons of milk powder, tons of steel and cement, everything was smashed, burned, and looted. We had planted three thousand trees, and these were ripped from the ground. Three thousand chickens were stolen or destroyed. Many widows' homes were destroyed.

All of this began in the morning of Eid, and lasted until the next morning. There was nothing left. Even concrete slabs had been smashed. When there was nothing left above ground to demolish, they ripped up tree roots to destroy. Police chased the looters away, then filled up their own cars with milk powder.

It was very evil, this stirring up of people that the Mujahideen had done.

These were widows of men killed in the *jihad*. The Mujahideen were not taking care of them, yet it disturbed them that someone else was.

Hoshey Afrasobey

I am the president of the Muslim Women's Society. I am originally from Panjshir, but I was raised and educated in Kabul. We came to Peshawar in 1983.

Our family was Mujahideen, with Gulbuddin Hekmatyr's party. My brothers were put into prison by the Russians. When they got out, they went to Peshawar. We left with them. I wanted to work for women and could not do so in Afghanistan. The police would not let us. They would catch us and put us in prison.

My husband fought with the Mujahideen. His job was in the battle. My brothers' jobs were to organize and do cultural work. In '83, '84, and '85, he was fighting against the Russians. This fighting was done like partisans. They had the support of the people. The people knew that the Russians didn't like Moslems. People took food that was meant for their children and gave it to the Mujahideen.

During this time, the fighting was good, and had good results for Afghanistan.

Some women in the villages were soldiers in the Mujahideen. They would help hide other soldiers in the Mujahideen. They would help hide other soldiers in their homes. They stayed in their own village, though, unless they went with a brother or a father. That was not really necessary, though. There were women in every village to cook and clean for the Mujahideen.

In Kabul, I would carry guns in my purse. I would deliver guns to other Mujahideen.

Our house was a safe house. One night a Mujahid was in our house, because he needed a safe place to spend the night. At that time, I was not married.

This Mujahid was injured. He had a head wound. At three in the morning, my father woke us up and said, "There are Russian soldiers outside in the street. They are searching the houses." During the night, Russian soldiers would often go into people's homes, searching for the Mujahideen, or material about the Mujahideen. My father told us to hide everything in a safe place. My brothers were in Peshawar, so I had a great deal of responsibility. The Mujahid was asleep in our guest room. We were scared, because if he was found, he would be killed, and we would be arrested. All night, we sat up and waited for the soldiers to come.

The Mujahid said, "If the soldiers come to your door, I will go into your bathroom." The bathroom had a small window he could climb out of. "I will tell the Russians, 'I come from outside, I am not from this house.' "

We lived opposite a school. We could see that the soldiers had gathered a lot of men from the houses and put them into the school. There were maybe fifty men.

The morning had come, and I made tea. I brought the tray of tea in to my father and the Mujahid, and the doorbell rang! I dropped the tea. The Mujahid ran into the bathroom. My father went to open the door, but when he opened the door, there was no one there! The doorbell was not working properly!

Even after all this time, I don't know why the soldiers did not come into our house. We believe that God was with us. The soldiers went to all the other houses, but they missed our house! The Mujahid came out of the bathroom, I made some more tea, and we all sat down and had breakfast.

It is a happy thing for me to remember. And that Mujahid is still alive, although his beard is now white.

My mother and cousin were always busy making safe hiding places in the house for guns and things, under the ground, behind walls, lots of places. One night, my mother had several books about the Mujahideen. Soldiers came to the door, and there was no time to hide the books. My mother put the books down the front of her dress, and then put her head scarf around her. The soldiers searched the house, but they could never find anything!

That time was a very good time for us, when the Russians were inside Afghanistan, and we were fighting them. That time was a good time.

Mallali (twenty-eight years old)

I was married for six years before I had to leave Afghanistan.

There was lots of fighting going on. I saw a lot of fighting with my own eyes.

I was right in the war front, where the Mujahideen fought against the Russians. Myself and two other women washed the clothes of the Mujahideen and cooked their food. We took an active part in the resistance of Afghanistan.

I saw many dead bodies. I saw the dead body of my cousin and of some other Mujahideen.

There were three of us women who cooked for six hundred men. We washed clothes for six hundred men. During the night, we carried a gun and took our turn at standing watch.

My brothers and some of my other relatives were at the front, and I wanted to be there to help them. The other men treated me very well. They respected me, and they respected the other two women who were working there with me.

Food was carried in to us from Pakistan on the backs of camels. We got sugar, tea, and beans this way. We also ate beef sometimes. We had to be very careful with these supplies, not to waste anything.

Watch duty at night was for one hour, then someone else took over. Each of us women took a turn. If we noticed something dangerous, we told the men. We were alone on a watch. Sometimes I was afraid of the darkness. Around that area, it is all mountains, and it is very dark during the night.

I saw some Russians once, during an attack. They killed two of my companions.

They trained us with Kalnishnikov's [rifles], but I never had to shoot.

I was in Pakistan when the Russians finally left my country. We came to Pakistan to get away from the war. We had had enough. Many of my relatives were still fighting.

My husband died twelve years ago. My daughter was three months old at the time. He was arrested in Pakistan. Gulbuddin's party arrested him and took him to their prison in the Shamshatu refugee camp, because he was against them. I never heard from him again. I tried for a long time to get information, but I couldn't find out anything. I even tried the Pakistan government. No one would give us any information, so we became sure that he is dead.

After he was arrested, we came to this camp. We have relatives here. Now I live with my mother-in-law and my father-in-law.

What I hope for my daughter is that she will finish school, then do something for her people.

I will not go back to Afghanistan. This camp is my home now.

Alima lives in Jalozai Refugee Camp.

Alima (forty-eight years old)

Life under the Mujahideen was worse than under the Russians. Under their control, there was no certainty that we would be alive from one day to the next. There were lots of rockets and bombs. You never knew when you were going to die. Many girls were attacked and abducted.

We lived in a fifth floor apartment. We had to carry water up from the first floor, because of bomb damage. There was no electricity, no fuel.

Sometimes people would be moving in a long line, from one part of Kabul to another, where they heard there was no fighting. Once I saw a line of about one thousand people. A rocket hit the crowd, and at the same time, a rocket also hit the building where we lived.

During the night, I couldn't sleep. I always thought a rocket would come. I had lots of reports of friends being hurt. Once, a rocket hit a pregnant woman. She died, leaving her five children alone.

A mother and her son were living with a relative of mine. Her son was killed by one of Gulbuddin's rockets. Every night, in the mother's dream, the son would come to her and say, "There's something of me in the yard." After three or four nights of this, the mother went into the yard and found a body part of her son's under a bush.

Two little boys were playing chess, and a rocket came and killed them on the spot. Another girl who had just become engaged was hit by a rocket and died. The shops were closed, and there was no way to buy her a coffin, so her family just wrapped her body in a cloth. Her fiancé wanted to climb into the grave with her.

One of the Mujahideen groups committed an atrocity against a Pushtun woman. She was on her way to the hospital to give birth. They said, "We have seen everything, but we have not yet seen how a woman gives birth." They took her and her husband to an army post, took the woman's clothes off, and watched her have the baby. She died giving birth. The husband took the new baby and left, but came right back again and said, "What life is this that you have left me with—you should kill me also!" And they did.

There was another woman who came to our apartment block from another building. Her husband had been killed by the Russians. A Mujahid came to the house and tried to rape her daughter. The girl resisted, so he killed her with eighteen strokes of the knife. He told the mother if she said anything, he would kill her, too.

In the old Russian embassy in Afghanistan, Hezbollah forces kept two hundred abducted women. All of these women were naked. After awhile, the people in Masaud's army went and saw the women there and told people about it. The government of France asked to have these women sent to France for treatment. The government of Rabanni refused to let them go. No one knows what happened to them.

The old Russian embassy had been turned into a command post for Hezbollah. They used the Culture and Art House, too. Women were also taken there, their breasts were cut off, and they died.

Under Gulbuddin, girls were abducted when they went out to get rice and sent to other parts of Afghanistan, especially central parts, like Razni. Eyewitnesses saw this and told about it.

Another crime of Hezbollah, they would abduct girls from Kabul. They tied their hands, taped their mouths, and sent them to other parts of Afghanistan. Someone saw two girls like this in a car, and stopped the car. There was a man driving the car who said he had driven twenty-three other girls like that. They had been abducted to be sold in Saudi Arabia. We didn't know their names.

The Hezbollah leader was once asked about his crimes. In reply, he said he once saw a six-month-old baby. He wanted to kill the baby, so he put the tip of his bayonet in the child's mouth. The child thought it was a nipple and began to suck. The leader's heart melted, and he decided not to kill the baby. This, he said, is a sign of his goodness.

Seema lives in Shamshatu Refugee Camp near Peshawar, Pakistan.

Seema (thirty-one years old)

My two brothers were with the Mujahideen, with Hekmatyr. They were in battle against the Russians. We are from Lagar Province. I also worked with the Mujahideen.

When I remember that time of fighting, I think, "How are we now alive and eating and everything?" That time was very bad for people, when there was fighting.

In our village, we had a big house. It was bombed, and my grandparents and four of my cousins died. In our religion, we wash the dead before we bury them. I have washed many bodies and dressed them for burial.

My mother and I used to cook for the Mujahideen groups.

Once, during a battle with the Russians, the Mujahideen inside a large compound were running out of bullets. I could tell, because they were firing their guns less and less.

I hid some boxes of bullets in a huge bale of reeds and plants, and started walking toward the compound. The Russians stopped me, and I told them I was taking food to my sheep, inside the compound. My heart was beating so hard! If the Russians were to search my bundle and find the bullets, they would put me in prison, maybe even kill me! But they let me go on my way. They didn't search me.

I stayed inside the compound until dark. We knew that the Russians were watching for us to bring our wounded out so they could capture them. But we fooled them again. We put mud all over a car, to make it harder to see, and we put the injured men inside. I walked far ahead with a small light. If the Russians stopped me, I would just look like a woman alone. The car, far behind me, followed my little light.

We got the men out of the compound, but unfortunately, they still died. We had no medicine. We poured hot oil on the wounds to stop the blood, but they still died.

My sister came from Kabul to join us in the village. She had some education, and she saw that Mujahideen had died without medical attention. This made her decide to become a doctor.

Another time, there was another battle in our village. We lost twenty-five Mujahid that time. We put the wounded men two to a bed and tried to care for them there, because we knew the Russians would watch us if we tried to take the wounded out. We did not eat for three days because we saw so many dead. All the dead were young men that we knew. This was our village, our home. The Mujahideen fighting in the battle were from our village.

We were very angry because the Russians were in our country. I knew that if my brothers and uncles were not fighting the Russians, I would fight the Russians all by myself. Just talking about the Russians, even now, gives me a headache.

I pleaded with my brothers to get me a small bomb, so that I could go beside a Russian tank and destroy it and myself. I would become "*shaheed*," a martyr. They would not let me do this.

I was taught to fire a gun by my cousin, in case I was ever left alone. We were allowed to clean and oil the guns, and to cook and clean the clothes for the Mujahideen.

We were very happy when the Russians left, and we were also very happy when the Mujahideen took power. I was in Kabul when that happened. I went into the streets to watch them come. My relatives did not want me to watch, they said it would not be safe, but I insisted that it was right for me to watch.

I became very sad when the Mujahideen began to fight each other. I was very surprised by their fighting.

The man who taught me how to care for guns came to my house the other day, looking for work. His foot was injured, and he could not walk very well. I became angry at his situation, and felt very sad for him.

Other Mujahideen I know have gone crazy. They are very sad, and they can't understand what has gone wrong in Afghanistan. Myself, I keep busy with my sewing. If I did not sew, I would go mad. I sew, and I teach others to sew.

I have never married. I live in Shamshatu Camp with my mother and others of my family. My sister is a doctor in Hyatabad, a part of Peshawar. One day I would like to go back inside Afghanistan and open a big sewing shop and school, because women in Afghanistan have no jobs. The hands of women in Afghanistan are tied now, and they cannot do anything, so my sewing school will have to wait.

Benazir and I visit Nasreen, Nasreen's sons, and her best friend Masuma in Nasreen's home. We sit together outside the one-room house, in the shelter of the over-hanging roof. Nasreen spends all of her time sitting there, as she is not able to walk. All day, everyday, she sits and looks out at the bare, cement courtyard.

Nasreen (forty years old)

I have three sons, ages twenty-two, eighteen, and sixteen. I am sick. During the time the Russians were in our country, there was much fighting. Our house was destroyed. My middle son and I were badly hurt. His foot is twisted. My spine is twisted. I am not able to walk.

My eldest son is not quite right, either, but he is still able to do some things. He takes me to the lavatory, he washes me. A son should not have to do these things for his mother.

When the Mujahideen came, they destroyed our house again. They stole everything from us. We are from the Old City of Kabul. The Old City no longer exists. It is now level with the ground.

Here is Peshawar, we have one room for three families. I've got an adopted daughter, a good girl. I found her on the street. She had no family, so I took her to live with us. She goes out to do washing in other people's home. Me, I sit here with my son, all day, everyday.

When I was younger, when I got married, I was happy. I had a car, a nice house. I thought that things would get better and better, that Afghanistan would become like Europe. There would be progress everyday. I liked seeing the younger generation go off to school and university. I thought, "One day, all of our nation's girls will be like girls in Europe and the U.S., with high education. They'd be doctors and teachers, and they'd be full of knowledge."

I never imagined everything in my country would be destroyed, that women would be so pushed back. I never dreamed the Taliban could happen. Afghanistan was going forward. And now look at us.

I've lost my husband. I live in poverty in a foreign country. I am like a beggar. In Afghanistan, I attended school up to the eighth class, then got married at sixteen.

In spite of us having such a poor life, please come to visit again. Stay for a longer time.

Masuma

I lost my husband last year. He was sick and nervous all the time. By the time we got to Pakistan, he was quite mad. After a few months here, he died.

Everybody here has depression, all the Afghans. Maybe a few Afghans have a good life, with enough money, but not many.

We had a very bad life in Kabul. We lost everything in a rocket attack. The rocket attack was followed by thieves who stole everything that had not been destroyed. The thieves were Mujahideen.

In Peshawar, the summer is very hot, and the air is very bad. I go from house to house, begging. I spend my life for nothing.

I lost two sons and one daughter in the rocket attack. When the rocket hit, we all ran in different directions, and I never saw them again. I looked and I looked, but we never found each other. Now I am here, and they don't know where I am.

We like to offer our guests everything, but we are quite sick and have no money, so all we can offer you is tea.

Masuma died a few days after this interview.

Benazir

Masuma died very quickly. We pray for her to have a good life in heaven. She died all of a sudden. She was on the phone with her children in America, then she hung up the phone and she died. She was always joking and laughing and then she died.

Katse

Masuma was my aunt. We left Kabul ten years ago. I have four children, two boys, and two girls. My husband sells things from a box along the sidewalk.

Our house in Kabul was destroyed by rockets.

I wash dresses for people to get a little money. I have completed grade twelve in school.

We are very hopeless about our country. There is only land and burnt places left.

We had to collect money from the neighbors to pay the cost of taking Masuma's body back to Kabul. A few relatives went with her. Seven Taliban tried to stop us. "Why do you come out at night from Peshawar? Are you sure that's a dead body?"

We finally got her through. She is buried in the middle of Kabul.

Nasreen

Masuma always came here to clean and cook for us, because I can't walk, and my sons are sick.

Masuma's Niece

Masuma was very kind, friendly, and cheerful. She often came to see us. She was a very good woman, and we were sorry to see her die. Now all the time we pray and remember.

NOTES

1. Edward Giradet and Jonathan Walter, editors, *Essential Field Guide to Afghanistan* (Geneva: Crosslines Communications, 1998), 214.

2. Philip Bonosky, *Washington's Secret War Against Afghanistan* (New York: International Publishers, 1985), 211.

3. Leslie Gelb, *New York Times*, May 3, 1983.

4. Michael T. Kaufman, *New York Times*, March 27, 1980.

5. Stuart Auerback, *Washington Post*, September 1, 1980.

6. Bonosky, *Washington's Secret War*, 163.

7. Ibid., 162.

8. Noam Chomsky, *Deterring Democracy* (Westport, CT: Hill and Wang, 1991), 118.

9. Bonosky, *Washington's Secret War*, 162.

10. Anthony Hyman, *Afghanistan Under Soviet Domination* (New York: Macmillan Press, 1982), 125.

11. Amnesty International, *Women in Afghanistan: A Human Rights Disaster*, London, Nov. 9, 1995.

12. Department of Legal Ruling and Studies of the Supreme Court of the Islamic State of Afghanistan, August 27, 1993.

13. Amnesty International, Afghanistan, *International Responsibility for Human Rights Disasters*, Al Index ASA, Nov. 1, 1994.

14. Ibid.

15. Ibid.

16. Amnesty International, *Focus Magazine* 25, no. 12 (December 1995).

17. Amnesty International, *Executions and Amputations*, A1 Index ASA, Nov. 5, 1995.

18. Amnesty International, *Women in Afghanistan: A Human Rights Disaster*, A1 Index ASA, Nov. 5, 1995.

19. Amnesty International, ASA Index, Nov. 3, 1996.

20. Giradet and Walter, *Field Guide*, 215.

21. Assad Ismi and Farhan Haq, "Afghanistan: The Great Game Continues" *Covert Action Quarterly* no. 59 (winter 1996–97): 47.

22. Giradet and Walter, *Field Guide*, 214.

23. Ismi and Haq, *Afghanistan*, 47.

24. Ibid.

25. Ibid., p. 48.

26. Ibid., 48.

27. Amnesty International, ASA Index, ASA, Nov. 3, 1995.

28. Giradet and Walter, *Field Guide*, 216.

29. Amnesty International, ASA Index ASA, Nov. 3, 1995.

30. *RAWA Magazine* no. 2 (January 1997): 99.

ROCKETS' RED GLARE

The 1997 movie "Armageddon" begins with a meteor shower raining down on New York City. Streaks of fire topple buildings, bore craters into streets, explode gas tanks, and pile cars on top of one another. Ordinary human interaction, with all its glory and banality, comes to a sudden, screaming end. The meteors hit arbitrarily, destroying everything they hit, without regard to beauty or value. A meteor shower is like a rocket attack.

Afghans have been subjected to rockets and bombs for twenty years. As the Americans did in the Persian Gulf, the Soviets waged much of their war in Afghanistan from the air. They bombed civilian targets, destroyed crops and irrigation works.[1]

Over the course of twenty years of warfare, roughly 50 percent of Afghan villages and 25 percent of Afghanistan's paved roads have been destroyed.[2] The bombing continued after the Soviets left. Thousands of people in Kabul have been killed in rocket attacks by fighting each other. Most of these attacks happened without any warning.[3] Since 1992, as many as forty thousand Kabul civilians have been killed, and half a million had to flee their homes.[4] There is very little of the city's infrastructure that has escaped destruction.

Afghanistan continues to be the most heavily mined country on earth. Forty percent of Kabul is infested with mines.[5] According to Handicapped International, in certain sections of southern Afghan, one child out of ten is a prime victim. More than half those injured in mines eventually die from their wounds.

Afghanistan has ten million land mines. Over 30 percent of the land mine victims are children.[6] Four hundred thousand people have been killed by land mines in twenty years of war.[7]

It is difficult to imagine what all this has meant to the Afghan people, to have their homes destroyed by rockets, to have their children blown up by land mines that look like toys, to have this go on for twenty years with no end in sight.

Lila (thirty-five years old)

We lived in one room in Macreon with a few other people. I was a teacher in Chessatun. When that was destroyed, we had nothing.

Dentist

My wife was killed in the bombing, along with my two sons. Her name was Fahima. Two and a half years ago, when the Taliban came to Kabul, there was a rocket attack on the city. I was away from the house at my job, and when I came home, my wife and children were killed.

My wife was very smart. She always got high marks in school. She was always very welcoming of guests, and was very good to me and the children.

Paregal

I have seven children. My husband was injured by thirteen bullets in his leg. The Russians shot him. He was Mujahid.

He sells notebooks on the streets of Peshawar. He gets a little money that way, but not very much. Life is very difficult here.

We come from Laghman. Our house was bombed. Everything there was destroyed.

Alia

We are from Laghman. My house there was bombed and burned.

My husband is here with me. He had a job, but not anymore. He has some psychological problems, and is not able to work.

I have four daughters, but no sons to go out and work for us. My children are not in school. There is no money for notebooks and pens.

Sobra (twenty-two years old)

My husband is sick from a rocket attack. I look after him. I wash clothes and embroider and sew to get money.

A few people live in this room. Their sickness is worse everyday. It is very cold and damp here.

My husband seems like he is very old. His knee was destroyed in a rocket attack. My father-in-law and my sister-in-law are also here. They can't stand up. They are very sick.

I attended school when I was younger and got as far as the fifth class. I was married seven years ago, when I was fifteen. My husband seemed younger then.

There is nothing left of my sister-in-law. She is only skin and bones. She can't walk. She shuffles to the bathroom on her hands and bottom. Once we were all young and healthy and had something to live for, and now look at us.

I am sick, too, but not as sick as the others. Mostly, I am tired.

We live in this one room. We had a very good life in Kabul. We had a house, a car, a telephone, everything. Everything was destroyed by rockets. What was not destroyed was stolen by thieves. We had nothing left. I had to beg for money for us to come here.

My husband's rocket injuries still give him pain, around his stomach and kidney.

I take care of three grown sick people, collect money, and look after my daughter. I go door-to-door looking for people to do washing for. Several people employ me. I am grateful to them. I work for them, but still I am grateful.

Fatima

I have four children. My husband cannot walk. His leg was destroyed by a rocket.

I work in rich people's houses to get bread and money. I take small meals to a school and sell them to the students.

We had a good house in Kabul, in the best neighborhood, but the houses were destroyed and looted. Now there is nothing left.

Laila

Kabul was very dangerous. Many houses were destroyed by rockets, many people lost family members. We came to Peshawar to escape the fighting.

I was in the twelfth class in Kabul. I left my studies, I left my friends, and two of my aunts. We were very poor in Kabul. My father wasn't working. We haven't been back there since we left.

Hozra (twenty-eight years old)

We came from Kabul six years ago.

I remember my daughter's birthday. My husband went to get her birthday cake, and there was a rocket attack. People saw him carrying the cake and said to him, "This is a very awful day, and you bring cake for your family! All the people eat blood, and you eat cake!"

For twenty years, Kabul has run with blood, like a river.

I have three children, two sons and one girl. One child is in school. The others will also go.

I don't like it in Pakistan. I would rather live in my own country, but I don't think things will get better in Afghanistan.

My brother has a shop in the Saddar bazaar. The police regularly take money from him.

There are fifteen people living together in three very small rooms. There are five families living in this one house. The rent is very high. It is difficult to manage with children. People in Kabul think we are rich because we live in Pakistan, but we have nothing to share. People in Afghanistan are very poor.

Hosnow (twenty-three years old)

I came here from Kabul seven years ago, from the Korte-e Paron district. Now it's all destroyed. It was once the best place in Kabul. There were wonderful cinemas, including the Cinema of Europe, very famous, near our house. There were wonderful shops and markets—beautiful homes with big yards. There were bookshops, too. I used to love to go shopping. We could walk along the streets whenever we wanted, without a *burqua*, with no punishment. Now, if you do that, you get beaten with a stick, and often much worse.

Zakia (fifty years old)

Fifteen days ago, I left Kabul. I came here to see the doctor. Soon I have to go back to Kabul. I was hoping to stay in Pakistan, but I have no money and cannot find a job. My husband came here with me. He also has no job.

We lost our house in Kabul in a rocket attack. We go from one place to another. If someone we know has a place to live, we stay with them for as long as we can. When we find a cheap place to rent, we go there for a little while, then we go back to our friends.

Our daughter lives with us. She is eight. I had three sons, but they are all dead, killed in one of Gulbuddin Hekmatyr's rocket attacks.

I used to be a teacher. I have graduated from the University of Kabul, but now I have forgotten everything. I feel now like an illiterate person, not like an educated person. I forgot everything because my nerves are so bad.

In 1951 the United States Air Force commissioned the Rand Corporation to study the emotional effects of bombing on civilian populations. Coming so soon after Dresden, Tokyo, London, Hiroshima and Nagasaki, there was an embarrassment of riches of damaged bodies and lives to study.

The study documented that people who live through air attacks suffer from tremors, extreme fatigue, and terrifying nightmares. When the air raid ends, people do not return to their pre-raid level of work efficiency. They endure depression, stammering, frequent crying spells, and feelings of being disconnected from reality.

Prolonged, repeated periods of aerial bombardment creates widespread reactions of fear. Some people become so paralyzed with fear they can neither think nor act. They become highly sensitive to noises and flashes of light.

More than one third of those who have been through repeated, large air raids suffer permanent psychiatric damage. They will never recover.[8]

NOTES

1. *Children in Afghanistan, in War and Refugee Camps*, A documentation of the international hearing held in Stockholm, April 4–5, 1987. Published by the Swedish Committee for Afghanistan, 1988, 160.

2. *HADAF*, newsletter of the Mine Detection and Dog Center, n.d.

3. Amnesty International, *Women in Afghanistan: A Human Rights Catastrophe*, May, 1995, AI Index ASA, Nov. 3, 1995.

4. Physicians for Human Rights (PHR), *The Taliban's War on Women* (Boston: Physicians for Human Rights, 1998), 22.

5. Ibid., 4.

6. *The Nation* (Islamabad), March 1, 1999.

7. Organization for Mine Clearance and Afghanistan Rehabilitation (OMAR), n.d.

8. Irving L. Janis, *Air War and Emotional Stress* (New York: McGraw-Hill, 1951), 72–100.

THE TALIBAN

The soldiers of the Taliban are very much a product of twenty years of war in their country. Many of them are orphans of that war. They grew out of the mud and hopelessness of the refugee camps in Pakistan, all along the Afghan border.

The word Taliban means student of Islamic religious studies.[1] They were educated at *madrasas*, religious schools, in Pakistan, although their education was largely limited to learning the Koran by repetition.[2] Most of the Taliban soldiers are unable to read and write.[3] Most had limited exposure to girls and women as they were growing up.[4] They were raised by men, men with a disregard for women that is cultural, religious, and, primarily, political.

The Taliban did not just spring from nowhere. They are not a spontaneous movement propelled along by the will of the people. They are a carefully, calculatedly, created force, nurtured and encouraged by Pakistan's security service, the Inter Services Intelligence Division (ISI).[5] Through guilt by association, it is also a product of U.S. foreign and military policy.

Gulbuddin Hekmatyr used to be the ISI's golden boy. For years, over the course of the Soviet occupation, Hekmatyr's Hezbe-Islami received more U.S. financial and military aid than any other of the Mujahideen parties, despite his bloodthirsty disregard for human rights.[6] After the fall of the Communist regime, the ISI waited for two years while Hekmatyr bombed the daylights out of Kabul but failed to take power from Rabbani, before switching their support to another group.[7]

Burqa shop.

The Taliban has close links with the Jamiat-e Ulena, Islam Party of Pakistan, an Islamic fundamentalist organization. It also has a close relationship with several Pakistani business interests, both legal and illegal. It is well funded, with support from both Pakistan and Saudi Arabia.[8]

The Taliban captured the city of Kandahar in November of 1994, and were joined by twelve thousand more Afghan and Pakistani religious students, eager to build on that first victory. Pakistan made them a present of a major munitions dump, containing nearly twenty thousand Kalashnikov rifles, one hundred artillery units, and a huge amount of ammunition.[9] The Taliban continued their march across the country, capturing Herat in September of 1995.[10] Their first task, wherever they went, was to close girls' schools and remove women from all areas of public life.[11]

In their battle for Kabul, the Taliban rained rockets and bombs down on the city, not caring where they landed. Thousands were killed and wounded. It triggered a new exodus from the city, with hundreds of thousands fleeing to Pakistan or internal exile. The Taliban had former President Najib hanging from a lamp post hours after they rolled into the city, having snatched him from the UN compound where he had been sheltered since his government fell in 1992.

Before the Taliban took over Kabul, 70 percent of the teachers were women, 40 percent of the doctors were women, over half the school students were females, and women were employed in all areas of the workforce.[12] Although there was some pressure on women to cover themselves, many did not, with no sanctions beyond random attacks on individuals.

The clampdown on women happened immediately. Announcements were made in the streets and on the radio that girls were no longer permitted to go to school. Women showed up at their workplaces to be met by armed men telling them to go home and stay there. A dress code for women came into force, with men carrying thick sticks wandering the streets, eager to beat the offenders.

Women were forced into the *burqa*, a garment many Kabuli women had never worn and did not own. The purchase of one cost the equivalent of two months' salary for many women. With their inability to continue their jobs, plunging them into poverty, one *burqa* often has to be shared by several women, creating another obstacle to them being able to leave their homes.[13]

Wearing the *burqa* is related to several health problems, including poor vision and hearing, skin rashes, respiratory difficulties, headaches, asthma, alopecia (hair loss), and depression.[14]

The Taliban closed the *hamams*, the bathhouses, for women in October of 1996.[15] They said that women going to public bathhouses is un-Islamic. In a city that has been devastated by warfare, the bathhouses were the only places women had access to hot water. For most women, it was the only place they had access to running water.

Taliban policies, coming on the heels of twenty years of war, have reduced most Afghans to abject poverty. With 400 percent inflation in 1996,[16] an astronomical unemployment level, and a ravaged economy, earning enough money to eat is a huge problem for most families. In families headed by women, now forbidden to hold jobs, the children must scramble for any kind of work they can get. Some have taken to digging up graveyards for human bones they can sell to bone brokers. The bones are taken to Pakistan for use in cooking oil, soap, chicken feed, and buttons. Disturbances in the ground caused by rocket explosions has brought human remains closer to the surface of the ground, making it easier for little hands to get at the bones.[17] The victims of the last battle are being used to feed the victims of the latest battle, all in the same war.

Through the Department of the Promotion of Virtue and the Prevention of Vice, the religious police, laws have been passed which restrict any freedom of movement and activity women have, and have put a stranglehold of gloom over the areas they control:

- Women are not permitted out of their homes without a male relative acting as an escort.
- Taxi drivers are forbidden to pick up women who are without a man. They risk punishment and the woman and her husband will also be punished.
- Music is forbidden. If music cassettes are found, the owner will be put in prison. The Taliban are so against music they have even "executed" musical instruments by hanging them from electrical poles![18] Television, videos, and cinemas are also forbidden.
- Men are forbidden to shave. Any men who do shave are put in prison until their beards grow to the proper length.
- Men must pray in the mosque and at the proper time, or risk prison.
- Women must not wear white socks.
- Women must not make noise when they walk, and must not laugh or talk loudly in the streets.
- Women must not do laundry in the streams.
- Women must not go to male doctors.
- Windows must be painted over to prevent women from being seen from the outside.
- No drum playing, no pigeon keeping, no kite flying, no photographs.
- Widows are allowed to receive assistance from aid agencies only through a male relative.[19]

These laws are enforced with beatings on the streets, and with harsher forms of punishments. The soccer stadium in Kabul is turned into an execution chamber every Friday afternoon. Crowds are forced into the bleachers to watch people being whipped, having their arms and legs cut off, or executed. Women are stoned to death for adultery, and homosexuals are killed by having a wall collapsed on them.[20]

Amnesty International has documented the Taliban throwing people into the prison for political reasons. University professors, community leaders, and former army officers have been tortured and killed. The

Taliban have also put children in prison in place of their fathers, who have eluded their grasp.[21]

Many of the punishments are focused on women. In December of 1996, the Radio Voice of Shari'a which is Taliban controlled, announced that 225 women had been arrested and lashed for violating the clothing laws.[22] A woman in Kabul in October of 1996 had one of her thumbs cut off because she was wearing nail polish.[23] When women are punished, they must still wear the *burqa*.

After the Taliban took control over Kabul, Glyn Davies, a spokesperson for the U.S. State Department, expressed hope that the Taliban might bring stability to Afghanistan.[24] The State Department hoped that the Taliban would assist the United States in containing Iran, since the Sunni Taliban is so rabidly anti-Shi'a, and make the region safe for investment, particularly the gas pipeline. Since that time, the U.S. government has, at least publicly, changed its tune. Pressured by groups such as the Feminist Majority, the Global Fund for Women, Physicians for Human Rights, and with stories confirmed by Amnesty International, the U.S. government closed the Afghan embassy in Washington[25] and added its voice to those around the world condemning the Taliban's treatment of women. Only three national governments have given official recognition to the Taliban: Saudi Arabia, Pakistan, and the United Arab Emirates.

Although the United States provides some humanitarian assistance to the Afghan refugees through nongovernmental organizations,[26] it continues to provide military hardware to Saudi Arabia and Pakistan, both of which have provided a huge amount of military hardware to the Taliban.[27] It is in the interests of the American government to say the right things to American feminists and the court of public opinion. It also serves their interests to keep Pakistan and Saudi Arabia happy, which helps keep the Taliban lashing the backs of women of Afghanistan.

Alima (forty-eight years old)

When the Taliban took over, we were in Kabul. We were there six months under the Taliban.

The Taliban ordered the people of Kabul to paint their windows, so that the women couldn't be seen. The Taliban also went into homes, took cars, TVs, radios, and satellite dishes.

We have not had to go to the stadium, but we have heard about it. There was an eighteen-year-old boy. The Taliban arrested him for theft and cut his hand off. He went home afterwards and killed himself by taking rat poison.

The Taliban gives beggar boys money and tells them to go into people's homes and spy: "Do they have TV? Do they listen to music? Do they have pretty girls?" The Taliban goes to the house and says, "We want to marry your daughter," and the family cannot refuse, or the Taliban will kill all the members of the family.

Afghanistan is a heavily mined country. Sometimes the Taliban collects people and makes them walk in mined areas to set off the mines, and to make the area safe for the Taliban.

Masuma

My youngest son saw the stadium with his own eyes. They tie the man to a pole, they cut off his hand, then they drive him around the stadium in a truck, holding up his arm with no hand on it, so everyone can see. Sometimes they make the man come on the loudspeaker himself, and have him tell the people of his crime. Women are also punished in the stadium, but with the *burqa* on. You can't see who the woman is.

Malakai (thirty-four years old)

My husband and I work at the Basic Health Care Clinic. It opened up just three months ago. We are caretakers and general helpers, and live in a room here.

We've been in Pakistan for three months. In Afghanistan, I was working in Kabul at the Ministry of Civil Engineering when the Taliban came. They hit and punished me. There were many educated people at the Ministry. When the Taliban came, they said to all the women, "Don't come back to work. If you do, we will beat you and put you in prison."

For a long while, we lived in poverty in Afghanistan. We were hungry all the time. We sold what we had—furniture, carpets, cushions—to get money to eat. When we ran out of things to sell, we had to come here.

For two years under the Taliban, we waited for things to get better, but it got worse everyday.

One day, I was in the market. I had the *burqa* on, but I was wearing the wrong kind of stockings. The Taliban started hitting me with a stick, saying, "Why are you wearing stockings like that? They belong to Christian women, not to Moslem women."

After the Taliban came, I couldn't go out to see any of my friends, and they stayed in their homes, too. When women go out, they all wear a *burqa*, so nobody can recognize each other! Even if my friend and I passed close beside each other on the street, we would never know it.

By my own eyes, I have seen a cut-off hand. Many die when their hand is cut off, because a main blood vein is severed, and they bleed to death.

I saw a dead body in the hospital. His hand was nearby. It had been cut off.

When I saw this, I fainted. I was sick for days. I cried and cried, and I want to cry now.

If the man lives after they cut off his hand, the Taliban parade him around for two or three days, holding up his arm, and shouting to people, "This man is a thief! Look what we do to thieves!"

I no longer wait for a better life in our country. The Taliban are like wild animals. They are not human. I no longer hope it will get better. All of our people will be separated from each other, in different countries, without homes, and without hope.

Salima (twenty-five years old)

I am from Kabul. I have been in Pakistan for about six years.

Three months ago, I went back to Kabul. The weather in Pakistan was very hot, and my mother was sick. I took my mother back to Kabul in the hope that the better climate would make her feel better.

One day, I went to the bazaar to buy some clothes for my small sister. I was standing before a shop to choose the color, when suddenly a Talib came. He hit me several times with a lash that he carried in his hand.

I asked him, "Why are you hitting me?"

He said, "Why did you come out alone? Where is your man? You have no permission to come onto the streets without a man." I became very unhappy. He kept whipping me, lashing me in front of the crowd. I was very upset, but I had no choice except to bear it. He kept whipping me for five minutes. There were a lot of people watching. They just stood and saw me get whipped. They were not able to meddle. If someone had meddled in my case, he or she would have faced the same fate. I felt myself very weak, very humble, just a woman, a low thing. I will never forget the pain of the beating, but the pain is something bearable. The insult is something that is unforgivable. But still, I will never forget the pain of a whipping by a Talib. When he stopped beating me, he warned me that I must never go out alone on the street again, then he just went on his way. He belonged to the religious police. These police are very famous for beating women. They drive around in special cars, wear black glasses and black turbans. Whenever people, especially women, see that kind of car, they try to disappear themselves. I was crying and crying after the Talib left. I was just on the ground and crying. People saw me, but no one helped me to my feet. I was afraid before the crowd, and because of that, I went home as fast as I could. I did not go out on my own again after that.

War has made all of our social problems more difficult. War is our most important problem. Now we are wandering in Pakistan because of the war in our country. It is the duty of women's organizations to let other women know, in other countries, to convey to the UN and other bodies what is going on in

Afghanistan. If the world community wanted to solve the problem of Afghanistan, they could. If they don't want to, they won't.

Noora

I'm from Kabul. I have been in Peshawar for six months. I was a student at the faculty of medicine, but, unfortunately, we couldn't continue our lessons when the Taliban came. One day, I was crossing the street, and a group of Taliban saw me. They ran after me, and they said, "Why are your trousers so tight?" and for this reason, they punished me and my friend who was with me. It was very bad. We were both wearing the *burqa*, but the pants, at the bottom around our ankles, were too tight. They started hitting us. I ran away, but they kept hitting my friend. When the school was closed, I had to just stay at home, and try to study by myself, nothing else. Sometimes I got very tired of just staying at home, and I would cry. There wasn't anything else for us.

Marzia (forty-three years old)

I came to Peshawar from Mazar-e-Sharif three months ago. I have moved around a lot. I lived in Iran for four years, then six years in Pakistan, then five years in Mazar, now I'm back in Pakistan.

During Taliban, and before Taliban, there was no safe place in Mazar, no security at all. Soldiers would abduct people, especially girls. They would rob houses, and fight between themselves, and innocent people would get killed in these fights. They'd go to rich people's homes and demand money. If the rich people refused, they'd arrest a member of the family. They'd go back in a few months and demand money again. If the family paid, they'd release the arrested person. If not, they would kill him. This happened to one of my neighbors. There was another man I know, a relative. He was traveling from Mazar to Kabul. On the way, the Jihadis arrested him, not far from Mazar. They kept him in a very dark room, for six months. After six months, they sent a letter to his house, demanding money. When the family paid, he was released. He told them the room was cold and dark. There was an old woman who brought him food. His hands and feet were tied. He died soon after he was released. There were a lot of girls who were abducted, and most of them never came back. Some of those who did come back were killed by their fathers or other relatives. Once, about thirty girls were taken by Dostum's men. After they were returned to Mazar, all of them were examined by a doctor. All of them had been raped. Some of them were pregnant. The doctor was shocked. No one knows what happened to the girls after that, if their families killed them, or what happened. Killing daughters is something personal, something private. It's not breaking the law at all. There is no law against it.

The father will kill his daughter with a gun, or with poison, rat poison. He may put the poison in her food. The other women in the family are powerless to stop him. Sometimes they agree with killing the girl. Even though the daughter was taken away against her will, that doesn't matter. If a girl is raped, it's a shame for the whole family. They have to kill the girl to get over the shame.

They say, "No one will marry her after she's been raped. Her life is over anyway." We were in Mazar for two months after the Taliban captured it. When the Taliban came in, the situation for people became worse than ever. At least before, women could go out. When the Taliban came, everyone was locked in their homes, especially the Hazaras [one of the ethnic groups of Afghanistan].

To deal with the Hazaras, the Taliban divided themselves into three groups.

One group took the Hazaras from their homes, and put them in prison. Another group took the Hazaras from their homes and killed them in the street. They ordered the families to leave the bodies in the street. A third group took Hazaras and sent them to the province of Faryab. There's a desert there. When the Taliban attacked Mazar before, the Hazaras fought against them, and a lot of Taliban were killed in this desert. To take their revenge, the Taliban took the Hazara people to the same desert, and killed them there. These prisoners were taken away in big containers, on trucks. They took only men, not women and children. Mostly they just killed men. They didn't need to kill their wives and children. Widows and orphans starve under the Taliban anyway.

The bodies were just dumped in the desert.

In Mazar, I saw many dead people. They were on the streets, and the dogs ate them. It was a scene I could not imagine. I was shocked by it, and so were most other people. One dog would take an arm, another dog would take a foot.

The people didn't dare to bury the bodies. They were forbidden.

After the men were taken away, it was the women who fought back. They went to the prison, took food for the men, and sometimes argued with the Taliban to release their men. They had to walk in the streets, which was very dangerous. There was no transport, so they used their feet, going from place to place to search for family members. At first, after the Taliban came to Mazar, women were afraid to leave their homes, but after two weeks, they had to go out. They had to get food for their children, if there was no man to get food for them. Many, many men had been killed or taken away. The Taliban kept telling people, especially women, that they should stay home, but the women refused their orders. They put on a *burqa*, and went out of their houses and got food.

I've left behind my brother and my brother-in-law. I've also left behind my close friends, Saeeda, Shekeba, and Nooria. We were teachers together. We were very close, and had been friends for fifteen years. Even here in Pakistan, I'm always replaying in my head the scenes I saw in Afghanistan. I often can't sleep. I see things over and over and over.

K. (twenty-nine years old, name withheld by request)

I have been in Peshawar for one year. We are from Herat. Living in Herat was very difficult. There was lots of fighting, and then the Taliban came.

I had a big problem with the Taliban, because I had been in Russia. They had information that I came into Afghanistan from Turkmenistan.

The Taliban bothered us a lot. They arrested me, and took me to jail. I spent three days there. It is a big problem for women to go to jail. I worried about what would happen to me. I worried about what other people would think of me.

There were other women in the jail, but I don't know what they were in for. I was held in a cell by myself. I was allowed to join the other women only for meals, but we were forbidden to talk. The guards were women.

The men, the Taliban, questioned me, but the women, the guards, beat me. The Taliban would question me, then the guards would take me to another room and beat me, then they'd bring me back to the men, and the men would question me again.

All the time, through the questioning, through the beating, I wore the *burqa*. They could not see my face.

After three days, they told me to go home and stay there. "Maybe we will come back for you," they said.

We left our house that same night, and went to a friend's house. We could take no luggage with us, so that no one, none of the neighbors would know we were leaving.

At four in the morning, we left our friend's house, and began the journey out of Afghanistan.

As soon as I was arrested, my husband began to make plans for us to leave.

It took us four days and four nights to get to Kabul. We traveled until eleven at night, spent the night in small rooms along the way, then got up early and traveled again.

I had a very small baby. It was only twenty-seven days old when I was arrested. The stress was very bad. I was not myself. I couldn't understand what people said to me.

My brother's wife had given birth just before I did, so she took care of my baby while I was in jail. She fed my baby from her body.

The Taliban said they would come again. I can't forget that. All the time, even now, I think they will come and get me.

In Russia, we were first in Moscow, then in Kiev. We went to Russia thinking that from there we could get to Europe.

Before that, we were living in Kabul. The Mujahideen came, and there were many problems.

We went to Moscow with a group of other people, and stayed in a small apartment. My husband was unable to find work. We gave a lot of money to someone who said he could help us get to Europe. We never saw him again.

After being in Moscow for awhile, we heard of someone who could help us go to Germany through Kiev. We gave that person money, too. He got us to Kiev, then he disappeared, just like the first person.

In Kiev, we paid to stay in an upstairs room in the house of some Russian people. It was very bad. We had to stay inside all the time. Once a day they brought us food. We were all very unhealthy, especially for my two daughters. It was very bad. We couldn't even look out the window for fear that the police would see us, and would see that we are foreigners.

Finally, I got so tired of it, I opened a window one day, so that the police would see we were not Russian. The police saw us, and they came and got us.

We were arrested, and taken by train to Turkmenistan. We went from Kiev back to Moscow, and from there to Turkmenistan.

We had to stay in jail for awhile in Turkmenistan, with the children, all of us in one cell, because we had no documents, and had to wait for the police to do the paperwork on us. It was not bad in that jail. The Turkmenistan police did not bother us. They left us alone.

Eventually, the Turkmenistan police handed us over to the Taliban. They got a receipt to be able to prove to their superiors that they took us back to Afghanistan.

I like Afghanistan, but there's nothing there for me now. We took only cash with us to Moscow, nothing from the house. When we got back to Herat after being in Russia, everything had been stolen.

I used to have beautiful things! People gave me many gifts for the house. All of them are gone now.

In Kiev, I felt very bad because I couldn't go outside. Everyday, I hoped this would be the day we would go to Germany.

We lived in two rooms, which we shared with two other families. Three families stuck together in two rooms for one year. We were all Afghans. My children were sick. We did not have enough to eat, we had no fresh air, and no exercise.

The police arrested all of us, but the other two families gave the police money, and were able to stay in Moscow. We had no money left, and so we were brought back to Afghanistan.

After a year in those rooms I could stand it no longer. I had no hope left that the smuggler was ever going to get us into Germany. And even if the smuggler did come for us, I was too sick, and my children were too sick, to make the trip.

I thought to myself that I could handle a new problem, but I could not handle *this* problem any longer. One year was enough. We could not even leave those two rooms to walk around the rest of the house. A Russian stayed in the doorway all the time, to keep us from leaving.

Now we are in Peshawar. I have traveled many miles, but life is no better.

Manija (twenty-eight years old)

I am from Kabul. I have been in Pakistan for two years. My favorite subject in high school was Persian literature, and I am a university graduate from the

School of Journalism. I was at the top of my class. Now, I do nothing, just cook and clean, which is nothing.

In Afghanistan, I wrote for a women's magazine, and for a few newspapers. Mostly, I wrote about social problems of women, the inequality between men and women. I also did a lot of interviews with a lot of artists. There were lots of artists in Kabul at that time.

I think the future of Afghanistan will be dark.

Zohra Rasekh, Researcher, Physicians for Human Rights

The Taliban will go to homes if they know a family has a daughter they like, and they demand marriage with her. If the family refuses, they threaten the family. If the girl refuses, they don't care, they marry her anyway.

In one case, the young girl refused to marry this guy. The family was afraid, and they said, "OK, marry our daughter." The girl herself, the night of the wedding, refused to go with this Talib, and a group of Taliban came and took her with them by force. She disappeared. Some of the family says she was killed. Some say she was taken to Kandahar. No one knows.

I hear also more and more stories of women being abducted, and then if they come back, their family kills them. It's hard to confirm these stories. The people directly involved don't talk to outsiders about this, because it is a big shame for the family.

NOTES

1. Physicians for Human Rights (PHR), *The Taliban's War on Women* (Boston: Physicians for Human Rights, 1998), 22.

2. Ibid., 23.

3. Edward Giradet and Jonathan Walter, editors, *Essential Field Guide to Afghanistan* (Geneva: Crosslines Communications, 1998), 173.

4. Gayle Kirshenbaum, "A Fundamentalist Regime Cracks Down on Women," *Ms. Magazine* (May/June 1997).

5. PHR, *The Taliban's War on Women*, 22.

6. Assad Ismi and Farhan Hag, "Afghanistan: The Great Game Continues," *Covert Action Quarterly* 59 (winter 1996–97): 47.

7. PHR, *The Taliban's War on Women*, 22.

8. Ibid.

9. Ibid., 24.

10. Ibid.

11. Giradet and Walter, *Field Guide*, 58.

12. Statement of Mavis Leno before the Subcommittee on Foreign Operations of the U.S. Senate Appropriations Committee, April 5, 1999.

13. World News Inter Press Service, September 18, 1997.

14. Abbas Fiaz, "Health Care Under the Taliban," *The Lancet* 349, no. 9060 (April 26, 1997): 1247.

15. *CCA Newsletter* 3, no. 5 (October 1996): 10.

16. Seamus Murphy, "A Market in Human Remains," *New York Times Magazine* (January 12, 1997): 30–32.

17. Ibid.

18. Proceedings from the First International Conference on Music and Censorship, Copenhagen, November 20–23, 1998.

19. Giradet and Walter, *Field Guide*, 255–257.

20. Ibid., 260.

21. *The News International* (Islamabad) March 11, 1999, 12.

22. Amnesty International, *Afghanistan: The Violations Continue*, June, 1997.

23. Ibid.

24. Ismi and Haq, *Afghanistan*, 46.

25. Mavis Leno, April 5, 1999.

26. Bill Clinton, March 3, 1999, taped message presented to feminist majority.

27. Mavis Leno, April 5, 1999.

CAMP LIFE

There are still 1.2 million registered Afghan refugees living in 170 refugee camps around Peshawar, according to the United Nations High Commission for Refugees. Many more Afghans are not registered, and live where they can around the city. Well over a million Afghans are internally displaced within Afghanistan.

Refugee numbers reached the high point at 1990, with 6.2 million people, largely in Pakistan and Iran.[1] They continue to be the single largest refugee caseload in the world, for the eighteenth year in a row.

Pakistan has hosted the single largest concentration of refugees in the world, 3.2 million at the peak, according to Pakistan's Secretary of the Frontier Mohammad Abbas.[2] At the high point of its funding, the UNHCR provided $55.6 million in humanitarian aid to the refugees in 1980 and 1981, and the World Food Program provided $160.9 million in 1982. Both the World Food Program assistance and the UNHCR Care and Maintenance Program ended in 1995. The ending of the World Food Program assistance, which included supplying wheat to the refugees, resulted in wheat shortages in Pakistan, causing riots at the beginning of 1997.

There was large scale repatriation of refugees back to Afghanistan between 1990 and 1995, when many refugees, country people who had come to Pakistan to escape the Soviet bombing, returned to what was left of their villages.[3] For many, there was not much to return to. Before 1979, 85 percent of Afghans were farmers. The war destroyed much of the irrigation system, land mines make much of the land unfarmable, and a generation of children, raised in the camps, have had no chance to learn agricultural skills. Factors like these have helped settle Afghanistan near the bottom of the UN misery list.[4]

Women in the refugee camps face a stricter version of *purdah* (seclusion from men) than they had experienced in the villages and the cities. Educated, urban women have found themselves and their activities severely restricted by the conservative tribal leaders and mullahs who control the camp. Those who continue to try to practice the social and cultural freedoms to which they were accustomed have to put up with ridicule and often threatening behavior from Afghan men.[5] For rural women, camp life has separated them from their extended families. Since they are living in close proximity to strangers, their men insist they remain almost constantly behind the walls of their home. Refugee women lead an artificial life, removed from much that is familiar.[6]

Camp life has not meant more security for women. During the war, most camps were controlled by one or other of the Mujahideen groups, and any aid that came into the camp went through the governing camp committee, made up of men who did not necessarily have ethical scruples. Husbands would often deposit their wives and children in the camps then return to Afghanistan to fight in the jihad. These unaccompanied women were at risk of attack, or of having to have sex with one of the commanders in order to get rations for her children.[7]

Many women in the camps suffer from post traumatic stress disorder, from a combination of shell shock, combat fatigue, the loss of their birthplace, being uprooted to another country against their will, and being dependent on hand-outs. The physically difficult life of the camps provides little relief and comfort to assist them in recovering from their trauma. In fact, camp life often adds to their trauma.[8]

Parents can easily become preoccupied with their own stress and sadness and pay inadequate attention to their children. These children can end up feeling very isolated and unloved. Parental violence against children increases with the length of stay in the camp. Hypersensitivity to noise, a common experience of people who have lived through a period of aerial bombardment, means that many parents insist their children be abnormally quiet. There is a high level of elective mutism among camp children.[9]

Children can react to the stress of camp life by exhibiting psychological symptoms such as aggressive behavior, irritability, intolerance, loss of energy, loss of interest in things and people, feeling suicidal, unable to concentrate, fear, insomnia, nightmares, panic, anxiety, depression, and social withdrawal.[10]

The conservative atmosphere of the camps forces girl children into *purdah* at an early age, sometimes as young as eight. They are forced to give up childhood play and remain in the house with their mothers.

Although there are some schools in the camps, there are not enough for all the children, and not all families can afford to send their children. Even if the school in the camp is free, the children in the family may be needed to contribute economically to the household, through begging or some other labor. Too many children live their whole lives knowing only their section of the camp, particularly girls, who are denied the freedom of movement their brothers enjoy. They do not know about other cities or other countries, they do not know about oceans or history or that human beings have walked on the moon. They are not being prepared to become the kind of aware, productive adults Afghanistan will need to rebuild itself.

Security in the camps is not good. Children have been stolen from them and from the streets of Peshawar. Some are held for ransom and then released. Others have disappeared forever. They are sexually assaulted, forced to smuggle narcotics, sold into prostitution, or trafficked to the camel-racing barons of Saudi Arabia.[11]

Some children, after they have been stolen, are made into professional beggars, their limbs deliberately twisted so that the child is permanently disabled.

Afghan children are also being kidnapped for body parts.

Samiullah, a small boy living in the Tahkal section of Peshawar, disappeared for ten days. When he was finally returned to his parents, he was alive but in pain, and had a scar on his abdomen. His parents took him to the doctor, who said that one of his kidneys had been taken out.

Sheela, an eight-year-old girl also disappeared. She got back to her home a week later, minus a kidney, and was dead within three days. She was taken on her way to school and thrown into a private car, according to witnesses.

Between March 1998 and June 1998, over forty refugee children disappeared from the camps and from around Peshawar. This figure does not include those who have turned up with internal organs removed. If forty children disappeared from Chicago over a four-month period, it would make headlines around the world. These refugee children have not made the news. Their stories have not been told.

Zohra Rasekh, Physicians for Human Rights

Life in the refugee camps is a very unnatural kind of life for women. The basic needs of life are not being met. They live under these makeshift tents, or in these mud houses. There is no shower, there is no civilized way of living. There is no education for their children, there is no work for them or for their husbands, there is no proper food or nutrition.

There are women who live in the cities in Pakistan. They may live in a home, but they share the house and sometimes the room with three or four other families, in order to afford the high rent. They have to cover themselves when they go out, because some Pakistani men consider all Afghan women to be prostitutes. They are in this waiting way of life, wondering when they're going to get out of Pakistan, when they're going to go back to Afghanistan. They're leading a temporary lifestyle which has become permanent. They have no future, nothing to look forward to.

For some women, there is not much difference between their lives in the camps and their lives in Afghanistan. In the southern part of Afghanistan, where the weather is hot in the summer, many people live in mud houses, and there are similarities for those people.

For urban women, life in these refugee camps compared to their lifestyles in Kabul and major cities, it's like hell. Imagine, there are all these women, and they are just stuck, like prisoners, inside these mud houses. I'm sure there is all kinds of crime going on. There have been cases of rape reported, and homes broken into.

The social life is terrible, although some women, some families, still try to do their best, even in that environment, to have some kinds of gatherings. I met a woman who was a beautician in one of the camps. She had these boxes of hair dye and things like that. I asked her what she did. She said, "We have some women who come here to have their hair dyed, or permed."

I asked, "You do this in a refugee camp?" I thought everyone should be depressed and upset.

She replied, "Well, you know, this is our life. We have to live it. Sometimes, for a change, women like to have their hair done."

Some women did talk about their husbands being abusive, but they would defend their husbands' actions by saying, "I don't blame him, because he has no job, he stays at home twenty-four hours a day, he sees all the poverty, he hears the children crying for food. He goes out of his mind, and he takes it out on me, but I can't blame him." Of course, there are also some abusive men who take advantage of the situation to be more abusive.

One of the camps I was in, Nasir Bagh, was better, comparatively, than Accora Hattack Camp. In Accora Camp, there is an area for new arrivals. They live in old tents. Many people don't even have a tent, and they have constructed flimsy shelters out of rags. Some of them have lived that way for more than two years.

As I was standing there, a group of women surrounded me, and they were telling me about their problems. One or two women said, "We don't have a place to go to the bathroom. So we wait the whole day, until it gets dark." Then they have to go to the edge of the camp, to the bottom of a hill, to empty their bladder. Imagine having to hold onto your urine for the whole day, everyday! That can cause bladder infections and other problems, as well as being terribly uncomfortable.

Sajida of the Revolutionary Association of Women of Afghanistan, RAWA, is my guide at the Jalozai Refugee Camp. Sajida is a confident, aware, intelligent young woman who attended an activist refugee school in Quetta as a child, and continues to be an activist as an adult.

Sajida meets me in Saddar Bazaar, and after a forty-five minute bus ride along the Grand Trunk Road, we negotiate a ride to the camp with a truck driver. We hop in the back of his truck and bounce along for awhile. The road to the camp goes through a brick-works. There is no topsoil on the ground. It looks as though it has been peeled away to get to the clay underneath. The whole area has the appearance of the surface of the moon. Already, in January, it is hot. By June, there will be little difference between the inside and the outside of the kilns. There is nothing beautiful about the landscape, nothing to relax the eye or mind.

The recent rains have created gargantuan mud puddles, and I have visions of having to get out and push every time the truck slows down to plow through the muck. A lone security guard waves us through the gate in the camp. Many of the men in the camp who have vehicles use them to taxi people back and forth from the Grand Trunk Road.

Jalozai Camp is an old, established camp. Although there are some recent arrivals from Afghanistan, they are assimilated into the community, not housed in tents apart from the community. The school has an excellent reputation. Some families send their children to live with relatives here, so that they can attend the school.

We get out of the truck in a clearing in front of Wadilla's house, where we will be staying for the next few days. Sajida and Wadilla know each other from RAWA. There are quite a few RAWA members in this camp. Wadilla is very happy to see us. Having guests is an important part of Afghan life, even though I know I will be a fairly burdensome one, not being able to speak her language, and eating food that she cannot really afford to share. I've asked Sajida already if I should bring food with me to ease the burden on Wadilla, but she says no, that it would be considered an insult. So instead, I have brought small toys for her children, and I take lots of photos of them.

Wadilla's house has three rooms, strung together like a train. In Afghan fashion, the rooms are bare except for mattresses along the walls and straw matting on the floor. Wadilla brings Sajida and me tea, then she leaves us to fetch her children. Sajida tells me a bit about the RAWA and the work they do in this camp.

Sajida

RAWA has thousands of members. Most are still inside Afghanistan.

We try to do education among the women here. For example, it is usual for men to hit their wives. Their wives, if they do not know about their rights, will say, "Men have the right to beat us, it has always been like this." We try to educate them about their rights. Sometimes we talk to their husbands, too. We ask them, "Why do you beat your wife?" This is sometimes enough to shame him into stopping the beatings, at least for a while. It does not always work. Some men hate even having the discussion with us. They don't think they should have to listen to women about anything. So it is both social and political education that we do.

All women have double tragedy, oppression from the government, and oppression from the men in their lives. Older brothers have the right to order little sisters around. Even younger brothers, when they grow up, have authority over their older sisters. It is very much a male-dominated society. Sometimes sons will beat their mothers and order their mothers around. This does not happen in all families, of course. There are advanced families where women have rights.

My family is advanced. Never in my life have I been limited because I was born a girl. Some of my friends are like me. Some grew up in very different families, and they have lots of problems.

Wadilla has come back in, with her three children. She pours me some more tea, and tells me her story.

Wadilla

My husband was killed by the Russians. We lived in the western part of the province of Helmand. I remember the Russians very well. I saw lots of them. I didn't just see their bombs.

My husband was killed by the government troops that supported the Russians. He was against the Russians. He was traveling one day when the troops surrounded him and killed him.

At the time, I thought my life had been destroyed too. I was left with three small children. It is very hard to live without a man in Afghanistan. At the time, I was twenty-four. The children were two months, two years, and three and a half years old. I spent a year not knowing what to do. My family helped a bit, but I had to learn how to run my own life. I thought I should educate my children, and I wanted to be educated as well.

We left Afghanistan and came to Pakistan. We were living in Peshawar, and I heard about a RAWA meeting, so I attended. I had been looking for a place to tell my stories and feelings and problems. I met other women at this meeting, and they gave me good advice. They invited me to join their literacy courses, and RAWA arranged for me to come to this camp.

I was illiterate before, but now I can read. I even teach others to read at the school in the camp. I have a house, a small salary, and I can run my own life.

Spurghai joins us. She is in charge of women's issues at the camp, a voluntary job that she created for herself. She spends her time meeting with women and helping them find solutions to their problems.

Spurghai (twenty-four years old)

I am from Kunduz, a northern province. We came to Pakistan in 1980, one year after the Russian occupation. I was only eight at the time, and don't remember the Russians. I am the youngest in my family. My father died when I was five.

I collect women for literacy courses, talk with women about their lives, about the importance of education. I also approach NGOs [nongovernmental organizations] to see if they will give us money for school supplies. Also, when women have family problems, I meet with them, and try to help them solve them.

For example, there was a woman who wanted to go to a literacy course, but she was not allowed to by her husband. I went to her house with a couple of other women. We talked to her husband and finally persuaded him to give her permission to take the course.

The camp council here supports our work, and they will often step in to help us with a man who is being particularly difficult.

Wadilla brings in the mid-day meal. A plastic cloth is spread on the floor. Pieces of nan are passed around, and platters of rice and meat stew are brought in. We all sit around the cloth and eat. The children sneak peaks at me for awhile, then forget about me and concentrate on eating.

The walls of this and the other houses in this camp are very thick, to provide some protection against the winter damp and chill and the summer heat. Everything is scrupulously clean, even in the Pakistani dust.

After lunch we start visiting some other women.

Shabnab lives with her family in a small, one-room house. There are many young children in the house, the offspring of her sisters and brothers.

Shabnab

My father fought against the Russians. Our house in Afghanistan was bombed, then bandits came and stole things from us. It was a very dangerous time.

I have never married. My sisters were still young when my mother died, so I had to look after them. Now my brother is sick, and I have to look after him. He won't get well. This is a big sacrifice for me, as I can't leave him alone for very long.

I attended the literacy courses here, and now I can read and write. I am also a tailor. People pay me a little money to sew clothes for them.

Naheed (sister of Zareen, twenty years old)

I was ten when I came to this camp, and attended school here. English, geography, and Pushtun were my favorite subjects.

Growing up, my friends and I would play hide and seek. Sometimes we'd make dolls and play with them.

I was married when I was fifteen. My family chose my husband for me. We were married right in this camp. We have no children.

I will probably stay in this camp for many years. I hope that Afghanistan will be free from the fundamentalists some day, and that the people there will be able to have a good peaceful life.

Happiness is for the future.

Zarmeena (sister of Zareen, twenty-four years old)

I live in Peshawar, and have three children. I came to this camp to be with my sisters over Eid. My husband is a shopkeeper. We were married in this camp when I was sixteen.

I only got to the third class in school. I'd like to go back to school, but, with the children to look after, it is impossible.

We go for a bit of a walk and come to a collection of rough yet sturdy wooden benches arranged in a grove of trees. There are women and girls there in tribal costumes that are different from ones I'd ever seen before. Sajida tells me they are from a district in Afghanistan quite far from here.

Bibihawa (fifteen years old)

I have been in this camp for twelve years. I have not been to school. I would like to go to school, but I have to earn a living. I make carpets at home, so, most of the time, I have to stay home and work.

My father has two wives. My mother gave birth to three daughters and two sons. My stepmother also lives with us.

When I'm not making carpets, I'm washing clothes, washing dishes, cooking, and baking bread.

For fun, I sit with the other girls, and we talk and tell stories.

I don't like weaving carpets. It is hard work, and I don't like it, but I have to do it. We are poor, and I have to earn some money.

An article called "Economic Activities of Afghan Under Difficult Conditions," by Mrs. Mazari, a Lecturer at the Faculty of Literature at Balkh University, talks about how female carpet weavers lose their youth, their eyesight, the feeling in their finger-tips, and are good candidates for tuberculosis and other illnesses.

Maryam (twelve years old)

I was born in Afghanistan. I am in the fourth grade at school. English is my favorite subject. For fun, I like to skip with my friends and play hide and seek. I want to be a doctor when I grow up.

She introduces me to her sister, Mossarrant, who is ten years old.

Mossarrant can't talk. I think there is something wrong with her tongue. She makes noises sometimes, but no one can understand her.

Shalah (seven years old)

I was born in Afghanistan and came here two years ago with my mother and father. When I grow up, I want to be a policewoman.

Nazira (twelve years old)

I've been at this camp for two years. My father and mother are still in Afghanistan. We lived in the central part of Afghanistan. My parents sent me to this camp so I could go to school.

What I remember most about Afghanistan is our house, and our neighbor-

Girl with baby brother on her lap.

hood. I miss Afghanistan, mostly because I miss my mother and father. They may join me here someday.

I like to study and learn new things. I'm hoping to be a doctor one day. I'd like to go back to Afghanistan and heal people there.

Leila (nine years old)

I've lived here for four years. I came here from Saram. I'm here with my family. I have two younger sisters. Altogether, I have seven sisters and two brothers.

I like to study and to play, and at night I like to watch TV, if the electricity is working. Sometimes there are programs for children. I like those.

Masuda (ten years old)

I know a little bit of English.

I've been in the camp for two years. I live here with my family. There are six people living in our one-room house.

My father died two years ago. He had a heart attack. After he died, we came to Pakistan, because my mother was not able to work in Afghanistan. The Taliban would not let her work.

I go to school here. I like learning English. When I grow up, I would like to be a teacher.

Wagma (fourteen years old)

I have been here for two years. Nazira is my sister. We live with our uncle. I remember Afghanistan, but all I remember is my house and the house of my relatives. We didn't have much to do with other people. We didn't go to school. We just stayed in the house and did housework. We saw our relatives, but we didn't really see anyone else.

I'm in school now, in the fourth grade. I like it a lot. I wish I could have gone to school for years already.

My sister and I never fight. It's good to have her here, since our parents are still in Afghanistan.

Lemba (seven years old)

I've been away from Afghanistan for two years. My parents are in Rawalpindi. They sent me to this camp so that I can go to school. I like to play volleyball, ping-pong, and badminton, but there are no play materials here. I like school. I would like to be a teacher, and teach big kids.

Obra (eight years old)

Lemba is my sister. We live here with our grandmother.

In my spare time, I like to play with my sister. We have one brother. He's younger. We don't play with him. Boys and girls don't play together. Boys play with boys and girls play with girls.

When I get old, I want to be a music maker. I would like to play the violin. I like it because it's difficult. I tried it once, in Rawalpindi. I like all kinds of music, and that's how I would like to spend my life, making music.

We spend the next few hours going to women's homes and hearing about their lives. Everywhere we go, we are given tea and something to nibble on, either candied almonds, or raisins and walnuts, or *samiyan*, which is dried, spiced noodles.

By the end of the day, my head feels like it's going to explode from all the stories. It is dark by the time we head back to the Wadilla's house. We use my little travel flashlight to light our way through the dark pathways. There is electricity in this camp, but it cuts off regularly.

The power comes on again after we get back to Wadilla's, and we eat our supper with the television on. The reception isn't very good, but I recognize Brooke Shields beaming at her tennis-playing husband. It is amusing to see that Pakistan's television commercials are as goofy as Canadian ones.

After dinner, Wadilla starts to cry. Sajida tells me this happens now and then, ever since she lost her husband. Sajida goes over to her and comforts her, massaging her with long, strong strokes of her hands on Wadilla's arms, until Wadilla is able to relax and stop crying.

Two days later, I head back to the Grand Trunk Road to catch a bus back to Peshawar. Sajida is staying on in the camp for the rest of the week, so I am on my own. A boy walks by leading a cow and an ox. A man keeps a herd of goats out of the way of the traffic. Everything is strange to me here, until I remember that I'm the strange one here.

Suddenly, in the sky, a hang-glider appears, the last thing I'd expect to see. A small truck stops, offering me a ride into Peshawar. I sit on a bench in the back, crowded in with six other women, all in *burqas*, and watch the hang-glider follow us into the city.

Freyba (nineteen years old) Tojobad Camp

Three years ago, I lost one of my feet in a rocket explosion. I was with my husband. We were taking my son to see the doctor when a rocket hit our vehicle. My brother-in-law and my five-year-old cousin were killed in that blast. Many children were injured. The other people coming along got me to the doctor. I was conscious, and in a lot of pain.

I was in the hospital for forty-five days, then I went home. But still, I was in a lot of pain.

I was in Kabul with this unlucky life. We had a lot of problems, especially poverty. Five months ago, we sold our things and came here. Now this is our life.

The ground in this camp is full of water. There is mud everywhere, even days and days after it rains. This house has made everyone sick. You can feel how damp it is. When rains, it's terrible.

My husband is now in Rawalpindi, working in construction. Many of the people here are beggars. Others wash the clothes of the rich Pakistanis. There is no school here, no teacher, no mosque, nothing. We pay rent to the Pakistanis. There are six families in this little house, which has three rooms. Nine people live in this room, ten or eleven in each of the other rooms. We pay fifteen hundred rupees each month, split between six families. There is electricity only at night. We pay for that, too.

We left everything behind in Afghanistan to get away from the fighting. It's not easy to leave everything and go to another country.

No NGO's come to this camp. No one helps us.

Farid

[Nasir Bagh Refugee Camp]

I lost my wife in a rocket attack on Kabul, one year ago. I came to Pakistan after that, with our two small children. My wife's name was Anohito. She was only twenty-five years old. She was young, beautiful, and had finished high school. I miss her very much.

School Master, Nasir Bagh Institute of Learning School

The school here began seventeen years ago. New students come all the time, from Kabul, from Mazar, whenever there is trouble.

Fifteen thousand families live in Nasir Bagh. It was a big desert at first. The government of Pakistan let us build a camp here. No one helped us.

Security is not good. Strangers blend in easily. Many people come here to steal, to kill, to take children. Girls will disappear and are never heard from again. It is a very big problem, and the thieves are helped by the Pakistani police.

Afghans go to have a job on the street, on busses, they are being taken, and the thieves flee with them. If the girls do come back, many kill themselves, or are killed by their families. Often the families move away, so that no one will know their shame.

Two weeks ago, thieves came here to take the children. They fought with the guards, and the guards killed one of the thieves. They got no children that time.

We get letters warning us not to educate girls. The letters are not signed. We will continue to educate girls.

Torpikai (twenty-four years old)

I am a teacher here at the school. I used to live in the camp, but now I live in the Bord section of Peshawar. It is too dangerous here. All the time, thieves were coming, banging on the doors, shouting.

I am single, living with my parents. We have been here for five years. We used to live in the old section of Kabul. It used to be very nice, but now it is all destroyed. I teach grade five science, literature, Islamic history, and Asian geography.

Alia

We are from Laghman. We came here as a group eighteen years ago. We came to Pakistan because of the war. Our homes in Afghanistan were bombed and burned. It took us seven days and nights to cross the mountains on foot.

My husband is here with me. He had a job, but not anymore. He has some psychological problems and is not able to work.

I have four daughters, no sons to go to work for us. My daughters are not in school. There is no money for notebooks and pens.

Zahmina

Six of my cousins were killed in the war with Russia, plus my uncle. Our village was bombed by airplanes and shot at by tanks.

About thirty families left Afghanistan together. Most of those families are here, in this area of the camp. We came out of Afghanistan on foot. It took a week, traveling day and night. We walked, and some donkeys carried what few belongings we had. It was a very difficult journey. The snow was very deep and very heavy. Some young children died. We left them there, buried in the snow.

My husband died ten years ago, only six months after we were married. I have no children. He had a heart attack and died.

When we first came here, we lived in tents. It was very hard, especially in the summer. Summertime in Pakistan is very hot. Finally, we got some foreign aid, and were able to build these houses. We have a water pump in this area, too, which makes things easier. Most of the foreign aid that was supposed to come to the refugees went to the Pakistan government.

What do we do for fun? We don't go out very often. We pray. We watch TV if the electricity is working. Sometimes we go into Peshawar, maybe twice a year. Money is the problem, money to get there and come back.

After it gets dark, one can come safely to this area, and no one can leave. There are a lot of robbers who wait for people in the darkness. One family I know of, my relatives, came here after dark, and they were shot at by people, by robbers.

Girls at this camp usually marry at fourteen or fifteen, sometimes as late as eighteen, but not very often. Families cannot keep daughters long. They can't afford to. Daughters just eat and do not earn money, so they have to be married very young. Sometimes husbands come from this camp, sometimes from another, sometimes they come from Afghanistan.

Noosala (nine years old)

I would like to go to school, if I could, but my father is very sick, and there is no money for school fees, or to pay for a way to get to the school. I spend my time doing housework and playing with the other children.

I ask her if she knows about other places. Does she know what oceans are?

I only know about places in Afghanistan, and in this camp. I don't know anything about oceans, or about other places in the world.

Afghani

I've been here for eighteen years. I got married here. My two children were born here.

My husband had a shop in the Bord section of Peshawar, but it burned down last year. There was a big fire. Lots of shops burned down.

My friend Bassoo is deaf. She came with us to Pakistan. Her husband is also a poor man. She was ten years old when she was married and has had ten children. None of them are in school. None of them have ever been in school.

Everything in Kandhi's yard is covered with mud, including the people. The recent heavy rains have made the roof of the house collapse. Everyone is pitching in to clean the mud out of the house and get the roof repaired before it rains again.

Kandhi

I am from Lagman. I've been in this camp for seven years. We left Afghanistan because of the war. My son was killed in the war. He was engaged to be married. His fiancée is still in Afghanistan. Our house was bombed, that's how he died.

We've been in the house ever since we came to this camp. We pay eight hundred rupees each month. The owner doesn't care that the roof was destroyed in the rain. He pays no attention to things like that. If the roof has collapsed, we have to fix it. The owner is a Pakistani man. He owns many of the houses in this camp.

My husband has no job. We have some land in Afghanistan that still gives us a little money, and sometimes one of the small businessmen here helps us out a bit.

Our life here is very bad. All we do is try to eat and keep ourselves alive.

I gave birth to triplets in this camp. One of them died, two are still alive. They don't go to school.

Two families live in this house, a total of fifteen people. We have no thoughts for the future. We just live day to day. I would like my children to be educated, but with my poor life, it seems impossible.

Such a long stay of such a large number of refugees has had a huge impact on Pakistan, especially the North West Frontier Province (NWFP), where most of the refugees are located. Large numbers of livestock have used up scarce grazing land, causing some areas to experience erosion. Water has become contaminated from the high number of people using it coupled with the lack of sufficient sanitary facilities.

Forests have been stripped, partly by the lumber Mafia, and partly to fuel the cooking fires of the refugees.

The labor market has also been affected. Refugees, desperate to make any kind of living, are prepared to work for lower wages and in any kind of conditions. In the first half of the refugee crisis, Afghans were helped with free accommodation and basic food, and, for a short while, a small allowance. This enabled them to work for even smaller wages. Also, the sheer numbers of ideal yet capable people has made Peshawar an employers' market.

Rents in Peshawar were also pushed up because of increased demand, plus the influx of UN officials, aid workers, and journalists. The war has also increased the number of weapons in the community, as everyone along the arms train takes their cut.[12]

After so many years, donor fatigue has created a drop in funding to refugee assistance programs. Some agencies that used to aid refugees are now concentrating all their energies inside Afghanistan. Very little aid goes to refugees now. A staff member of the International Committee for the Red Cross considers Afghanistan and the refugees to be their largest under-funded program.[13]

The government of Pakistan makes regular threats to force the refugees back to Pakistan. In August of 1998, the North West Frontier Province's government closed down four Afghan universities in Peshawar, in a move designed to make Afghans less comfortable in Pakistan.[14] In surprise raids, the police forcibly evicted the students, broke furniture, and sealed the buildings. Although they were allowed to re-open almost a year later, their continued existence is not guaranteed.

Afghans are being blamed for a high crime rate, with the senior superintendent of police in Peshawar saying that 90 percent of the crime in the city is committed by Afghans.[15] Pakistanis are tired of Afghanistan's battles being fought in the streets of their cities. The Peshawar newspapers regularly carry stories of one Mujahideen party assassinating members of another Mujahideen party.

In March of 1999, the NWFP government announced they would soon begin to confine all Afghans to camps, to make it easier to send them back to Afghanistan, as soon as the time comes.[16]

The "New Arrivals" sections of Accora Hattack refugee camp are crowded with tents, both the official UNHCR canvas tents and makeshift tents made of rags and plastic sheeting.

I am visiting this camp with Homa Zafar of the Cooperation Center for Afghanistan. No sooner do we get out of the truck than we are surrounded by women in desperate need. They press in on us to get our attention. Homa explains to them that I am just a journalist, I have no power to get them food or jobs or medical attention, but that does not seem to matter. They tell me their stories faster than I can get their names and faster than Homa can translate.

Mogol

I am an old woman from Kabul. I came here almost one year ago, and we have nothing, no shelter, nothing else. We have nothing to eat. We left Kabul because of the war and bombing. Many people came and took all that we have. Our house was destroyed.

No Name

I have nothing to eat, and I just gave birth to two children.

No Name

They distributed blankets to the others, but we received nothing. Recently there was very bad cold weather, and we had nothing to cover ourselves.

I am from Kabul. I left because of the war. Our house was completely destroyed in the bombing. My husband was killed and also my son-in-law was killed.

I have been in this camp for six months. We have nothing to do here. If we receive food from Shelter Now International, we eat. If not, we go hungry.

No Name

I have lost four people in my family. Here I have nothing. I built this oven, and bake bread for people.

I was out working in the wheat field at home in Afghanistan, and when I came home, I saw that a rocket had destroyed my house. Four people inside the house were killed.

No Name

I am a widow. I have lost my husband, and my child is sick and I have no money to take her to the doctor. Nobody is asking about us. Nobody is taking care of us. I also lost my sons in the bombing. All I have left is this small girl, and she is sick.

No Name

We have come to Afghanistan with just what we are wearing. We have nothing. My daughter-in-law gave birth to her child in the truck on the way.

No Name

It is almost one year that we are here, and so far, we have received nothing from UNHCR.

No Name

I have lost my two sons. I have come from Afghanistan. I have nobody, and no help to live here. I came here five months ago. I am just living and begging.

The UNHCR gave us this paper to get a tent, but we have received no tent

Tent city at Accora Hattack refugee camp.

yet. Come to my place and see how I have to live. All these people are helpless.
I am not the only one. We all have nothing.

Bozga

I left Kabul one and a half years ago, because of the bombing and the war. I
have lost five people from my family.

Gulmakai

I have been in this camp for six months. I come from Mazar-e-Sharif. When
the Taliban came to Mazar, there was fighting and a lot of killing. We had to
flee. We took nothing with us. And so we came here.

   I am an educated person. In Afghanistan I was a nurse, but here I am jobless.
I am living in this desert.

   When the Taliban came, the situation became so much worse that I prayed
to God that this situation would never come even to our enemies. The mothers
didn't take care about their children. Everybody was just taking care about
themselves and was just running, trying to run out of Mazar. Many youngsters

were left there. The Taliban destroyed many houses and they killed many educated people.

There are seven people in my family. In the fighting in Mazar, I lost my grandmother, and two of my uncles' families, completely. When we went to bury the bodies, we couldn't find some of the bodies' heads, we couldn't find some of the bodies' hands. There was very bad killing. We just buried our dead and fled the country.

My two brothers go around Peshawar and beg. Because I am a young daughter, I must stay close to home.

No Name

The only thing we receive is food from Shelter Now. Can you give us money?

No Name

The people who are powerful, they receive everything. Because we are poor, we receive nothing.

Zelaiha (seventeen years old)

I came to this camp fifteen days ago from Kabul. I am here with my husband and my two-year-old son. I am seven months pregnant with another child. There is nothing in Kabul, no jobs, no work. Life was so difficult in Kabul for women and for young boys under the Taliban, so we left the country and came here.

The time in this camp has been the most difficult time in my life. We have nothing. My husband works in a bakery, and they pay him only fifteen rupees a day. I can't feed us on fifteen rupees a day.

Rosta

I just gave birth last night to a son. I have been in this camp for three months. I have four other small children. We are from Kabul. My husband sells fruit along the streets of the camp. Living in Kabul is difficult, that's why we are here. If life was easy in Kabul, don't you think we would have stayed there?

No Name

I am a widow. It's almost one year I am living here, receiving nothing. I need shelter. My husband died twenty years ago, of a sickness. I am living with two daughters and two of my sons. I lost one of my young sons in the war. I am from Kunduz.

IN IRAN

In 1990 Iran led the world in hosting refugees, sheltering 4.5 million Iraqis and Afghans within its borders.[17] Many were provided with green cards, which gave them access to subsidized food, free schooling, and free health care. Others received short-term work permits, giving them official permission to be in the country, even though there were limits to the types of jobs they could hold.

Iran also benefited from the refugee population. The Afghans worked for low wages and long hours, further bolstering an already booming economy. Afghans could be found working as day laborers in construction and in the brick kilns. Children held jobs in pistachio-shelling factories. Women worked in clothing factories, did various types of needlework, and also cooked and cleaned for wealthy Iranians.[18]

Afghan women who headed their families had a greater chance of becoming independent than their sisters in Pakistan and Afghanistan. The greater availability of jobs, plus free education, meant that many women were employed and going to school for the first time in their lives. Having left family and in-laws behind in Afghanistan, these women were finally free to make decisions themselves about their children and their time. This freedom made it very difficult for them to consider returning to the restrictions of Afghanistan.[19]

While the economy was good, Iran was in no hurry to rid itself of its refugees. However, when the economy took a nose dive in the early 1990s, and the refugees showed no signs of wanting to go home on their own, the government tried to encourage them.

No more green cards were issued, only temporary papers. Greater restrictions were placed on the types of jobs Afghans could take, and returning Afghans were presented with an incentive package to see them through the first two months back home. Initially, the temporary cards, first issued in 1993, were only good for three months. These were extended several times to allow Afghan children to complete their school year.

Life became much more difficult for Afghans in Iran. The police became more enthusiastic in rounding up and deporting those without documents, and people were finding it difficult to manage economically. Jobs were scarcer, and rents, even for cramped, inadequate quarters, were expensive. Still, people were in no hurry to leave. The situation in Herat, where many of them were from, was even worse. The city had been devastated by bombing, and the economy was in ruins, with virtually no jobs available.

Refugees had generally been settled into the cities of Mashad and Tehran, rather than in refugee camps. In 1995, the situation began to change. In an effort to control and contain the refugee population, the government housed more of them in camps. One camp was built between Mashas and the Afghan border. Eight thousand people were moved there, and were provided with some basic food and supplies. Exit was controlled through an iron gate. Those with work permits could go out to their jobs, but only in government vehicles.

When the Taliban took over Herat in 1995, repatriation efforts slowed down, but further restrictions were enacted. Undocumented refugees were arrested and placed in detention camps to await deportation. Those living in the cities were confined to certain parts of the city. Anti-Afghan feeling was rising among the Iranian population, who blamed the Afghans for economic downturn. Refugee-free zones were created in the cities.

In August of 1998, the Taliban took Mazar-e-Sharif, and things went from bad to worse. The Afghans killed an Iranian journalist and seven Iranian diplomats. The Talibans systematically butchered the Hazaras and Shiite populations, causing further anti-Afghan feeling among the Shiite Iranians.[20] Hostilities escalated, and that autumn saw the Afghan/Iranian border crowded with hundreds of thousands of heavily armed troops, ready to go to war.

As many as thirty Afghans were killed in random anti-Afghan violence in the cities of Mashad, Isfahan, and Tehran in October of that year. Refugees in Iran called family members in Pakistan to tell them of threats to their lives.

The government newspapers condemned the killings, saying that there was no difference between the killing of the refugees and the killing of the Iranian diplomats. They urged the Iranians to be hospitable to the Afghans and to stop harassing them.[21]

In late November, hundreds of thousands of Afghans were given three weeks to return to Afghanistan.[22] Although tensions at the border are no longer as high as they were, the situation is still not good, and anti-Afghan feeling continues to grow among the population. With life in Afghanistan as oppressive and impossible as when they left, it is difficult to imagine a bright future for the Afghan refugees in Iran.

NOTES

1. UNHCR, *Refugees Magazine* 2, no. 108 (1997).

2. *CCA Newsletter* V, no. 5 (October 1998).

3. United States Committee for Refugees, *Country Report.*

4. Ibid.

5. *Journal of International Affairs* 47, no. 2 (winter 1994): 557.

6. Kathleen Howard-Merrium, "Refugee Women and Their Struggle to Survive," in *Afghan Resistance: The Politics of Survival*, edited by Grant Farr and John Merrium (Lahore: Vanguard Books, 1998).

7. Amnesty International, A1 Index ASA, Nov. 3, 1995.

8. Mohammad Azam Dad Far, "Refugee Camp Syndrome," in *Children of Afghanistan in War and Refugee Camps: A Documentation of the International Hearing Held in Stockholm, April 4–5, 1987*, published by the Swedish Committee for Afghanistan (1988): 65.

9. Ibid., 67.

10. Ibid., 67.

11. *CCA Newsletter* 5, no. 3 (June 1998).

12. *Silent Voices Magazine* 1, no. 3 (June 1998).

13. U.S. Committee for Refugees, *Country Report*, 1999.

14. *CCA Newsletter* 5, no. 4 (August 1998).

15. *Frontier Post* (Peshawar), January 18, 1999.

16. *Khyber Mail* (Peshawar), May 4, 1999, 1.

17. UNHCR, "An Iranian Surprise," *Refugees Magazine* 2, no. 108 (1997).

18. Martin Regg Cohn, "Afghan Refugees Find Increasingly Cold Comfort in Iran," *Toronto Star*, Nov. 8, 1998.

19. UNHCR, "An Iranian Surprise."

20. Cohn, "Afghan Refugees."

21. *CCA Newsletter* 5, no. 5 (October 1998): 6.

22. *CCA Newsletter* 5, no. 6 (December 1998): 8.

HEALTH

Twenty years of war has left Afghanistan in ruins as a nation. Those who have survived are in a state of chronic, preventable ill health, which will have far-reaching implications on the society, even if justice were to come to the country immediately.

The war and the chaos that comes with it has crippled the health-care delivery system. With the Taliban persecuting educated people—a persecution that continues and expands the repression begun under the Mujahideen—many of the few remaining trained medical personnel are leaving the country, if they can. Women who are trained and could be of use are largely forced to remain at home. Although some women are permitted to provide health care for other women, the hospitals and clinics set aside for female patients are few and ill equipped.

Present day Afghanistans, in addition to dealing with problems today, have inherited health problems from the past. An estimated seven hundred thousand Afghans are disabled, with one out of every ten people having a disabled family member. One quarter of those who are disabled lost their limbs through land mines and missiles.[1] The millions of land mines still in the ground, and those that are being newly planted, kill or cripple ten people a day, still, in Afghanistan.[2]

Land mines can blow off a foot or a whole leg, and blast dirt fragments into the genitals, bones, and internal organs. Fragmentation mines project a burst of fragments in the shape of an arc and can tear a person to shreds. Some mines are designed to maim, others are designed to kill.

There are bouncing mines on springs that jump to waist height before going off, which kill their victim virtually every time.[3]

The rest of the disabilities are a result of polio, tuberculosis, blindness, deafness, mental retardation, or cerebral palsy.[4] Most of these cases could have been prevented with proper nutrition, adequate hygiene, and a workable basic health care delivery system, which largely do not exist in Afghanistan.

Destruction of the infrastructure, including water pipes, has resulted in only 39 percent of urban residents and 5 percent of rural residents having access to safe drinking water.[5] The percentage of people with access to proper sanitation is even lower.[6]

Afghanistan was once self-supporting in food, but that ended when the war began.[7] Land mines have made many once arable lands unavailable, and land that has been cleared for planting has, in many places, been given over to opium cultivation. Afghanistan is now the largest producer of opium in the world.[8]

Many Afghans suffer from chronic malnutrition and stunted growth.[9] In centers such as Kabul, food is available, but unaffordable. Many people are out of work, and inflation has sent food prices soaring as much as 500 percent in one year.[10] UNICEF estimates that one in five Afghan babies have low birthweight as a result of their mothers being malnourished. Low birthweight makes them more likely to become blind, deaf, mentally retarded, or have cerebal palsy.[11]

The rate of mothers who die while giving birth is the second highest in the world, after Sierra Leone. This is caused by malnutrition in young girls resulting in small pelvic size and obstructed labor; early marriages and frequent, closely spaced pregnancies; and infections, such as tetanus, that could be prevented if proper drugs were available. Almost all births in Afghanistan are home deliveries, without trained medical personnel being there.[12] There are other complications caused by war and the present regime. One pregnant woman had her baby on a street in Kabul, while her husband was being beaten by the Taliban for trying to take her to the hospital.[13]

Women make up 70 percent of those reported to be suffering from tuberculosis. Effectively treating the disease takes six to eight months of medication. Although the drugs are available, extreme poverty means that the medication is usually stopped long before it should be. This creates a strain of drug-resistant TB.[14]

Many patients have been tortured by the guards and suffer broken bones, extensive bruising, and fractured skulls resultant from severe beatings. Some torturers will pour fuel on their victims and set them on fire, resulting in severe burns.[15]

The Taliban's restrictions on access to education has resulted in a lack of basic knowledge of health and hygiene among children, so that even the limited healthy choices that are available to them are not being made. Destruction from bombs, missiles, and land mines has created a need for over a million new homes to be built. Afghans who are living in the only shelter they can find—often tents or bombed-out buildings—suffer from malaria, cholera, parasites, and respiratory infections.

In Pakistan, although there is the possibility of greater access to healthcare for Afghans, many people cannot afford to see a doctor or pay for medications. The poor nutrition and sanitation problematic in Afghanistan carry over to most of the refugee communities in Pakistan, and the hot, unfamiliar climate adds additional problems.

There is an exhaustion among Afghan women, a bone-tiredness from trying to keep their families fed, their husbands sane, and everyone alive through two decades of war. Many Afghan women in Pakistan have come to a dead end. There was no future for them where they were, no possibility for a decent life where they are, and little or no likelihood for them to ever be able to go anywhere else.

Dr. Zarlasht has come out of Afghanistan to attend a health seminar in Peshawar. She works secretly as a doctor in Kabul.

Although some women are officially permitted to work in some health clinics, the women who do so are still at risk of being brutalized by the Taliban. Female doctors and nurses are often beaten, or forced to watch their colleagues being beaten. Hospitals are under constant watch by these armed men who represent the Department for the Promotion of Virtue and the Elimination of Vice.

Dr. Zarlasht

I am from Kabul. Secretly, I work as a doctor in Kabul.

My sister is also a doctor. She works in the north of Kabul. She also works secretly. The Taliban doesn't know about either of us.

Go ahead and use my own name. I am not afraid. The Taliban are not able to read English books, so they are not able to understand if I appear in your book. They are illiterate in their own language—how can they read English?

My house is very far from the clinic. I have to catch a bus. When the bus is empty, I must pay enough for five or six people, just so it will take me. I have to wear the *burqa*, of course, and I have to ask the bus driver very politely to take me. I ride on that bus for awhile, then I catch another bus. I leave my home at half past six in the morning, and I don't arrive at work until nine. That's two and a half hours, one way. I work until one-thirty, then I start for home again, so that I arrive home before dark. Lots of problems. I get very tired, traveling all that way for only a few hours of work. But all the time, I keep risking it.

The women who come to the clinic are very happy to have me working there. They need to have a doctor for their children, for themselves.

There are too many diseases. There is not enough for people to eat and drink. Often they eat only bread, nothing else, and sometimes not even bread. It is not enough for the body. This is the main reason they get sick.

The climate in Kabul is very nice, and people do their best to look after themselves. They are very clean and tidy. The main problem is that there is nothing to eat. There are no vitamins in the diet. They don't have enough money to buy anything better, and there isn't enough food around, even if they had money.

All Afghan women have depression. When we look around, there is no education, no house to live in, no money, no people, nothing. How can we have a good life? How can we be healthy people?

Everyday we see worse and worse around the city, along the road, in the house.

I am in Peshawar now for a few days for a workshop, along with other women doctors who have come out of Afghanistan. We all came here secretly. The seminar is on family planning.

The Taliban has punished all the doctors and all the people, but they don't know about me and some of my colleagues. We will probably get our turn to be punished!

The *burqa* makes me very tired, especially the way it covers my eyes. A screen is in front of our eyes, and that makes it difficult to see. You have to look at things close up and far away at the same time. It is very difficult.

By my own eyes, in the middle of Kabul, I saw two feet and one hand hanging from a post. After I saw these things, I began to hate seeing meat in stores, because meat is also hung from hooks in shops, and it reminds me of the hands and legs.

The Taliban are happy with each other, but nobody else is happy in Afghanistan.

The Taliban soldiers carry a stick in their hands, and hit people and force them to go to the mosque. It doesn't matter if they are clean or not. They must leave their shops open, they must leave their *karachis*, with cigarettes or something for sale, and go to the mosque. The Taliban hit them and say, "Go quickly!

Don't Wait! Don't lock your shops!" They won't listen to one word from anybody. They just say, "Go!"

I have a friend who is married. She was talking with a man in the street, a friend of her family's. They were talking with each other. A Talib came and asked her, "Who is this man?" She said, "He is a friend of mine." The Taliban said, "It is no good for you to talk to a man in the street. Now you must get married!" She said, "I am already married! I already have a husband! This man is a friend of mine."

The Taliban said, "No, you must not talk to this man! What business do you have to talk to this man!"

The Talib then took both of them to the courtyard to get married, and so they were married! After they were married, the Talib let them go. My friend and her friend laughed about it, and my friend went home to her real husband.

Once I went to a shop to buy a pair of shoes. The Taliban came by and hit the shopkeeper. "Why do you sell shoes to a woman? Her husband or brother must get shoes for her!" They hit the shopkeeper, and I ran away. I see things like this all the time in Kabul.

I am obliged to go back to Afghanistan when the seminar is over. It is my duty. Also, I like to help Afghanistan's poor people.

I hope one day my country will get better, and when it does, I would like to invite you to visit me there.

In the back of Hyatabad, on the edge of a mud-house and rag-tent settlement, the Basic Health Care Center for Afghan Refugees has just opened a new clinic. It is largely funded by Afghans living in Germany.

Dr. Kotsea (thirty-two years old)

I trained at Kabul University, and came to Peshawar during the time of the Mujahideen, six years ago. Now I work at the Basic Health Care Center for Afghan Refugees.

Life in the camps is hard on women's health. It's very difficult to live like that, but they are poor, they have no choice. Most have no electricity, no gas, no clean water. It's very hot in summer and very cold in winter. They get a lot of diseases, skin diseases, stomach diseases, heat stroke, cholera, malaria.

Camp life is very difficult. I think, myself, if I go there to live, after two or three days I will be dead. Many people die there.

Fatima (thirty-five years old)

I had a baby four years ago, but I am still sick. There is pain where the baby was. I come from north of Kabul, fourteen years ago, because of the war with the Russians. I live in Tajobad, the refugee camp near the clinic. Before the clinic, I had to go to a clinic in Hyatabad. It is a long walk. Someone told me about this new clinic and I'm happy. There is free medicine, and it's very close to where I live.

Macia (twenty-eight years old)

I have been here for one year. We left Kabul because of the fighting. All of my family are here, my husband, son, and daughter. We have no money to send them to school.

Life was a bit better before the Taliban. Under the Taliban, it is very bad. They are always hitting women. We can't go out, can't get jobs. We have lots of problems.

I came to the clinic today because I am sick. Can't you see it in my face? I'm very sick.

Dr. Rona

I am a doctor at the clinic attached to the Afghan Institute of Learning.

Infectious diseases are our greatest problem. The next is birth spacing, women having too many children too close together.

Many women want just three or four children. They come here to discuss family planning. We can help them get an IUD, birth control pills, tubal ligations. The treatment is very low cost, but we can serve only a very small number of the women we would like to serve.

Osia

I am a Health Educator with the Afghan Institute of Learning.

We train women to teach other women about hygiene, food poisoning, seasonal diseases. TB is bad in Peshawar and in the camps, and so is viral hepatitis. It gets especially bad in the summer, because of the heat, the bad water, and living so close together.

Dr. Mohd

I am a dentist at the dental clinic for Afghan Refugees.

The first reason they get pain is from bad nerves. Many have lost teeth this way. The second problem is from a poor diet. There is not enough food, and especially not enough food with vitamins. The third problem is that they are not able to keep clean. They are not able to brush their teeth properly, and there is no clean water to rinse their mouths with. But the main thing is nerves.

It is very sad here. Often they cannot afford any medicine or proper food, and the only thing that will stop the pain is for me to take their teeth out.

Sometimes a woman comes here, says her face is in pain. She has pain in her teeth, her ears, and so on. After talking to her, she tells me that her child is crying all the time, and there's not enough food to feed the family.

Because of this tension, she gets pain in her face. It's difficult to remedy, because the problem is more economic than dental.

Another time, I met a woman who was sick and in pain all the time. She told me she was married eleven years ago, but still has no child. Her husband yells at her and hits her all the time. That's why she has pain in her teeth.

When the Russians were in Afghanistan, this clinic was funded by Norway, Sweden, and France. When the Russians left, the funding left.

As far as I know, there is no dental treatment for women in Afghanistan. None at all.

There is one place for men to wait and to have their teeth examined, and there is a completely separate place for women. We sit in the women's waiting room, simple wood benches under an awning, and listen to the women who are waiting to see the dentist.

Shilah (twenty years old)

I come from the countryside, near Kabul. The war was bad there. Our house was destroyed. There were lots of rockets. I came to Peshawar one year ago with my family.

I graduated from high school before the Taliban came.

My husband is now in Australia, in Perth. He is trying to bring me there, but it will take another one or two years for the papers to be fixed.

I came to the dental clinic because of my bad nerves. I get pain in my teeth when I think too much.

Gulalai (thirty-five years old)

I am originally from Wardack Province, but we moved to Kabul. I got married eleven years ago, but still have no child.

We left Kabul during the time of the Mujahideen. There were rocket explosions in our area, and we fled. When we came back, our house was still standing, but we had been robbed. The furniture, the rugs, everything was gone. Soon after that, another rocket came, and this one destroyed the house.

Guljan (fifty years old)

We came from Kabul three years ago. We lived in a very nice section of Kabul. Everything there has been destroyed.

We lost everything. Whatever the rockets didn't destroy was taken by thieves.

Now I am a widow. My husband was murdered by a rocket. He was on his way to Mazar, and he was killed. I have two sons. Both are with me in Peshawar. They sell things from a small box in the street, gum, cigarettes, things like that.

It is difficult to build a country again after it has been destroyed. We pray that things will get better in Afghanistan, but we don't think that they will.

Lohmia (fifty years old)

[*She cries and talks in a whisper. Benazir can barely hear her to translate.*]

Everyone's story is the same. I live with my niece here in Peshawar. My house was also in Kabul. It, too, was robbed and destroyed. I have nothing. I am very disappointed with life. All I have are my tears. I don't know if it is day or night. I don't know if it's dark or light, warm or cold. I don't know anything, just that I'm breathing. I don't want to say anything else. Just, I cry.

Paregal (forty-two years old)

I am from Jalalabad, and have been in Peshawar for two years. We left because of the fighting. There was too much war, too much poverty, no peace.

I got nervous and suffered mental problems, as did my son. Now I am sick. We had a very good life in Jalalabad, but the war didn't let us stay.

When I think too much, I get pain in my teeth and my head. It's hard to live here with no money, no job. My husband was an office worker in Jalalabad. He made just enough for us to live on. We had a good house, right in the city, but it was destroyed by bombs.

Jalalabad used to be very nice city. It was a little hot sometimes, but very nice. It had lots of schools, hospitals, very good shops that were full of everything, the roads were paved, there were lots of cars, busses, and trucks. We had TV, radio, electricity, telephones, all modern things. Now, there is nothing left. It is very bad. It looks like a cemetery.

I would like to go back, but what I would see would just make me sick again. I would like to leave Pakistan, but where could I go with no money? I don't like staying here. Peshawar is a dangerous place, full of murderers.

When the rockets started coming, we heard a terrible noise, so we fled to the desert, running away from the bombs. My nerves got so bad, my whole face was frozen from fear.

I am here in Pakistan with my mother and my husband and five children. My mother helps to look after us, as my husband and I are sick. My oldest child is thirteen. He works making carpets, to bring in a little money.

Dr. Naureen

I am a doctor at the Red Crescent Clinic for Afghan Refugees. We deal with eyes, ENT, orthopedics, paralysis. We visit different camps and refer patients to specialists.

The health problems we see among the refugees include malnutrition, anemia, vitamin and mineral deficiencies. This happens mostly because of lack of food, and multiple pregnancies. When the mothers are breastfeeding, and not in good health, naturally the children also suffer.

We see a lot of injuries in women that are a result of beatings by their husbands. Battering is really very common around this part of the world.

In the camps, hygiene is one of the biggest problems. The women are usually not aware of hygiene, and they don't have the facilities to keep themselves clean. They don't have any soap, they don't have a change of clothes. They wear one suit of clothes all the time, even for months, and they don't take a bath for months. Similarly, their children are also living in the same condition. So hygienically, they are very poor. In women, this can lead to lots of gynecological problems, like vaginal infections, and things like that. They can get diarrhea from eating contaminated food. Children can get diarrhea and diseases from playing in dirty water, also middle ear infections. The ear drum gets perforated and when dirty water keeps going there, it never heals. Deafness can result.

Parasites are also a problem, and they can result in anemia and malnourishment because of malabsorption.

We give advice on better hygiene and good health, and on providing clean food to themselves and to their children. We can advise them to the extent that whatever little they can do, they should do. They can prevent their children from playing in dirty water. They can prevent their children from eating dirty food. They can do this even within their limited means.

Land mine injuries usually require amputations. Also there are burns. With the hygiene problems, it is impossible to keep their wounds clean, and they get infected.

There are also contagious diseases, such as malaria, typhoid fever, polio. The biggest cause of this is poor hygiene, many people living together in small spaces. There is vaccination that takes place against polio, but most people are not aware of it. Also, they are not aware of how polio can damage a child.

Those with Down's syndrome and cerebral palsy are generally neglected. The children are wholly dependent. They cannot even go to the toilet on their own, so they are just a burden on their parents. The family, rather than helping the child, feel it is a burden so it generally gets neglected.

Rape is something which normally people don't talk about. It happens, but no one talks about it. Fathers kill daughters who have been raped. They are uneducated men. They follow their forefathers, who were just brutal. They feel their daughter has destroyed the family honor, even though it was against her will. Instead of blaming the person who was responsible for it, they kill their own daughter.

Incest is *not* talked about, but we know that it happens. A girl in the house might be raped by her father or her older brothers, but she would never speak about it.

War has caused Afghan women much physical stress and mental stress. They have no home of their own, they have lost their house, they have lost their country. That causes a lot of problems, but most of their problems are caused by their society structure. That's what I think. Of course, war had made it impossible for their social structure to improve and advance.

At the Japanese Hospital and Physiotherapy Center, women sit and stretch out on clean, white-sheeted mattresses on the floor to have their aches and pains attended to. It is a friendly, relaxed atmosphere. Women listen in on each other's conversations with me, while the doctors apply their treatment.

Head Doctor (male), Japanese Hospital and Physiotherapy Center (JIFF)

Many of the people who come here were injured by gunshots during the war, and their injuries still give them pain. Land mine injuries are mostly treated at the land mines hospital near Jalalabad.

Near to this clinic is an office of the Taliban. They come to us for treatment sometimes.

Everything is free here for patients, which is why we are so crowded. Many of the women who come here are ill from their heavy workloads.

Dr. Saraya

I am from Kabul. My husband and I left in 1996, two and a half years ago, two months after the Taliban came. I was working in the hospital of Indira Gandhi in Kabul, but the Taliban made me leave that job. They announced on the city streets and on the radio, "No women come out of your homes." All the time, I was shut up in the house. I was very scared. I thought a lot about my job, about all the sick people I was unable to help. I was very unhappy and very angry.

We had lots of problems on the road to Peshawar. The Taliban were every-where. Many times, they stopped us, searched us, took money from us.

Women come here with many injuries. Some have pain in their back or their legs, elbows, shoulders, hands. Afghan women do lots of heavy work, and this causes pain. Some have been beaten. Afghan women have many children, and this also causes pain.

Rozia (thirty years old)

I am from the center of Kabul. We came to Pakistan seven years ago. We left because of the war. Our house was destroyed. We lost all of our things because of bombs and rockets.

I had four children. Three died, now I have only one. They became sick here, from the climate. We had no money for medicine or good food. The ones who died were seven, three, and two years old.

Now we live in Peshawar, in one room near Saddar Bazaar. My husband works in a shop with Pakistani men. He gets a small amount of money for us to live on.

When we go to the bazaar, the Pakistan men call out, "Afghan! Trespassers! Go back to your own country!"

My one remaining child is nearly four now, and he is sick all the time, too.

Future? I don't know. I am disappointed in the right now.

Ishai (fifty years old)

I am from Kabul. We've been in Pakistan for two years. We came here because my daughter and son were doctors and had a pharmacy in Kabul. The Taliban hit and harassed them, called them Kafir, nonbeliever. We waited for things to get better, but they didn't.

Rockets damaged our home, and thieves would come and take things.

I have no education. I am illiterate, but all my children have been to school! I have five daughters and two sons. Three of my children are still in Kabul. Three of my girls have higher education, from Kabul University. They are doctors. My husband is an educated man. I came from a province where girls are not educated, but in spite of that, I talked to my girls all the time about the importance of their education.

We are obliged to live in Pakistan. What does it matter if we are not happy?

Malalai (thirty years old)

I come from Pol-e-Komri, in the north of Afghanistan. We came here two months ago for treatment at this clinic.

Life at home is very bad. There is war, poverty, all the time people are crying. There are no jobs. All life there is very difficult.

I am married. I have no children. I came to Peshawar with my husband. He is a shopkeeper in Pol-e-Komri. We will stay in Peshawar for only a few days more, then we must go back.

All the population of Afghanistan cannot go abroad. Some of us are stuck there.

The Russians were better than the Taliban. The Taliban cuts people's arms and legs off. Punishment is the Taliban's gift to Afghanistan. We are crying all the time, especially old people. Why will the UN not help? We are human beings! Someone's got to help us!

I went to school to the eighth grade. I married twelve years ago. All of my marriage I have been nervous, so I have not had any children. I had a heart attack, and I came here for treatment. I had a bit of jewelry that I sold to get here. Most women in Afghanistan have no money, so when they get sick like I am, they just die.

People sell what they have to buy food. When they have nothing left to sell, they become beggars. When they go home from begging, their children have died, because they have no food.

Nafisa (forty-eight years old)

I am from Kabul. I've been in Pakistan for two years. We came here because the Taliban punished women. My husband died in Quetta three months ago, of a heart attack. He was sad all the time, always thinking sad things, then he had a heart attack and he died.

In Kabul, my husband was manager of a dental clinic. Here, my sons are tailors. I am always looking for work washing clothes or cooking for someone.

In Afghanistan, I was working in a hospital, doing mending. The Taliban came to our workplace and said, "After today, you women are not allowed to come to work. You must stay home."

So I stayed home. Finally, we left.

Zaibo (sixty years old)

My name means "beautiful." I come from the Old City of Kabul. All of the houses are now destroyed. Just dirt remains.

I came here to Peshawar five years ago. I go from house to house, doing laundry and cooking for rich Afghans. There are a few wealthy Afghans here.

I'm sick now because my house is wet and cold. My hands and feet hurt. I'm not able to stand up very well.

There are eight people living in my house. All women, no men. I had a son, but he is in prison, I think, in Kabul. He went missing during the Mujahideen, five years ago. There are no other men. I live with my daughters and daughter-in-law, and grandchildren. My daughter also tries to find a job, but the best she can do is laundry, like me.

My hands feel a bit better from the treatment, but my feet don't get any better. I still can't walk or stand up very well.

My granddaughter is here with me. Her name is Samina.

Samina (seventeen-year-old granddaughter of Zaibo)

I am in class eleven. Life here in Peshawar is better than it was in Afghanistan. I lost my father in Afghanistan. We have many problems.

My father's name was Ahmad Shah. He was an engineer. He used to make artificial legs, for people who had lost their legs in the war. He was a very friendly man, very kind to his family.

My mother is now a cook in a clinic in Shaheen Town. My sisters have graduated from school, my younger brothers are still in school. I would like to become a doctor and help my people. If only it is possible.

Zabida (seventy years old)

I am from the countryside near Jalalabad. I have bad pain in my shoulder.

I left Afghanistan twenty years ago, because of the fighting. I have three sons. Two are here in Peshawar. One is in Afghanistan. He is a member of the Taliban.

[*I ask how she feels about him being with the Taliban.*]

He is a learned man, not one of the mob.

[*The other women laugh at this.*]

The treatment here makes me feel a little better, but I am very old. I won't get much better.

NOTES

1. Edward Giradet and Jonathan Walter, editors, *The Essential Field Guide to Afghanistan* (Geneva: Crosslines Communications, 1998), 148.

2. United Nations Mine Action Program, n.d.

3. Giradet and Walter, *Field Guide*, 68.

4. Ibid., 148.

5. Ibid., 196.

6. *CCA Newsletter*, 5, no. 4 (August 1998): 13. The World Health Organization reports worsening outbreaks of cholera and acute gastroenteritis in some parts of Afghanistan. Six hospitals in Kabul reported, over the course of one week in August 1998, fourteen hundred cases of acute diarrhea, gastroenteritis, and cholera. In Bamyan Province, in an area housing thousands of internally displaced persons escaping the fighting in the north, that same week of August saw 328 cases of suspected cholera, including twenty-eight deaths.

7. Ibid., 14. A Taliban blockade has resulted in approximately one hundred deaths from starvation in central Hazarajat. Tens of thousands more could be facing the same fate.

8. Giradet and Walter, *Field Guide*, 206.

9. Ibid., 206.

10. Ibid., 206.

11. Ibid., 202.

12. Abbas Faiz, "Health Care Under the Taliban," *The Lancet* 349, no. 9060 (April 26, 1997): 1247.

13. Giradet and Walter, *Field Guide*, 202.

14. Faiz, "Health Care Under the Taliban," 1247.

15. Giradet and Walter, *Field Guide*, 194.

CRAZY IN THREE LANGUAGES

Shukria's Story as Told by Nasrullah, Her Husband

People call my wife crazy in three different languages.

My wife is thirty-three years old. We have been married for ten years. She was well when we got married. We were married in Kabul. She was neat, clean, and looked after the children. Now, she's always thinking that everyone is her enemy.

In August of 1992, she became ill. The fighting was going on between the Jihadi factions. One night, she just started talking to herself, saying, "Why do you want to kill me? Why do you want to kill my children?" She talked to herself all night.

When the Mujahideen came, we were living in Kabul. We had to keep moving to different places, because rockets kept coming. My parents and relatives were not very good to my wife. They were not kind when she became ill.

For some time her brothers wanted to put her into a mental hospital in Jalalabad. For awhile she was in a hospital here in Peshawar. She got electric shock. That helped a bit, but not for long. Also, she could not bear to be apart from the children, so they had to stay with her in the hospital, which was not good for them.

The medication she's on has bad side effects. She can't keep her tongue in her mouth, and water comes out of her mouth all the time.

My wife has removed the children from school, saying, "Our enemies will get you, so don't go." She rushes after the children when they leave the house to play with their friends.

My wife's behavior disturbs the neighbors. She talks all the time, very loudly, and she screams, too. We have to move every two months because the neighbors treat us meanly because of her behavior.

The neighbors threw dirty water at my daughter. She had a cut on her head, and it turned into a large, infected abscess on her head. There were even worms in the hole in her head.

My wife's illness affects the children very badly. She beats them. She does not allow them out of her sight. They are stuck with her all day.

The children fight a lot. They say bad words to their mother, but if I punish them, she gets upset. Whenever I go out, I worry about what's going on at home.

Last month, the landlord took our eldest daughter because I couldn't afford to pay the rent. He kept her as a hostage, until I found the money. She is only nine years old.

My wife can no longer cook properly. She can't keep the children clean, she can't keep the house clean. She tears up anything that's left lying around, extra clothes for the children, school books. The few official papers I have left, I must carry with me everywhere, or she will tear them up.

My hope now is to go to any western country that will have us, where my wife can get proper care, where the children can go to school, where I can work. I was trained as a lab assistant in India, and I have also been a teacher.

When my wife was well, we used to laugh a lot. We were happy. We do not laugh anymore.

A recent study of women's health in Kabul by Physicians for Human Rights showed that 81 percent of the Afghan women interviewed reported a decline in their mental health in the last year. Thirty-five percent had mental health problems so severe they significantly interfered with their daily activities. Ninety-seven percent of those interviewed were struggling with major depression.[1]

After twenty years of war, and with no relief in hostilities and repression in sight, these statistics are not surprising. Extreme, unrelenting poverty has removed the possibility of material comforts being able to make their lives easier, and Afghan women are forced to try to keep themselves and their families together under tremendous hardships.

In Afghanistan, freedom of movement for women is severely curtailed. Officially not allowed outside without a male relative escorting them, those who do, out of necessity, go out alone are at risk of being beaten in the street. Their lives are closed off and walled in. There is no possibility of a leisurely walk to relax and relieve tension. Regulations around clothing means that women must always be aware of themselves, careful that no ankles are showing by accident, and that no sound is coming from their feet. No sunshine can touch their faces. Even inside their homes, they must paint their windows so that no men can see in and be distracted from their prayers. It is no wonder women are depressed.

In Pakistan things are different but not easier. Work and recreational opportunities are limited. Many women wear the *burqa* in Pakistan out of choice, due to harassment from Pakistani and Afghan men if they walk about with their faces uncovered. Women in Pakistan interviewed by the Physicians for Human Rights had even greater mental health problems than those in Afghanistan. Ninety-eight percent of them had severe depression, anxiety, or post-traumatic stress disorder.[2]

For most there has been no way to escape and forget the traumas they have lived through in the war. In Afghanistan, signs of destruction are everywhere, and many still live with mine fields, rockets and artillery attacks, and the sound of gunfire. There is no opportunity for distraction through work, education, or recreation. The Taliban has outlawed music, television, and any sort of gatherings of groups of women. Most women are entombed within the walls of their homes.

Most also have personal grief to deal with. Almost everyone has lost one or more family members during the war.[3] There has been no quiet time to help them deal with their grief, no time when fear has let up enough for them to be able to properly mourn and heal.

Long-term bombardment has meant that most Afghans have been displaced from their homes at least once over two decades of war. During the Soviet occupation, the countryside was the most vulnerable. After the Communist regime fell, Kabul and other cities became the main targets. Eight percent of the women in the Physicians for Human Rights study has to move at least once, and frequently more than once within Kabul between 1992 and 1996.[4] Displacement increases problems such as poverty, illness, and emotional stress. Women who had left Afghanistan for Pakistan experienced the additional stress of living in a strange country, one that no longer welcomes Afghans, with a different language and culture and an unfamiliar climate.

In 1997 a UNICEF study of the psychological difficulties of the children of Kabul showed that three-quarters of the three hundred children they interviewed had lost someone from their own family between 1992 and 1996. Almost half had lost a parent. They had all seen war violence with their own eyes, and had heard the anguished sounds of war with their own ears. Half had seen people die during rocket attacks. Ninety percent believed that they, too, would die this way.[5] These children are living in a state of chronic trauma with no end in sight.[6]

While living in refugee camps and communities has given Afghan women a refuge from the day-to-day problems of war and the constant tyranny of the Taliban, life in the camps creates other problems. Camp life is an unreal life. It is a life of waiting. For most, it means a life of nonproductivity, of being dependent on other people's help, as the traditional paths to self-reliance are unavailable.[7] Most lead monotonous lives, with scant possibility for future chances and happiness. Many women are kept indoors by their husbands, who have no other way of asserting what they see as their rightful role as head of the family. It is impossible to guess at the level of wife abuse. With no positive change to realistically look forward to, many refugees drift into permanent states of pessimism, hopelessness, passivity, and depression.[8]

Children suffer greatly when their parents are psychologically traumatized. Many homes in the camps are headed by women who have been widowed, or whose husbands go back to Afghanistan for a large part of the year to try to work their land. Economic hardships aside, these women, struggling with their own traumas, are hard pressed to provide an emotionally healthy home for their children.

Unless and until there is a decent, just government in Afghanistan, one whose structure and mandate can give people something to hope for and productive work, Afghan women will continue to experience a high rate of mental health problems.

Needa has recently come out of Mazar-e-Sharif, where she experienced the traumatic events that took place after the Taliban took over the city in August of 1998.

She came to the attention of Annemie, a German psychologist living in Peshawar, and underwent therapy with Annemie to help her come to terms with the horrors she saw and went through.

I meet Needa in Annemie's living room, surrounded by beautiful Afghan quilts, needlework and artifacts. The room is comfortable and calming.

Needa (twenty years old)

I have been in Pakistan for five weeks. I came here from Mazar-e-Sharif. I am here with my whole family.

When the Taliban came, a lot of people ran away into the mountains. The

Taliban went into the houses, took people out, and killed them. That's why I started having problems.

I saw a lot of dead bodies. I saw how people were beaten up and mistreated. I saw how the dogs were eating up the dead bodies. There was such a bad smell in the city.

The dead bodies were in the streets for about two weeks. The Taliban wouldn't allow the relatives to bury them, so they were all swollen up and stinky, and animals started to eat them.

The Taliban started killing people immediately after they took control of Mazar. In the first days, they killed everybody who appeared on the streets, even other Pushtuns. After a few days, they stopped killing just anybody, and concentrated on killing Hazaras, and Uzbecks, especially the Hazaras. The Taliban had been in Mazar before, and the Hazara gave them a difficult time and killed them, so the Taliban was now killing the Hazaras in revenge.

Until the Taliban came, it wasn't a great life, but we had enough to do, we had work and schools. When the Taliban came, everybody had to sell everything just to make ends meet.

In the first month, when the Taliban was still going into people's houses to take people out and kill them, we left our house and ran away to a refugee camp a few kilometers away from Mazar.

There were all kinds of different tribes living there, including Hazaras. There were more women than men, because the Taliban had killed many of the men. There were around twenty thousand people in this camp.

We lived in a tent with mud walls around the bottom of it and just the canvas above us, nothing else. It was very dusty and dirty. We had to go a long distance to get there. There was no electricity. We had to carry water a long way. There was no food. Often we went hungry to bed.

Step-by-step, we sold things, clothes, carpets, to buy food. There were no shops at the camp, so we had to walk six kilometers into the city to do some shopping. The women in my family did the shopping because it was too dangerous for the men to do it. The Taliban mostly arrested and killed men.

When things calmed down a bit, the Pushtun people could re-open their shops, but only them.

As soon as we stepped out of the tent, we had to have the *burqa* on. I had never worn it before the Taliban came.

Those who had money could run away. They had a way out. Those who didn't have money were stuck there. I became very, very upset. It made me sick. I became emotionally very unstable. This continued until I came to Pakistan.

Some of the bodies had only a head left, or just the upper and the lower body, but everything in the insides was gone, only the bones left, no meat.

The first time when the killings happened, when the Taliban were killed by the Hazara, someone came and put the bodies in a truck and took them away. But this time, the bodies were lying in the streets for about two weeks.

The journey to Peshawar was very difficult. We went from Mazar to Pul-e-Komri in a hired car. Everything we had, we sold, so that we would have money for the trip. From Pul-e-Komri, we went to Kabul, and from Kabul we went to Peshawar. We traveled for two nights and two days to come here. It was very cold. It was the middle of winter when we fled. We arrived in Peshawar just before Eid [the day of feasting that comes at the end of Ramadan]. I had never been in Pakistan before. It's OK here. At least there is peace and not so much killing going on.

Going to school and learning—these used to be my favorite things. I am not really a houseperson. Housework is not what I want to focus on in my life. I would rather study than get married.

Annemie, Psychologist

When I first saw Needa, she was already a little bit better. The switchover from Afghanistan to Pakistan had a kind of a healing effect.

Before she came here, she spent about three months totally withdrawn. She couldn't sleep. Whenever there was a sudden noise, she would just scream. Her mother described her as "uncontrollable." She was hysterical. She couldn't hold her urine, and she wet herself all the time. She was just a totally different girl than she used to be.

This came about after she saw the bodies being eaten up by dogs. This must have been such a trauma to her, to see bodies. She said some had only the head, some had arms and legs but no stomach. The bodies were lying in the streets for a couple of weeks. It must have been terrible because it was hot, and the sight and the smell must have been horrible.

I think even in Afghanistan, people were listening to her in the beginning, because they were shocked about her symptoms, and they loved her, but the more she was difficult, they withdrew from her. They were fed up. They told her to be quiet. They were disturbed, and when you get disturbed your compassion ends and you get irritated, so they were irritated with her, and they had no compassion for her anymore. They would still talk about compassion, but I don't think it came from inside anymore. They were really irritated, and I think that had aggravated her whole problem, because she had nobody really to talk to.

What I said to her the first day I saw her, in front of her family, was, "What you have experienced is a very dreadful thing, and your reaction is a totally normal one. You are totally normal that you actually reacted to stress like that. You are sensitive, and you are normal, and the way you reacted was normal." I think that was a revelation for her, that she was actually normal, because everybody considered her to be crazy.

The other people in her family did not have the same reaction she did. They thought she had just gone "off." None of the other family members saw what she saw. She was the one who would go out of the house to the market, to run errands. It must have affected the others as well, because everybody was living in that stressful situation, but they weren't exposed to the full horror of it like she was.

She came here twice a week for four weeks, then once a week for another month. I would just let her talk, to again and again repeat that story, what she saw. I encouraged her to express her feelings, to tell me how other people reacted to her. We looked at it from all angles. We worked it through.

The only thing now is occasionally she gets tension headaches, because she is worried about the family's economic situation. The family has no income, and they often go to bed hungry. There are two families that live together in one room, with seven small children, and that of course, worries her.

Mostly, I counsel expatriots, people who have been in Afghanistan as aid workers, and have become traumatized by the war or by things they have seen in Afghanistan.

I assist Afghan women on a more informal basis. One Afghan woman was having a terrible time with her husband, he had gone totally crazy, but we finally got him to a psychiatrist, and he's under medication now, but when he takes it, he sleeps for twenty-four hours and when he wakes up, he can't even move. His mouth hangs open, and the saliva runs down his face. That's what the psychiatrists do here, you know, just knock 'em out! It solves the problem by keeping them quiet. In this case, I'm quite happy about it, because at least his wife can get some rest now! Before taking the medication, he was a nightmare! But now, the kids have to feed him.

So I have Afghan women like that, especially with psychosomatic disorders. They don't come to me for therapy, for counseling, but they come to talk. I just listen to them, I comfort them, I advise them where to go, what to do. Like yesterday, I had a woman sitting here. She was also from Mazar, and I said to her, "What at the moment, is your biggest struggle?"

She just broke down and cried, and I put my arms around her. Sometimes it helps to be held by somebody. Then we talked a bit and she said, "You know, I had such expectations about my life, what I could do and learn, to study and move on in life, and it's all finished. Life has gone over me. There's no hope. There's no future." Then she said, "Honestly, I really struggle with self-pity."

So you could call that counseling, but for me this is just everyday things, women coming to my door, pouring out their hearts, struggling. They are here everyday. I enjoy working with Afghan women, but I don't have a scheduled working time, and certainly I don't charge them for my time. I am just available to them. Word gets around.

Most of the women are drained of love. They are not valued, they have no rights, and to have somebody who actually listens to them, appreciates them, cares for them, holds them, cries with them, is a revelation, even a revolution for them.

One of the programs for women that has been shut down by the Taliban is a grass-roots mental health project. It had given women of the area a rare opportunity to get together with other women in the village, without men, to talk about their lives.

Four of the workers from that project are taking advantage of this Taliban-created holiday to come to Peshawar for more training. Annemie has been putting together a week-long seminar, which she will lead, that will help them hone their skills as counselors and group facilitators.

We gather in Annemie's backyard, and talk while the shadows lengthen and the insects buzz around our heads.

Soila

One of our topics is about opium. We put on a drama showing the bad side-effects of smoking opium, and they say "From this day, we will stop smoking it." After they stop they can see that they begin to feel better. We are dealing with people who are addicted. So we try to get them to substitute something for opium, like almonds, "When you think about wanting to smoke opium, make yourself a cup of tea or a dish of almonds, and that will help."

Although one lady tried this with her husband, he wanted to smoke opium, so she prepared something for him to eat. He ate what she prepared, then started smoking! So, it is not easy!

The Taliban doesn't know we are in Peshawar. We left Herat secretly.

On the way here, I cried a bit. It was a very long distance. I thought it would take us two days, but it took us five days. We didn't really sleep in all that time. I was very emotional when I arrived.

In Herat, the Taliban closed down the *hamam*, the bath house for women. After it was abandoned, some women got the key from the owner and went there secretly to wash themselves. Some neighbors informed the Taliban on them, and the Taliban came and beat the women, and their brothers, and the owner of the *hamam*.

I have a message for the world's women. I think they forget Afghanistan's women. At first when the Taliban came, I heard that foreign women were interested in Afghanistan, but now we have been forgotten.

Sheree, Program Manager

We have come to Peshawar to get more training in things like post-traumatic stress, conflict, psychosomatic illness, and suicide. It is difficult to deal with these problems. Some women with post-trauma needed in-depth counseling, but we don't have time to do that in our groups. Some women don't like to do counseling with one person only, so they prefer being in a group.

Women get better in our groups because they have a chance to come out of their homes. The women in the group remain close friends after the group ends. It is a very important thing that women come together and meet with each other. This is an opportunity for them to leave their homes and get together. Even if they are relatives in the same village, they often haven't seen each other for several years.

Some husbands don't allow their wives out of the house, or there is a quarrel among the men in the family, and her husband doesn't permit her to go to her relative's house. But in the group, they can see each other.

Some women are of different parties. They may be relatives, but they still belong to different parties. They had conflict during the war, and after that they were denied permission from their men to see each other. This is a problem that is caused partly by the war and partly by the structure of the society.

The women always dress up to come to the group. This is an opportunity for them to take care of themselves. This is a very good chance for them. Most women keep animals in their homes and do a lot of work, and this time in the group is like a holiday. They don't want to be ashamed in front of the other women.

They learn from each other, practical things like cooking, and other types of support. There was one very poor lady in one of the groups. All the women collected money and gave it to that poor lady. Her son was in the hospital with TB, and her husband was dead, so she was all alone in the hospital with nobody. It was very sad. Even we counselors gave her money.

Also, we have a chip-making project for the poorest ladies, who have no other source of income.

All of the women get lessons in leadership, then by turns they lead the group. It is better than having just one leader, because all women can then feel they can do things. Then they decide as a group what they want to discuss.

We tried it at first with group choosing one leader, but after a very short time there was a lot of jealousy, and the leader started thinking she was much better than the other women. It caused problems in the village. It is better to share the leadership.

I am not married. I haven't found the right man. But even if I *was* married, I would continue my work!

The Taliban coming to Herat has changed my life. Before, I didn't wear a *burqa*, but now I have to wear one. It is very difficult for me, because I wear glasses. Every time I wear the *burqa*, I get a headache, and I get depressed. When I am at home, I don't feel like going outside everyday, because of the headaches.

One day I left my home and went to the market. I went into one shop to buy some things, but the Taliban came and beat me, just because I wanted to buy some things! They don't like women going into the shops.

I was angry when they beat me, but I didn't cry. I didn't fall down. I kept standing while they beat me, then I went on my way. It was nothing. I was laughing because I didn't feel any pain. I wore thick clothing under my *burqa*, so they didn't hurt me. But I was very angry.

Annetesat (twenty-seven years old)

I have been a mental health worker for two years. I grew up in Herat City and had never been to the villages, so it was very interesting for me to work there. At first the work was difficult, but gradually we got more experience, and the work became easier.

Economic problems are the hardest ones for me to help the women deal with, that and suicide, of course. When a woman says she is thinking of suicide, it is very difficult, because we should contact her family, and that is not always possible. Also, sometimes we hear of her suicide thoughts just as we are leaving the village, and we are not able to stay and help.

Sometimes a suicidal woman's family will protect her and look after her, but sometimes they won't, and we are not able to stay and protect her.

The group meets for two hours twice a week. We begin the meetings with a drama. We wrote little plays about different topics, and we put the play on, and then the women discuss it. The topics are about depression, anxiety, suicide, conflict, bereavement, psychosomatic illness, things like that.

The women have a good time at the meetings. They say, "We grow up at these meetings." They say, "I was very sick, but I know myself that I am getting better, and anytime you have a group, I am ready to attend." They wait for us to come each week.

This is a very new thing for the women in the village. They have never before met in such a group. They are so eager to come, even through three or four feet of snow.

I am single. I graduated from the teacher training institute. I took various subjects, such as psychology, English, Russian, literature, and science. I studied there for four years.

Some of the women in the group will tell the group that their husband beats them, and all the women know already. They say, "She has a very bad husband." Some women hide their private lives from the group, because they fear the other members of the group. They are afraid that word will get back to their families.

When a woman tells us she is being beaten, we ask her, "What is happening when the man is beating you?" The group discusses the situation, and the woman who is beaten also takes part in the discussion. Sometimes they come up with good ideas, sometimes they don't but at least she has talked about it.

Fulmae

Some women have so many problems that they want to kill themselves. When we go to the village and have discussions, they become very happy, because it is a chance to go out and get together.

In our program, we would go to villages, and let the women there know we were starting the groups. We would first have to meet with the *shura*, the group of men that run the village, and ask their permission for us to do such a thing. We told the *shura* that we had some questions for the women about mental health problems. We asked the men of the *shura* if the women in the village had depression or other psychological problems. They would say yes, and also that they didn't know how to deal with the problems. There was no doctor and no hospital for the women. When we said we could help, they wanted us to come to the village and do our program.

This year, there was a problem in the village where I was working. A woman wanted to come to our group, but her family didn't want her to. They said, "You should stay at home." The woman cried a lot, and she threatened to kill herself unless she could come to our group.

I and another counselor went to her house and spoke with her mother-in-law and eventually she was allowed to join the group. She became very happy.

The family had objected because they didn't like the women in the family to go out of the house, or to have any rights. The women suffer a lot because of economic problems and family problems.

Usually, families all live together, sometimes as many as twenty-two people in one room. It is very difficult.

Our groups are divided into three age groups, the oldest, the middle, and the youngest.

The youngest women are aged fourteen to eighteen. Their problems are mostly because they are unable to finish their education, and also because they know they would soon be forced to marry. It is difficult for them.

One of the women in our course was forced to marry at eighteen, and she said, "I don't want my husband. I don't want to be married." She wanted to kill herself. One of our counselors spoke with her, and eventually she accepted marriage. There was no way around it for her, other than killing herself. We said, "It is not good to kill yourself. Maybe things will get better in the future." So she made the choice to live, and to live with being married.

We are having to counsel women with major problems in a situation where we cannot bring justice to them. That is very difficult.

It is common in Herat for women to kill themselves by pouring kerosene on themselves and setting themselves on fire. They also do it by eating a large amount of opium, which poisons them.

The older women have resentment because of how they have been forced to live their lives, depression because they have lost a member of their family or their property in the fighting.

Zohra Rasekh, M.P.H., is a senior health researcher for Physicians for Human Rights. In 1998 she spent several months in Afghanistan and Pakistan interviewing Afghan women for a report called "The Taliban's War on Women: A Health and Human Rights Crisis in Afghanistan." The report is available from Physicians for Human Rights.

Zohra Rasekh

My parents are Afghan. I was born elsewhere, but lived as a child in Afghanistan.

It was quite a devastating experience, to go back to the place where I once lived, and see something totally, totally different, negatively different. I saw destruction. Everything in the country is ruined. Things were absolutely upside down from what I remembered. When I lived there, I was old enough to remember what Kabul, our city, looked like, especially the area where we lived, and it had all been destroyed.

I was very open about what I was doing in Afghanistan, because for scientific research, I couldn't just go there, talk to some people, and come out. The methodology required some proper sampling. I had to go through open ways. I got a visa as an American researcher. Of course, I didn't give out all of my plans of why I was there. For example, I couldn't say, "I'm going to interview women." That would have absolutely kept me from getting in. Expatriots are not allowed to talk to Afghan women. I said I was doing a health research project.

I had a lot of difficulty getting a visa, but after a month of trying, while I was in Pakistan, I got lucky. They had turned me down three times, and the fourth time, suddenly somebody that day was in a good mood and didn't ask too many questions. I got my visa purely by luck and by chance.

I was in Afghanistan for a little over two months. I stayed in various places, because it was not safe to stay in one place all the time. I mainly stayed in the guest houses of some of the humanitarian organizations. As an expatriot, I was not allowed to stay with local people. If I had been caught staying at a local person's house, that person would be in trouble.

Mental health problems were reported more among the women I interviewed in Pakistan than in Afghanistan. The reason that I see for it is this: Women in Pakistan were those who couldn't take it any more in Afghanistan. They were up to their foreheads with financial difficulties, pressure of Taliban, education problems, work problems, all of these problems they were experiencing. So, they got up and left. This is why women reported more mental health and other types of health problems, because they were the ones who were affected very much.

In Pakistan, they are free to move around, they can go to school, they can work, if there is anything available, but there is no availability. They are stuck in this country where they are not really considered refugees, they get no help, they are on their own. They have tremendous difficulties, financially, the climate change, the hot temperatures. That explains why there is such a high rate of mental health problems. There is this double burden of the things they have suffered in Afghanistan, and the things they are suffering in Pakistan. They left one place, hoping things would get better, only to face more problems in Pakistan.

Psychologically, all human beings are that way. We think that if we change where we live, our problems will leave us.

In this case, the problem of Taliban goes away in Pakistan, although the Taliban has many people in Pakistan as well, but by and large, that problem is gone. However, the problems of poverty and everything else stay with them. They move from one camp to another, from one city to another, and they lose their minds. I sympathize with each one of the families who are living like this, because it would make me go insane.

I have heard of mass suicides, of whole families taking poison. I have heard that some women drink caustic soda to kill themselves, which is the most painful type of death.

Overall, I see a high rate of severe mental health problems among Afghan women, based on the findings of our research. In two years, 80 percent reported a decline in their mental health. Twenty years of war, including the Soviet invasion and the chaos of the previous government, did cause problems, but not to the extent that has happened under the Taliban. The pressure on women that the Taliban has created, psychologically, financially, physically, you name it, is incredibly severe.

This extreme pressure has not been felt by all Afghan women. There are women in some rural areas whose lifestyle has not changed very much under the Taliban. They never did go to school, they never did work outside their homes, they did cover their faces, although it used to be by personal choice, and now it is forced.

But the intellectual and educated female population is devastated. The pressure is so high now that women are committing suicide. I think the rate of suicide will increase if the situation in Afghanistan does not improve dramatically and soon. I think that there will be more mass suicides, that women could kill their children then themselves, because they can no longer feed them, and can no longer stand the pressure.

When I asked Afghan women about their hope for the future, most of them said, "We have faith in God." That's actually one of the things I think is keeping these women alive, a hope in God. Otherwise, there is no hope. The only hope they have is that God will change the situation.

The Islamic Relief Mental Hospital is a shed at the back of a shady flower garden, behind another building on Chinar Road in Peshawar. There are three whitewashed rooms, two with desks and chairs, and one with a small cot and shelves full of files. This is the combined record-keeping and electroshock room.

The doctor lets me look through some of his files while I wait for him to be free to talk with me. The intake questionnaire has questions I've never seen on similar questionnaires in Canada: What is your tribe? How many family members have you lost? How did they die, in battle, by execution, as a result of torture, or by natural causes? Are any of your family members missing? In what year and month did you migrate? How many people are you responsible for? Do you receive help from any organization? How do you feel about being helped? Are you a Mujahid? How active are you now? Have you lost your home in a rocket attack?

I read some of the women's case files. "Depression, restlessness, anger, insomnia, wish for death, loss of interest, loss of energy." "Anger, restlessness, obsessive thoughts, compulsive acts, sadness." A woman who is thirty-two suffers from continuous weeping. A sixty-five year old woman has headaches, loss of energy, and anger. A forty-year old married woman has anger, irritability around noise, sadness, body aches, and spends too much time thinking. An eight-year-old girl has begun falling and having fits of weeping.

I cannot even imagine what these women have had to live through to this point.

Dr. Mohammad Zahir Sharifee

I trained as a psychiatrist in Afghanistan twenty years ago.

Four or five years ago, 250 patients per day passed through this clinic, all psychiatric patients. Now, many patients are too poor to come here.

The patients I see these days are almost all very seriously ill. Because of poverty, their families wait as long as possible before they bring them here for treatment. I see patients with depression, anxiety, mania, hypomania, multiple personality disorder, schizophrenia, psychosis, epilepsy, mental retardation, Parkinson's dementia, and senile dementia.

Of the illnesses related to war, depression is the most common, particularly among women. They have the stress of being stuck inside their homes, the pain of having lost children during the war.

During the war, and up to now, many people have depression, morbid grief reaction after the death of a loved one, epilepsy due to trauma, post-traumatic stress disorder due to bombs and guns.

The cultural reaction of Afghans to psychiatric illness is very bad, because of lack of education, especially those who have no education because of the war. They think that the ill person is inhabited by fairies.

There is an increase in depression among women living under the Taliban. Women who would like to work, to walk in the city and buy things from the shops, do other things, cannot, because the Taliban prevent them.

There is a high rate of suicide among refugees. In the last fifteen years, I have seen many cases of depression with suicidal tendencies and attempts. The family of a suicide experiences great shame. People say that a person who commits suicide was not a Moslem, and that causes the family shame. Those who kill themselves use a gun, or a knife, or poison.

There is a lot of violence in the home, a lot of stress living in the camps.

The family is run like a dictatorship by the men in the family, especially among noneducated Afghans. They keep wives and mothers and sisters and children under pressure. They don't like their women to talk to another person, or go to the park, or go to a picnic, or even just go out for a walk along the street.

I would say that half of Afghan women's psychiatric problems are due to the family culture, and half are due to the war. Of course, twenty years of war has meant that fewer people have been educated, and lack of education only strengthens the male dictatorship in the family.

Women who are educated know different things, and can solve their problems. The uneducated women are treated like animals. They are not allowed to speak with anyone, often not even relatives, and they are under the total control of their husbands.

There are many factors that contribute to psychiatric illness, such as no education, bad economic conditions, bad culture, troubles, family problems, and social problems.

We give ECT [electro-convulsive therapy, also known as shock treatment] to patients who are more agitated or aggressive, or profoundly suicidal. It works well.

We need many things at this clinic, especially for poor Afghans. They cannot purchase medicines, so they remain sick in their houses. Their problems are very bad by the time they come here. Their families bring them in.

Sultana is here for shock treatment. She has been brought here by her husband, a tall man with a long beard and a turban. Sultana is dressed in red and green tribal dress, her head draped in a green scarf. She sits in a chair beside Dr. Sharifee as he talks to her for awhile in Dari, then tells me in English a bit about her life. He says she talks to herself, cannot sleep, laughs inappropriately, and gets angry frequently. She has a low tolerance for noise, becomes very sad, and will start weeping and not be able to stop. He tells me she also has paranoid ideation, and worries that her husband will take another wife.

I ask her to tell me about herself. Dr. Sharifee translates.

Sultana (thirty-five years old)

I have six children. I live in Tojobad, near one of the refugee camps. We pay three hundred rupees each month to some Pakistanis.

I became ill two years ago. My mother-in-law died then. My father died during the war. The treatment makes me feel better.

I am here today with my husband and my brother's wife. My husband works as a day laborer.

I've never been to school. My children don't go to school either. I don't see the reason for it.

We left Jalalabad thirteen years ago, because of the fighting.

We finish talking and another woman comes in, dressed in black. The doctor introduces her to me as Sister Masooda. He tells me that she is not educated, but she is very wise. She has been assisting him with the female patients for eight years. Her husband died many years ago of a heart attack, so she is the sole support of her children.

The doctor stands up and so does Sultana. She has done this before. We go into the shock treatment room. Part of the roof is coming apart, and we can see the sky and a piece of rusty metal roofing. The doctor draws the curtain across the doorway, leaving Sultana's husband outside.

Sultana, a short, slight woman, climbs up onto the cot. She stretches out on her back. Sister Masooda folds Sultana's arms across her chest, and both she and Sultana's sister-in-law lean their weight into Sultana's body. She moves around a bit, but I can't tell if that's from discomfort or protest. The doctor inserts a piece of rubber into her mouth so she doesn't swallow her tongue. The women get a firmer grip on her as the doctor prepares the electrodes attached to the small brown box at the head of the bed.

It happens fairly quickly. Sultana's slender body arches from the electricity going through it, and continues arching, even after the voltage has stopped. Sister Masooda rolls Sultana onto her side, and her sister-in-

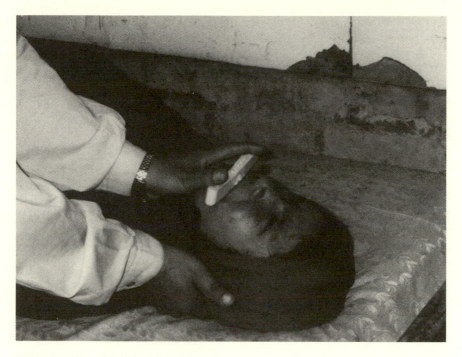

Sultana undergoing shock treatment.

law places a cloth under Sultana's loosely open mouth. Sultana shudders and shakes for some time before her body finally is still.

Lela *(fifteen years old)*

[Jalozai Refugee Camp]

I am from Fara, in Western Afghanistan. In 1994, my father was killed by the Mujahideen.

In 1997, this is what happened to my mother. She was alone at home. My brothers were away, and I was at a neighbor's house, with my smallest brother, washing clothes to get money. Some armed men came to my house, found my mother alone, and raped her.

When I came back to the house, I found my mother unconscious. The neighbors told me the story. After that, my mother became like you see her, very depressed. She doesn't want to talk to anybody. She had lots of psychological problems.

After that, we came to Peshawar. When we first came to Peshawar, we didn't have any place to live, so we lived on the streets for a week. It was the summertime and very hot. We didn't have a thing to eat or to help us to live. My younger brother was begging, and my older brother was trying to find work. I stayed with my mother, who was not well, mentally. We slept on the sidewalk in a corner of the bazaar. After a week or so, someone told us about this camp, and helped us to get here.

All the time, my mother is very sad. She doesn't want to eat, so we have to feed her by force. Sometimes, she can't even recognize her sons and daughters. She doesn't want to talk with anyone.

She hasn't seen a doctor. We don't have enough money.

Before this happened, I had a good relationship with my mother. We talked all the time.

When my father died, my mother was shocked by his death, but it was not like this. My father was a shopkeeper. The Mujahideen came to the house and took him. After that, we have had no news from him. We didn't even see his dead body.

Before my father died, my mother was very happy and in good condition.

My life has changed a lot since my mother was raped. I am also very sad, because my mother often does not recognize me. It is very sorrowful for me. Often, I cry.

When my father was alive, I went to school. After he died, I stayed home. Now, especially, I can't go to school because I have to take care of my mother all the time. My younger brother goes to school, though, here in the camp.

My mother cannot do anything around the house, and she doesn't want to do anything.

I don't know about the future, except that I'll have to look after my mother. If my elder brother can find a good job, maybe we can afford treatment for my mother. If that happens, maybe I can go back to school.

NOTES

1. Physicians for Human Rights, *The Taliban's War on Women* (Boston: Physicians for Human Rights, 1998), 49.

2. Ibid., 49.

3. Ibid., 50.

4. Ibid., 50.

5. Edward Giradet and Jonathan Walter, editors, *An Essential Field Guide to Afghanistan* (Geneva: Crosslines Publications, 1998), 126.

6. Giradet and Walter, *Field Guide*, 127.

7. M. Azam Dadfar, "An Analytical Review of the General Causes of Physiological Problems among Afghan Refugee Children," *The Impaired Mind Magazine*, published by the Psychiatric Centre for Afghan Refugees (March 1988).

8. M. Azam Dadfar, "From Mental Peace to Impaired Mind," paper presented at the Third International Seminar on Afghanistan in Oslo, September 28–October 1, 1989.

EDUCATION

The Prophet said, "The pursuit of knowledge is obligatory for every Muslim, male or female."[1] Education has never been Afghanistan's strong point. An 80 percent illiteracy rate for women would be classified as progress, but it has only been in the last few years that education for women has been forbidden by law.[2]

Before Taliban, education was free for boys and girls, but, outside the cities, this had little impact on the lives of girls. In the rural areas, poverty meant that schools were poor and poorly equipped. In addition, conservative families preferred to keep girls at home.

After the 1978 revolution, the government began a mass literacy campaign which raised the ire of the local Mullahs. The government, acting clumsily, had tribal women sit in classrooms with male teachers. The men in the community became furious with what they saw as a direct threat to their authority and their propriety over their women. Many schools were destroyed.[3]

During the Soviet occupation, Mujahideen groups destroyed two thousand schools. Over fifteen thousand teachers fled with their lives. People equated keeping their children out of school with supporting the jihad.[4]

In Kabul, before the Taliban came, the schools were coeducational, and 70 percent of the teachers were women. One of the first acts of the Taliban after taking power was to lock girls out of the classroom.[5]

Haji Khulimuddin, the Taliban's religious affairs minister, made an announcement of the school closings and threatened with punishment anyone who disobeyed his ruling. The Taliban also shut down vocational training projects for girls.[6]

The Taliban has given several excuses for their ruling. They've said that, after the war, their first priority is to save lives, and once security improves, girls will once again be educated. However, Kandahar has been under Taliban control since 1994, and the schools are still closed.[7] They've said that they have insufficient resources right now to educate girls, but they have also closed down privately run home schools that cost the government nothing.[8] They have also said that their front-line soldiers would not be able to concentrate on killing people if they knew that women were walking the streets on their way to school.[9]

Three-quarters of the teachers were women, and with them forbidden from working, the male teachers have to cope with class sizes as high as two hundred.[10] Many women who were teachers are now beggars or have fled the country.

Kabul University once had nine hundred lecturers and was linked to universities all over the world. It was destroyed by rockets, but a group of professors had begun the process of rebuilding. They collected a quarter of a million books, and got student enrollment up to ten thousand, four thousand of which were female. The Taliban shut it down.[11]

Mori, Kindergarten Teacher, Nasir Bagh School

I have been teaching here for four years. We have some special problems in this school. The first problem is that the ceiling collapses when it rains. You can see the holes. Another problem is the salary, it is very low, only eight hundred rupees per month. It is difficult to live on that. Also, part of the economic problem is that there are almost no teaching materials. It is hard for me to ask the children to bring something from home, because their families are very poor.

The kindergarten classes are held in a room made of mud around the walls of the school compound. We go from class to class to class, meeting the children and their teachers.

The rooms are dark. Straw matting on the earth floor creates a place for the children to sit. The children remove their sandals at the edge of the matting, to keep from getting it too dirty.

In one classroom, the children are standing in a circle, playing a hopping game. In another, they sit in small groups, counting out things, such as pebbles, dried split peas, toothpicks. Some use the pebbles to form the shapes of letters.

The children are crowded into one corner of the room. Part of the roof has collapsed from the recent rain.

Mina

I started teaching here three years ago. It is difficult to teach without materials. It is much better for the children to be able to show them something new while I explain it to them. It is not good enough if I just talk to them.

Mina has decorated her classroom with a map of Afghanistan and hand-drawn alphabet charts in English, Dari, and Pushtun. She points out one little girl who is deaf. There are no special services available for her.

Mina gets the children to their feet and has them show me what they have learned. They hold up their little fists with the thumb sticking out. "See," Mina says, "they make Afghanistan with their hands." I look again, and their hands do resemble the shape of their country, with their thumbs representing the province of Badakhshan.

The children recite numbers in English and sing a song about teachers: "We respect our teacher, she is like our mother, she is kind, she is kind, she is kind."

The teachers have to be very creative to make teaching tools for their children. Often, they have only garbage to work with. One teacher has strung bottle caps through a string to amuse a child who is not mentally capable of joining with the others. Pictures from old magazines are pasted onto paper and hung on the walls.

In one class, the teacher asks a tiny little girl to sing for me, and she belts out earnestly, "The cruel people killed people in Afghanistan, they murdered many people, and God should send them to hell."

The Afghan Institute of Learning does many things. It runs and supports preschools, primary schools, and secondary schools for forty-five hundred refugee children and provides literacy classes for adult women. They train three hundred female teachers a year to be primary school teachers, and they update the education of women who have already been teaching for a few years. They also provide health education to women in the camps.

Nasifa, Principal, Afghan Institute of Learning

Our children are very hopeless now, psychologically. If we take proper care of them, we think they can have a very good and bright future. In Peshawar, funds are not available for schools. If only funds could be made available for children's education and entertainment, the children are very keen to learn. But the economic problems are so bad.

In families where the economic problems are not as bad, the children are very interested in studying. Among the poorer, the children see no point in education. They want to work and get money instead.

Kadija

I am the manager of the preschool education program. The role of preschool education is very important. The children who go through our preschool program are always at the top of their classes at the next grades. This is because our teachers are well trained. They are very creative, can do everything with the children. They are specialists in teaching young children. We have a six-month training program for preschool teachers.

Sadaf (four years old)

> [*singing*]
> This is a country, but it is not my country.
> It is beautiful but it is not my home.
> Paris is beautiful, but not like Kabul.
> We are homeless.
> We want our country.
> Afghanistan is the best.

Farwah (three years old)

My doll is very beautiful. She is dancing. My mother is very beautiful, too. When she is happy, she dances.

Gohar (four years old)

I like to cut and paste pictures best. I am pasting a picture of a ball, because it starts with "B." The ball is orange.

The Rehabilitation Agency for the Development of Afghans, Orphans, and Widows (ROAOW) has a small handicraft school. It has two classrooms, one with portable, nonelectric sewing machines, and a smaller

Girls singing.

one, where students stand around a high counter to get instruction from their teacher. Students here learn both tailoring and embroidery.

Sewing Workshop Teacher

I teach forty students how to cut and piece dresses, also tailoring. Students from here become self-employed, and can get good incomes. Many students came here when Peshawar University for Afghans was closed by the Pakistan government. They come here to learn to sew, so they can work. All their education has brought them nothing.

Frazon (sixteen years old)

I came to Peshawar only one week ago, from Kabul. I was not happy at all in Kabul. I wasn't able to go out. I was sick of staying at home. I came here to Peshawar to be able to go out sometimes. I am staying with family here. The course is four months long and costs five hundred rupees. When the course is finished, I'll probably have to go back to Afghanistan, but at least I will have had a break. It is up to my family what I'll do. I cannot just decide for myself.

I have no way of taking care of myself without my family. Back in Afghanistan, I may be able to work secretly, but no one has any money to have clothes made.

Benazir and I trudge for an hour through the Board neighborhood of Peshawar. Board is an Afghan shopping area of labyrinth streets and crushed-together shops selling everything from cloth to jewelry to food. Outside stalls crowd into each other on both sides of the putrid canal that runs down the middle of Board. Several restaurants are clustered on one side, with long charcoal grills for cooking chicken and shish-kebabs, and huge, round, flat pans for frying patties. Goat and sheep carcasses hang from hooks in the hot sunshine, the heads of the beasts arranged on trays below. Peddlers push *karachis*, carts on wheels, filled with oranges and other items for sale. This is the cheapest place in Peshawar to buy food. It is also the best place in town to purchase a *burqa*. Several stalls in the labyrinth specialize in them.

The Board is a busy place, filled with Afghans selling, buying, looking, begging, and visiting. Many Afghan doctors have set up practice in the little rooms above the shops. Benazir is not sure of the address, and we take many wrong turns on the advice of people who aren't any more certain than she is. Finally, some distance from the main cluster of shops, we find what we are looking for: the Afghan Women's Medical University.

The school, like all the other Afghan universities in Peshawar, was shut down by the North West Frontier Province authorities in 1998 as part of their plan to make life less comfortable for the Afghans in Pakistan. The students campaigned and finally won the right to go back into the building, unofficially, to continue their studies independently.

The university is part of a clinic and is different from any university I have ever heard of or seen. It is one room, the size of a smallish high school classroom back in Canada. A table at the front serves as the teacher's desk. Most of the students' chairs are falling apart, and none of the students have desks to write on. To accommodate everyone, the chairs are squished together tightly. There are no books on the shelves, no instructional posters on the wall.

The students are on a break when we arrive, and they are eager to talk. Most of them speak English, so Benazir sits back for a long gossip with the professor, one of her former students, and the medical students and I huddle together as they tell me about their lives.

Malalai (twenty years old)

I came to Pakistan four years ago, from Kabul. There was fighting, and rockets. I had graduated from high school and started university when we had to leave. I have friends who are still in Afghanistan. We used to play in the snow together.

The Pakistan government said we had no right to continue our education, so they shut our school down. Once a week after that, we came to the school, met with the principal, and tried to get the school reopened. We talked to journalists, to the BBC, and to Voice of America. We asked them to talk to the UN, to find out why the school was closed. The principal struggled on our behalf.

This university is not legally open. We're not officially supposed to be here. We don't know when they might close it again.

Shauzia

I am from Logar Province. We left because of the fighting. There are eight in my family. All of us are in school. From the beginning, my parents wanted all the girls to be educated. My mother is a high school graduate and my father went to university.

Naderijan (twenty-one years old)

I'm from Wardack province. I came to Peshawar with my family eight years ago. We had been living in Kabul, where there was a lot of fighting. It was very confusing during the bombing. When I left for school in the morning, I was not sure if I would come home alive.

Sultana (eighteen years old)

We came to Pakistan eight years ago, because of the fighting between the Mujahideen and the government. I have brothers now in the U.S.

In Kabul, I played with my friends a lot. We played games, or played with our dolls. Sometimes I went skiing.

Homaira (twenty years old)

Here, we have a lot of problems. We have an incomplete lab. We cannot work in a real hospital, just a clinic. For more than three months now, all the universities for Afghans have been closed by order of the Pakistan government. Now we come here to study on our own.

Fayeba (twenty years old)

Three months ago, I went to Afghanistan for one week. It was very damaged. Everything was destroyed. Women were in *burqa*. We had historical places. Now they are all destroyed. The University of Kabul has been destroyed. There are animals living there now in the ruins. There are no hospitals. The library is all gone; the museum is all gone.

Wearing the *burqa* is not the main problem for women in Afghanistan. It is difficult to see and to breathe when you wear one, but the main problem for Afghan women is education. The Taliban and other fundamentalists want women to remain uneducated so they can be used. When women get educated, they will develop their own lives and will fight for their own rights and own purpose.

Farishda (twenty years old)

I am from Kabul. We left in 1996. I left to save my life. Kabul was very bad. There were lots of rockets. J was not happy to come to Pakistan. For every person, their own country is best. I choose to study medicine to help Afghans and other people.

Waheeda (twenty-three years old)

Education is very important and badly needed in Afghanistan, especially for women. If you educate a man, you educate only one person, but if you educate a woman, you educate all of society, because she will educate her children.

As soon as a mother has a little education, she realizes how important it is for her children, including her daughters, to study. Her daughters then become less likely to be married off when they are too young. A lot of families are not educated, especially in the villages, and the women begin having babies when they are just twelve or thirteen.

I came to Pakistan eighteen years ago. The trip took a week or ten days. Before the Mujahideen, it was very difficult to come here. We came on foot. My sister and I traveled with a woman who knew our family, and with guides. If the government found people leaving, it would kill them.

This university has just one classroom. Before the closing, there were fifty students. Now there are thirty. During the closing, some people got married, left town, or went to foreign countries.

[*Next to the classroom is the laboratory. It is too small to accommodate more than four students at one time. The shelves contain a few beakers and test tubes, and not much else.*]

Our laboratory is really part of the clinic. It is not complete. There are important things missing. We have only one working microscope. We learn from books only. The lecturer photocopies pages from textbooks for us. Sometimes we can use medical books in the library. Next semester, we will do practical work, if the University is reopened.

Qamar Safi, Principal, Fatema-Tu-Zahra Girl's High School

I came to Peshawar fourteen years ago, from Mazar-e-Sharif. I got my degree from the School of Science in Kabul.

Mazar used to be a beautiful city. The people there were hospitable and educated. Lots of women didn't wear the *burqa*, they were independent. Now, with the Taliban there, women can't leave their homes without a man.

Although I went to school in Kabul, I would go back to Mazar to be with my family. When the Russians were in Afghanistan, they would come to Mazar in tanks. Men in the families there ran away to avoid being arrested or taken by force into the army. Both my uncle and brother ran away.

I started out here in 1986 as a math teacher. Now I am the principal.

There are 650 students here, mostly girls. The classrooms are very hot in the summer time, and we are very short of books and science equipment. It is also hard for the girls to get here everyday. Most students are very poor, and it is hard for their families to afford transportation. Also, security in Peshawar is not good for Afghan girls.

Aziza (forty-eight years old)

Seven years ago, I left Kabul. I started to teach as soon as I left Peshawar.

There are special problems in this school. It is very difficult to have enough books and stationery supplies. It's hard for the students to pay the fees. Economic problems are so hard.

We are happy to teach the younger generation of Afghans, even though the salary is small, just one thousand rupees a month. We get no salary during vacation.

I am married, and have four children. My daughters attended the University of Kabul, but now just stay home and study by themselves. My husband works in a Pakistani shop for a small salary.

Yagada (fourteen years old)

We need some help. The weather is very hot, and we need fans in the classroom.

I have been living in Pakistan for seven years. I used to live in Afghanistan.

My country has very nice weather, and the people were very friendly. We had a good life there, but now things are very difficult. I had lots of friends in Afghanistan, but some of them are dead now. Some of them came to Peshawar, but they are too poor to go to school.

My father is a shopkeeper. In Kabul, he was a supervisor and a teacher. My mother was also a teacher in Kabul, but now she's jobless.

My friends and I like to get together and talk, play some games, talk about famous people. We play a game where one person says a word like "cat," and the next person has to say a word that begins with the last letter of the previous word.

Tasmina (fifteen years old)

I have been in Pakistan for four years. We used to live in Logar Province.

Before the Taliban, my life was very nice. We lived together, my whole family, my uncles, my aunts, we all were together. When the Taliban came and the war started, we all spread out to different places. We now are so far from each other. It's very hard for us.

I would like to be a kind, generous person, but now I cannot be, because the situation is not good for us. But I would like to be that sort of person.

Mariya (fifteen years old)

I would like to talk to you about the problems we face in our schools, and in other situations. We only read books. There is no chance for us to do experiments, like in chemistry, or biology.

We came to Peshawar ten years ago. We would like to go back to Afghanistan.

Kostra (fifteen years old)

We have been here for eight years. Living in Pakistan is very hard, but when we hear of people in Afghanistan who cannot go to school, we thank our God that we are here and can study. When we see our other people here who are not studying, who are just like broken people, putting their hands out in front of other people for some money, especially when they beg from Pakistani people, it is very hard for us.

When we study here for our future, we also study for our parents' future as well because they don't have any other way to feed us. We have a hope for ourselves that we will become something for them and we will do something for them and make their life a little better.

I'd love to go to other countries but it's very hard for us. It is difficult to study in Pakistan because everything costs money. The person who has money has everything. The person who has no money has nothing.

I come from Kandahar. We were very happy there. We had a house which is now destroyed. If we go back to Afghanistan, we have no place to live.

Peshawar is a dangerous place for Afghans. Children get kidnapped. A child of seven was kidnapped recently, and when the child was returned, it had only one kidney. The kidnappers put five hundred rupees in the child's hand and let it go. So it is very hard for us to go to school. From the time we come to school until we go back home, our parents are very worried about us.

Homaira (nineteen years old)

I am from Kabul. I have been in Pakistan since 1982. My family left Afghanistan because of the war. We came here to save our lives.

This school has no library and no laboratory.

Feyba (seventeen years old)

I am from Kabul. I have been in Pakistan for six years. I am here with my mother and two brothers. We left because of the war and because there was no possibility for an education or a good life. The schools were closed because of war.

My father died before I was born, in a rocket attack. He was an engineer. My brothers were too small to work and find money for making a living, so we lived with my uncle's family.

Living under a war was hard because we could not go out of our house, especially during the time the Mujahideen came, so it was all the time bullets and rockets. We often did not dare to go out even for food.

Life in Pakistan is very hard. When we come out of our house to go to school, we have to face so many problems. Society is so hard and everyday we are scared.

We don't feel easy, walking around, because the men are so rude. When uneducated men see a woman going out, they say things, they question why women go out, so we feel uneasy about it. Men, mostly, but Pakistani women also say things.

I had friends in Afghanistan, but now they've all gone to different places, so I don't know where they are.

I heard that the government wants to put us all into camps. That would be so difficult.

Education means everything to me. I would like to say to other girls around the world that if they have the chance for an education, they should work as hard as they can, because not everyone has the chance they have.

Weedah (seventeen years old)

I am in class twelve. I want to be a doctor, but I know I won't be.

Our house was in Kabul. There was war and life was very difficult for us, but we tried our best to study, and to move ahead in life by studying. When the Taliban came, they closed all the schools for girls. People faced a lot of difficulties, especially no rights for women, and shortage of food. Some people have died because of lack of food.

Once I was punished by the Taliban when we were still in Kabul. I was wearing the *burqa*, but my hand was showing. They hit me with very thick sticks. I could still feel the pain many weeks later. I was walking along the street, and there was a car full of Taliban. They stopped the car very near to me, and two of them came out, and said very bad words to me, words that it is not right for a woman to say. They hit me very hard. I dropped to the ground and they hit me while I was on the ground and I couldn't move for some minutes. There were lots of people around, but they couldn't do anything, because they would be hit, too.

I cried very much. When I got home, I was still crying. My mother asked, "Why are you crying?" I said, "I was beaten by the Taliban," and everyone said, "That's something very normal. You don't have to cry about that." Lots of people are punished, and it becomes something very normal to them. No one will help someone who is being beaten. Even if a husband and wife are together, and the wife is beaten, the husband will run away and leave her there. They cannot help their wives. They cannot tell the Taliban, "Don't hit my wife!"

I had friends in Kabul. They were very interested in learning, but now they are stuck in their homes. Some of them got married. They got married because of lack of food. Also, a Taliban man will go to someone's house and say, "If you don't give your daughter to me to marry, I will punish you and I will take you to jail." There is no way for the father to do anything. They must give their daughter to him.

This happened to one of my friends. We had been friends since we were small children. Now she is married to a Talib. The Talib took her to a very bad place. He said to her parents, "Your daughter no longer belongs to you. She belongs to me now, I can take here wherever I want." Her father and mother were crying very much. Her mother said, "It would have been better if my daughter was killed by a rocket in front of my eyes than married to this kind of person."

My friend was eighteen when she got married. I don't know where she is. Not even her parents have any information about her. The last time I saw her, she came to see me. She said, "I am about to marry a Talib. I am forced to do this. If I refuse, they will kill my mother and father. It's better to marry that Talib than kill my father and mother."

I don't want to get married, but people say when Afghan girls finish school, they have to get married.

People also say that Afghan girls should marry an Afghan man who lives in a foreign country, because if they marry an Afghan man in Pakistan or Afghanistan, he will not be able to give food to his family. Even if the man is very old and uneducated, but in a foreign country, they should get married.

Zahra (fifteen years old)

I am from Kabul. I have lived in Peshawar for seven years. In Kabul, we had all the facilities for life, our own house, everything, but here we do not have all the facilities. I was eight years old when we came here. That is the only time that I have traveled.

When we first came here, it was so hot that my whole body soon became covered in rashes. After being here for a few years, I am getting used to it.

There is nothing easy about living in Pakistan. Everything is difficult, especially for women, because the society does not respect women. I never talk with Pakistani women. The men on the street say nasty things to me.

I like everything about school. I think education is life. I have many wishes for the future. I am not without hope. I want to be a doctor, and maybe, one day, have my own hospital.

Waheeda (twenty-two years old)

I come from Lagman. We came to Pakistan six years ago because of the war. It was not possible to live there. We couldn't even go out of our house because of the fighting. For six months, we kept moving from one house to another, one street to another. Everywhere we went, there was war. There was a lot of shooting, rockets, bullets. There was death in every step. So, finally, we decided to come to Pakistan.

You can see a lot of Afghan beggars here. They were not always beggars. Life has made them beggars, society has made them become beggars.

I am not married. I have been a teacher at this school for four years. When we first came to Pakistan, I stayed in my house for a whole year. It looked very strange for us, to see women in Peshawar cover their faces. After the Mujahideen took power, we began to cover our heads. But in Peshawar, lots of women had their faces covered, so we tried to look like everyone else, not different. We covered everything but our eyes. The Taliban make women even cover their eyes!

The students here are very interested in getting an education. They want to become something. They have lots of economic difficulties, which makes them very hopeless. It is hard for many of the students to get here each day, to afford the bus fare.

Their future and my future looks like a dark place.

NOTES

1. Muslim Women's League, MSANEWS, Feb. 3, 1997.

2. Physicians for Human Rights (PHR), *The Taliban's War on Women* (Boston: Physicians for Human Rights, 1998), 3.

3. Edward Giradet and Jonathan Walter, editors, *An Essential Field Guide to Afghanistan* (Geneva: Crosslines Communications, 1998), 171.

4. Ibid.

5. PHR, *The Taliban's War on Women*, 75.

6. *CCA Newsletter*, 5, no. 3 (June 1998): 14.

7. Giradet and Walter, *Field Guide*, 173.

8. *New York Times*, June 17, 1998.

9. Giradet and Walter, *Field Guide*, 173.

10. Ibid., 172.

11. Ibid., 174.

CHILD BRIDE

In Afghanistan, each member of the family is valued according to what they can contribute economically to the household. Girls are valued for the price they can fetch on the bridal market.[1] In Afghan culture, the groom pays the bride's father for the right to marry his daughter. The money is supposed to compensate the parents for the money they spent raising her, and for the services she will no longer be able to provide for them. In return, the bride's family would generally provide the new couple with some household goods.[2] A man must often work for many years to afford the bride price, so frequently a young woman will marry a much older man.

Few families allow their daughters a choice in who they marry. Negotiations are held between the father of the bride and the father of the groom. Sometimes there is an exchange other than money. A father might exchange his daughter for another man's daughter so that their sons can marry. Marriages are also used to cement family relationships, settle a feud, or expand a family's holdings. It is not uncommon for cousins to marry.

Many women are married when they are in their early teens or even younger. The Taliban has encouraged this practice, both through direct statements that girls are ready for marriage at age eight and through the impact on families of their policies. Poverty means that families no longer can afford to keep girls at home very long, and the lack of educational opportunities reduces girls' employment options to cooking, cleaning, and having babies.

In October of 1978, the Communist government passed laws in an attempt to reform these practices. It raised the minimum age of marriage to sixteen, and lowered the allowable bride-price to a nominal sum.[3] The purpose of the decree was to "remove the unjust patriarchal and feudalistic relations which exist between husband and wife."[4] It did not work.

Educated women were pleased with even these modest reforms, but local Mullahs saw it as a challenge to their power and authority, as did male heads of families. This decree was brought out at the same time as the decree that all girls should be educated. Fathers were terrified that their daughters would disobey them and thereby bring shame upon the family.

Protests broke out, which grew into armed revolt. Teachers and government officials were assassinated.[5]

Under the Mujahideen and Taliban rule, marriage reforms, which had never really caught on, went out the window. Women are considered to be the property of men, their fathers, or husbands, or even brothers.

In the marriage ceremony, the bride is asked three times if she agrees to the marriage, but saying no creates several real problems. She will bring about disgrace to her family, she will cause trouble between her family and the groom's family, and she will be causing problems for her own future. There are few, if any, options for most Afghan women outside of marriage. She cannot move out of her father's house, live on her own, and manage her own life.

Men are entitled to take more than one wife. The second wife, usually younger, is frequently treated a little better than a slave by her new family.

Shaima (twenty-four years old)

I was eleven when I got married. I am from Maidan, the countryside near Kabul.

I have been here in Peshawar for one month, living with my mother and sister and three of my children. My other child is still in Afghanistan, staying with my sister-in-law. I will have to go back to Afghanistan soon.

Life in Afghanistan is very hard. I am a widow. I have nothing. Sometimes I wash clothes for other people for a little money. It is difficult to do that, because the Taliban wants us to stay at home. When we go out, they punish us. They say, "We hear your feet! You are making too much noise!"

I know other widows in Afghanistan, lots of widows, very young ones, whose husbands were killed in war.

Zohra Rasekh, Physicians for Human Rights

Because of the poverty and devastation, parents have to get rid of their daughters as fast as possible. The families can't afford to keep the daughters, who will never be able to work outside and bring money into the house.

The Taliban says it's good, it's Islamic, to marry your daughters off while they are young. They say, "Don't keep your daughters too long at home. After age nine, they should be married!"

This is child abuse, to have a ten-, eleven-, twelve-year-old girl married to someone, a man who is generally a lot older. Men marry not in their teens, but in their twenties or older, and they can have several wives at one time. These young girls are basically raped, but that's not talked about.

There are a number of gynecological problems from such early marriages and childbirth.

Women who get married at an early age have a higher chance of cervical cancer, for example. Psychologically, especially if they are forced, there is a chance of suicide, a chance of mental problems, such as depression and anxiety. Plus, there is the problem of a child raising a child. The impact on the child of this child is also another problem, because she doesn't know how to take care of herself, let alone a child.

Malalli, Parvin, and their daughters live in Jalozai Refugee Camp.

Malalli (twenty-eight years old)

I was twelve when I got married, right after my first period. When my period came, I didn't know what was happening. It was a complete surprise to me.

I didn't know beforehand that I was going to be married. It was my parents' decision. I was in Kabul, visiting relatives, and when I came home to Nangahar, my parents told me I would be married the next week.

I was not happy about it at all. I was in the seventh grade of school, and I wanted to continue my education. The marriage was completely against my will. I was not allowed to continue my schooling.

I did not have the courage to refuse. If I had, everyone would have been very, very upset. In all parts of Afghanistan, it's not good for a girl to refuse to marry if plans have been made for her.

My husband was my cousin. If I had refused to marry him, my father and uncle would have fought against each other. It would not have been good for my father's relationship with his family. My husband was twenty-five when we got married.

After I was married, I was very, very sad for the first two years. After two years, I got used to it. What else could I do? This life became a habit.

After I was married, I was not able to do any of the things I used to do before I was married. My husband was not strict. He was a little broad minded, but his parents were very strict with me. They didn't let me go to other people's houses. They kept me at home, doing housework all the time.

Five years after the wedding, I gave birth to my daughter, Nadia. She is now twelve years old, the same age I was when I got married.

When I look at my daughter, I do not even consider her getting married. I want her to finish her education.

Parvin (twenty-four years old)

I am also from Nangahar. Malalli is my relative, my sister-in-law.

I've been in Pakistan for thirteen years. I got married at eleven. My husband was twenty-five. He was my relative. He did not have any other wives.

My daughter was born when I was twelve, but by that time my husband was dead. He fought with the Mujahideen and was killed eight months after we were married. I was a widow at twelve.

After he died, I came to Pakistan, and since then, I have lived here in the camp with my in-laws. I make handicrafts, and I take courses for adult women at the school.

My daughter goes to school. I don't want her to marry for a long, long time. When she's ready to marry, I'll let her choose her own husband. Right now, she must continue her education. She wants to be an engineer.

Nadia (Malalli's daughter, twelve years old)

I like going to school. My best subject is English. There are eighteen students in my class. All girls. We go to class from nine to twelve everyday and study five subjects each day. In the afternoon, we study and do our homework.

With my friends, I mostly like jumping rope and sitting around and talking.

I never think about getting married. I want to be a doctor.

Shauzia (Parvin's daughter, twelve years old)

Nadia and I have lived together all of our lives. We're like sisters. We sleep in the same room. Sometimes we fight over whose pencil it is, and things like that. Mostly, we get along.

Married? [She giggles.] No, no, I don't want to be married.

Homa Zafar, Editor-in-Chief, Sadaf Magazine for Women

We have lots of problems in marriage. We have a multicultural country. In each part of Afghanistan, there's a different law for marriage.

For example, some tribes of Afghanistan just trade women. In some tribes, when somebody kills somebody, the grieved family can take the other family's daughter as payment for the killing. Even if the family of the killer has only a five-year-old girl, she must go to the other family. A thirty or forty or even fifty-year-old man can get married to a child because of taking revenge for the murder. The girl must bear the punishment for a murder she did not commit.

Only in the capital city of Kabul, I think, could women or girls make a decision about marriage. In other provinces, the parents always choose the groom. That can make the relationship between the wife and husband very bad.

We don't have a proper society. For example, a woman could be forced to marry a man that she doesn't want but her family wants. He may be nothing that she wishes, from a cultural point of view, personality, everything, yet she will be forced to live with him for the rest of her life.

It makes for much fighting in the family, and gives children a bad picture in their minds about marriage and family. That has a very negative affect on the children, and also on society.

One of the difficulties we are having now is forced marriage among the educated people. Many families, because of economic problems, are giving their girls to Afghan men who live abroad in Canada or America. We call this "parcel marriage." The husband living abroad pays the family in Afghanistan or Pakistan for a wife to go abroad with him.

Many, many cases of this type of marriage are unsuccessful. For example, there is a fifty-year-old man. He sends his age-twenty photo of himself from abroad. The girl's family sees it, and accepts him, the money is accepted, the arrangements are made, and he is just coming here for the marriage. Suddenly he is here and he is an old man, and the girl says, "I don't want to get married to him," and the family says, "But we are Afghan," so she must marry him. Sometimes, the bride is kept away from the wedding, because she doesn't want to be married to this man. The wedding ceremony takes place without her there.

In other cases, the man from abroad will come here for the wedding, and then decide that he doesn't want the woman he's married to. After the marriage, he goes back home, and never comes back for his wife, never sends letters. She stays here just like a widow. There are lots of cases like this.

We had sometime ago in our magazine an article about an Afghan girl who sent a letter to her mother from Dubai. She wrote that, "My husband sold me here, and now I am in a place that every night I am dancing, and I have been raped a lot, and the people I am living with, they are taking money from me." We hear of these things happening in other Middle Eastern countries. The men come here, get married, take their wives to another country, and sell them. They pay much less for a bride price than they get when they sell the woman.

The mother who received the letter brought it to our magazine, and said, "Please print this. All families should know that they shouldn't give up their girls to receive money, to relieve their poverty, because this is what can happen to them."

Dr. Naureen, Red Crescent Clinic for Afghan Refugees

Early child marriages affect women's health very badly. Because they get married at an early age, they have their first baby at an early age, and usually they have multiple pregnancies. It really affects their health. They get anemia, they have abnormal labor, difficult labor.

Because of multiple pregnancies, the abdominal muscles become lax. They lose their tone. Whenever they get a new pregnancy, the child adopts any position, possibly breech. And that causes lots of problems, because they normally deliver at home.

Early pregnancies in a young girl, thirteen or fourteen, she can get cervical cancer later in life.

Child brides certainly have to face extra stress, physically and mentally, both. She has to face a new family, a whole lot of people to do work for. She just serves them, you know? She has to look after the needs of her husband. And then she gets ten or twelve children, and all of that really impairs her physically, mentally, or emotionally.

If she's a young girl, if she gets married at thirteen, they expect her to bear a child at fourteen, within a year. Sometimes she's not able to. A woman may take a few years to get her ovulation going correctly and become fertile. So when she gets married early and she's not able to have a child, she has to face even more stress. Her husband might go for another wife, and then she has to suffer all her life.

There are usually so many children in the house, ten, twelve, even fourteen children in the house, so they just want to get rid of them.

Also, the money a father receives for his daughter from her new husband is usually badly needed by the rest of the family.

Girls generally get no education at home about their own bodies, about menstruation, babies, sex. Even among educated families, they don't talk about such things. A girl might get information from her friends, but not from her parents. When a girl gets married, she often does not know what to expect, and that's one of the biggest problems.

It is party time at Jelozai Refugee Camp. One of the local girls is getting engaged, and many people in the camp are celebrating.

The celebration is spread out among several houses, the men in a place separate from the women. Sajida, Spurghai and I cross an open field past a handful of cows grazing, goats snuffling through garbage, and boys playing cricket. There is a playground, but the January rains have made the ground around it too soggy. The swings are shaded by big trees, and will be full of children as soon as the ground dries out. We step over a stream of muddy water, shoo some chickens out of the way, and pass through a narrow, curtain-covered door. We are at the women's gathering.

Little girls swarm around us in the courtyard; palms are marked with henna as part of the ceremony of the event. They are dressed up, in their best clothes. One little girl clomps along in her mother's shoes.

Like many houses in this camp, the courtyard contains several low, mud buildings, and a vegetable garden, although it's too early in the year for it to be cultivated. The children urge us to the doorway of one of the huts. Inside is a single long, narrow room, chock-filled with women sitting on mats on the floor. They greet us warmly, and invite us in for tea, although that's just a formality, as the room couldn't possibly hold any more bodies. Spurghai tells them we'll see them later, at the ceremony.

"Which one's the bride?" I ask Sajida.

"She's in another house, by herself," Sajida answers. "The custom is that the girl doesn't talk on her engagement or her wedding day. She should be very shy and quiet on that day."

We wander around the camp for awhile, looking at things, talking with women, then it is time for the engagement ceremony.

This takes place in another house. There is already a crowd gathered by the time we get there. Boards have been placed over the mud, providing a dry sidewalk to the porch. The women are gathered on the porch and near the house, the men are at the back of the yard, near the wall. Chickens and children are everywhere.

"The bride is only thirteen," Sajida tells me, and my stomach turns to ice. At thirteen, my biggest worry was passing eighth grade home economics. "The groom is twenty-eight. He already has one wife, and they already have three children. This girl will live with his first family in Jalalabad. He's taking her back to Afghanistan."

Bunches of blue *burqas* hang on the porch. Many of the groom's relatives, and the bride's, have come out of Afghanistan to attend the ceremony. We meet the groom's aunt, who is only able to stay in Peshawar long enough to see her nephew engaged. Her sons have not been able to find work in Pakistan, so she must go back.

She goes through the crowd and comes back in a minute with the groom's first wife, Waheeda. She's twenty-three, but looks closer to forty. I ask if she was surprised to learn that her husband is taking a second wife. She tells me she was. I ask if she is sad about it. No, she says, she is happy.

"She's not happy," interjects the aunt. "She has been crying for days." The other women who are gathered around us, listening, nod in agreement. I'm not sure if they are agreeing that Waheeda has been crying, or if they are saying that they would certainly be crying in the same circumstance.

I don't get a chance to find out. The banging of a drum outside the courtyard walls heralds the arrival of the groom.

First through the doorway is a video cameraman, walking backwards, taping the event. An old woman beating a hand-held drum leads the marriage procession. The groom and several family members come next, and right behind the groom is a woman holding a Holy Koran over his head. A man dances in front of the parade as it makes its way up the board sidewalk to the porch. The groom looks solemn, but the other men and women in the yard are laughing and singing. Someone tosses out candies and one-rupee coins, which sets the kids scrambling.

The procession goes inside the house to fetch the bride. Women and children crowd onto the porch, peering through the window to see what's happening inside. Some of the little girls are wearing lipstick for the occasion. They look like little girls anywhere look when they've been playing around with their mother's make-up bag.

"The bride's father got 150 thousand rupees for his daughter," Sajida tells me. That's around three thousand dollars. "That's a very high price, probably because the girl is so young."

The door opens and the cameraman backs out, and the bride and groom take their place before a red-blanketed bench on the porch. The bride's family press their faces to the inside of the window to watch the proceedings.

The bride's face is cast downwards. She is dressed in a frilly, long pink dress, a flowered head-dress on her head. Her hair is done up in massive curls, and she is very heavily made up.

The drums keep playing. Waheeda, the first wife, dances before the couple, to show an approval the aunt says she does not feel.

Not once during the ceremony does the bride raise her eyes.

The next evening, the bride's father gives me permission to talk to his daughter. Sajida and I sit with Norzia on a mat in a room lit by a kerosene lamp. The camp's power is off again. Norzia's uncle sits across from us on another mat. Norzia looks to him before she answers most of the questions. She becomes more comfortable as the interview goes on.

She is wearing a simple *shalwar-kameez* (baggy trousers and loose, long shirt) and a plain, green veil over her hair. The make-up has been washed off, and she looks like a regular child.

Norzia (thirteen years old)

I'm from Laghman, an eastern province of Afghanistan. I've been in Pakistan for six or seven months. My mother and father are here with me. I still have friends in Afghanistan. I miss them.

We had to leave because of the war. It was difficult to live in Afghanistan. There is no school. The Taliban shut its doors. My younger sisters went to that school, before the Taliban came. I did not go to school. There is a school here at the camp, but I don't go to it, either.

My engagement party was yesterday. It took me three hours to get dressed. My dress came from Jalalabad. The party was my adventure.

I will be married in a few months I don't know exactly when. They haven't told me. It will be after the next Eid.

[*"It is a religious point," the uncle says. "Between Eids, people cannot marry. The next Eid is coming up in two months."*]

I have six sisters and three brothers. Only one of my sisters is older than me, and she's not married, because she wants to get an education.

Once I am married, I will not be able to get an education.

After I'm married, I will live in Jalalabad, in the same house as my husband's first wife and her children. I've met the first wife. She is ten years older than I am. I will be a housewife, looking after the house, and taking care of the children.

[*I ask, "Do you hope to have children of your own?" Her uncle responds, "Of course she will have children!"*]

In Jalalabad, I will have to wear a *burqa* if I go out. I've worn one before. It's hard to see through.

Jalalabad has good weather, better than Pakistan.

The man I'm going to marry was our neighbor in Afghanistan. He is twenty-eight years old.

What will I do with my free time? I will not have any free time! I don't have any free time now. I just do housework. All the time, I just do housework.

Two of my friends are also engaged. They are the same age as I am. It is usual in Afghanistan for girls to get married at my age, although my mother was twenty-two when she got married.

It depends on my parents whether I marry or not. It doesn't depend on what I want or don't want.

Norzia stands next to the man her family has engaged her to. Waheeda, the first wife, dances before them.

I didn't know anything about the decision my parents made for me to be married. I didn't know at all. They didn't ask me any questions about what I wanted. After they made all the arrangements, then they let me know.

If they had asked me before, I would have refused, because of my young age. It is not possible to refuse now, after the arrangements have been made. But this is not what I want.

"That's enough questions," her uncle says. We say thank you and goodbye. She walks with us to the door in the courtyard wall, and waves as we walk away. The next day I ask to interview the girl's mother. The father says, "No."

NOTES

1. Nancy Peabody Newell, *The Struggle for Afghanistan* (Ithaca, N.Y.: Cornell University Press, 1981), 79.

2. Ibid., 82.

3. Anthony Hyman, *Afghanistan Under Soviet Domination* (New York: St. Martin's, 1984), 88.

4. Ibid.

5. Newell, *The Struggle for Afghanistan*, 84.

MOTHERS AND DAUGHTERS

Twenty years of war has created many husbandless wives, fatherless daughters, and brotherless sisters. In a culture where women are considered to be the outright property of the men who control them, women without men are especially vulnerable. They are rendered completely invisible.

Other men have been damaged, physically or mentally, and their care places an additional burden on the wives and daughters who care for them. In addition to somehow providing economically for their families, these women must also cope with a man in the house who, deprived by tragic circumstances of his traditional role, has no outlet for his frustrations but the women and children around him.

Under the Taliban, mothers who may be educated professionals themselves are in a quandary over how to raise their daughters. Should they teach their daughters as much as possible about the world, so that the girls will be equipped to play an active role in it when the situation in Afghanistan improves? Or, in the absence of any sign of positive change, do they raise their daughters to have the lowest possible expectation of life, to spare them the anguish of what is likely to be inevitable disappointment?

In this chapter, we meet several extraordinary mother/daughter teams living in a variety of circumstances. Each one of these women has been directly affected by the long years of war, and each has learned unique ways to survive and to maintain some sense of who they are.

In a plaza on Jamrud Road in Peshawar, up a back staircase and down a dark hallway or two, Maria operates a beauty parlor with her daughter, Wajma. Two plain chairs face mirrors that are hanging over a long counter. Spray bottles, scissors, and combs are arranged in neat rows. On the walls are large posters of Afghan women with elaborately styled hair.

Maria insists that Benazir, her former teacher, needs a hair cut. Benazir leaves the couch where she and I have been sipping tea and eating cookies and sits at the counter, getting a free haircut and translating while Maria talks.

Maria (forty-three years old)

I was a student of Benazir's in high school. We are from the middle of Kabul.

My husband is a very famous writer and poet. He is here in Peshawar with us. The Taliban don't like learned people.

We were waiting for King Zahir Shah, hoping that he would come back to take control of the country, but we were waiting for a long time.

The first few days of the Taliban, we saw things through the window. We didn't go out. We understood that those people are wild, that it was not good for us to go out. They would punish us and they would hit us.

Our country, our city, completely changed.

Kabul used to be very nice, very clean. All young men and women wore suits, and they were very tidy all the time. They went to their schools and universities, and to their libraries. They were walking very nicely in the streets. The capital city of Afghanistan was very nice, very similar to the other capitals of the world. But now it is all clay, just a piece of land. There are no learned people left.

I will do any kind of work anywhere, if I can only go abroad.

When it gets hot here, it gets very, very difficult for us. Maybe this year we will die, all of us. It gets very hot, like hell. I am obliged to do work all of the time, during the day and during the night. All the time is like night for us. If we do not work, how can we live? So every day, every night, we do work here.

But still, we are happy here because there are no rockets, there is no killing, no blood, nobody hits us, so at least it is a peaceful life.

If someone comes here to kill us, some people will come to ask, "Why did you kill this person?" In Afghanistan, there is nobody to ask why.

This is peace for us. This is our definition of a good life.

We have only two rooms. We all live in one room, and this beauty parlor is the other room. We live in the room next to this one.

I work to make pretty the women who come. Also, brides come here to have their hair made beautiful.

Wajma (daughter to Maria, eighteen years old)

I work with my mother here in this shop. This kind of work is OK. It's better than nothing.

I wanted to study at the Faculty of Literature, especially English literature. My father is a writer, a poet, so I'd like to follow him.

My father writes all the time, poetry, history. If he publishes, he gets some money.

I am eighteen years old. All of my life, I have heard bombs and rockets destroying people and houses. My country has always been busy with fighting.

It is not difficult to work with my mother. She is like a teacher, she is training me.

Maria

If I'm not here, I can trust my daughter to do the work perfectly.

We didn't like the Russians, although they were not as bad as the Taliban. I had two brothers-in-law, one was a doctor, one was an engineer. The Communists arrested them. One, the doctor, was doing an operation. The Communists took him from the operating room. We still haven't heard from him. The engineer disappeared, too, after one week in jail. I am still very unhappy, and will remember this as long as I am alive.

Farzona (twenty-five years old)

I'm married, and we have a son who is six years old. My husband doesn't work. He sits at home.

We know the boss, Maria, from Kabul. That's the only reason my husband lets me work. We need money now, to live, and to pay for an education for my son.

Many Afghan women with a high education have no job and no good life, so why should we waste our time getting a high education?

(Shanaz lives in one room in Hyatabad, Peshawar, with her husband and six of her seven daughters. The room is furnished with carpets and cushions. More rugs are on the walls, as decorations, and as reminders of the few belongings they were able to bring with them when they left Afghanistan. Several of her daughters are with us. They go in and out of the room, fetching tea and small dishes of walnuts while their mother talks.)

Shanaz (forty years old)

We are from Kabul. We had two beautiful, big houses there. Now they are all destroyed.

My husband was a carpet merchant. I have seven daughters.

We came to Pakistan seven years ago, after the Russians had left. Rockets came during the night. They destroyed everything, and we had to move to my brother's house. The fighting was between the Hazaras and Gulbuddin. We had two houses, in different sections of Kabul. There is nothing left of either of them.

I am crying now because my husband is no longer a normal man. He is sick, always talking to himself. He is a young man, but he looks like he's a hundred. If he dies, how will we manage?

Under the Russians, two of our shops burned, with all the carpets inside. We lost everything. I must try not to think about it, because I always cry, but I can't stop thinking about it. We had so much. We had money and servants. Now, we live in this one room. It is a struggle each month to pay the children's school fees.

I still have dreams about our old house, filled with our belongings and our servants, and then I wake up and see that I am in Pakistan, and have nothing left.

In Afghanistan, I was always busy looking after the children, looking after the house, supervising the servants. I used to enjoy watching television, and I loved being a hostess when family or friends would come for a visit.

Now, when I see poor people, people leading a poor life, and cannot help them, I feel sad. When I was rich, I helped people, with food, with money, with clothes. There were often poor people around the house, and I gave them money. Or we'd be at a wedding, and there would be poor people there, and I'd invite them to my house so I could give them something.

During Eid and the New Year, I was always helping people. Now at Eid, I cry. I can't even buy new dresses for my own children.

We rent the room here from a Pakistani landlord. He came to us and said, "You have to pay more money," This made my husband's sickness much worse. He is now working in someone else's carpet shop. He only gets paid when he sells a carpet, and he doesn't sell very many. But it gets him out of the house.

Anohita (twenty-one-year-old eldest daughter)

I'm always thinking about when we'll have peace and can go back to our country. There, we had the best climate. We were very healthy. Here, we are homesick, we are physically sick, and we spend our lives in poverty. I study, but not very hard. I am too sad.

I am the eldest, and I like to try to control all the children, and be a teacher to them. When my mother goes out, I take her place, and tell the others what to do. I'm proud of being able to do that.

The future belongs to God, and to my parents. They will decide what I am to do. I would like to be a journalist, but there is no place to study that here.

At first, I used to write on my own, but now, I have no hope that it will go anywhere, so I stopped. Sometimes, I don't like to live.

I make fancy beadwork and try to sell it. When I sell something, the money goes into the household. There are so many children in the family, and because I am the eldest, I must help out.

Hawajan (sixteen years old)

I was small when we left Afghanistan. I don't remember much except for the noise of the rockets, and how afraid I was.

The attack on our house came early in the morning, while we were having breakfast. I was drinking tea. We ran outside in our nightdresses, no shoes, no head covering. The rocket landed on one side of our house, and the ceiling came down. We were in the street. There was lots of shouting and running and dust. There was no place to flee. The airplanes were bombing everywhere.

We had a very big dog. He was very small when we got him. I fed him milk like a baby, until he got big. He was killed in a rocket attack. I still get sad when I think of him.

In the future, I would like to learn as much as possible, and get a higher degree. I would like to learn English better, so that I can read English literature and understand it perfectly.

It is good to have so many sisters. We talk all the time. There was one sister I fought with, but she got married and lives away from here, so I'm happy about that. She ordered me around all the time, so I'm happy she's gone.

Zobiadah (thirteen years old)

Our country is very beautiful, but all I remember are the planes and bombs and rockets. That's all I remember.

We would like to learn, but our school is very poor. I'm not able to ask my parents for money for fees and stationery.

I have friends here. I study with them, and we talk about our country. Sometimes we go to Khyber Park together.

I want to become a good doctor, and treat Afghans in our own country.

Hamida (eleven years old)

In school I learn English and Arabic and the other subjects are in Farsi. I am in grade five. I like to learn Persian poems by heart.

I like having so many big sisters. Usually, they are friendly. We all share the housework. Sometimes my oldest sister tells me what to do, and I don't like it, and I don't do it, and she hits me!

We don't have a kitchen here, just a gas stove on the verandah. We carry water there from the bathroom.

I also like to sing. I love music.

Nilofar and her mother and her sister live in a second floor apartment above a shopping plaza in Islamabad. There is a "Titanic" poster on the wall. It is January, and it is cold inside the stone building. Nilofar offers me a quilt to wrap up in while we talk.

Nilofar (twenty-six years old)

I was twenty when I left Afghanistan.

I was very little when the Russians came to our country. I saw lots of fighting. Many people died.

Lots of people went to Russia to study. My brother studied economics there for four years. When he came back to Afghanistan, he was called for military service, so he fled to Pakistan. My mother refused to let him join the army. From Pakistan he went to Holland.

Three or four of our relatives died in the army. They were fighting against the Mujahideen.

My father died when I was nine. That was also the year when the Russians invaded. We weren't allowed to go outside and play. Even at school, we couldn't play outside.

I watched on television as the Russians left. They looked happy to go. The Russians lost a lot of people in Afghanistan, so they were happy to go, and we were happy to see them go.

We came to Pakistan because of the dangerous fighting that started up after the Russians left. There was lots of fighting in the streets, lots of people hurt and killed. My uncle looked after us after my father died, and he decided we should go to Pakistan.

We came to Pakistan by truck. Lots of people came with us. Their homes had been destroyed by rockets, so they came to our house with just what they were wearing. That's all they had left. My uncle owned a truck. Everybody climbed in, and we came to Pakistan. We had some pillows, mattresses, rugs, some water, some food, and not much else.

There were lots of people walking in the road in front of the truck, trying to get out of Afghanistan. Soldiers were everywhere. They kept stopping us and checking the truck, and checking everybody in the truck. I was very scared.

We were planning to be here for only six months. It has now been six years. If there is ever peace in Afghanistan we would go back. After all, that's our home. But I think we will be here for a long time.

It is difficult to live in Pakistan. When we get sick, we have no money to pay for doctors. The Pakistani men constantly harass Afghan women. I can't go to the bazaar by myself because of the men.

We do nothing for fun. There is no fun in our lives.

I hope peace comes to our country, and that there will be no more problems in our lives. If not, I would like to go to some other country so that I can work and complete my education, and walk around on my own without being bothered by men. I hope to bring happiness to my family, especially to my mother.

I don't want to marry because then my mother would be alone. There is no one else to help her. She has diabetes and is not able to work. She also has rheumatism. After my father died, she was sick a lot. The weather in Pakistan in not good for her.

Nilofar's Mother

When Najib was in power, we lived without any problems. When the Russians came, we were sad. Lots of people died. There were too many rockets and bombs. People went underground, to cellars, to escape the bombs. Lots of young and old people died.

After that, my brother decided to go to Pakistan for ten or twenty days, to see if we should stay there.

My husband was a bank worker. He died when the children were little. There was no other man to help us.

After the Russians left, everyone was happy, then people began to fight each other. There were many different groups with many different ideas. Everyone wanted to be King.

Faranos, Nilofar's Sister

I was in class seven when the Russians came, thirteen years old. I hated them coming, everyone wanted freedom.

We were afraid of talking about it in school, afraid the police would take us. We had to study politics.

People didn't accept the Russians. There were big marches in the street against the Russians. After one of the marches one day, the police surrounded people, arrested, jailed, and punished them. Sometimes the police would put cigarettes out on somebody's skin.

There was fighting in the provinces. People were killed. They took girls and destroyed everything, the houses and livestock.

The day the Russians left, people were very happy, because my country wanted freedom.

I was very surprised by the fighting when the Russians left. After that began, we saw no good days.

Before the Mujahideen came to Kabul, women could wear whatever we wanted, jeans, T-shirts, whatever. I wore lots of pants and shirts. Now, in Pakistan, we have gotten used to wearing *shalwar kameez* and the *chador* [baggy trousers under long, loose shirt, and head covering].

People like to wear what they want. Nobody likes someone telling them what to wear.

Behind Islamia College is a neighborhood of winding streets, small shops, and mud-brick houses.

Anisette and her daughter Huda, who is deaf, live in a small shop. A square of cement provides a stepping-stone over the fetid open sewer that runs rancid along the street.

Anisette is a warm, welcoming woman who ushers us into her family's small room with a smile.

Anisette

Nobody knows about what my daughter can do. She knows many things, but she cannot speak. If she lives abroad, people will respect her. She could be a very famous artist.

My husband was a lawyer under the Russian occupation. They didn't influence him. He was independent. He both defended and prosecuted people. He knew about political prisoners at that time. The government had good laws for taking care of prisoners, but it was just for show. In practice, there was not enough food, water, or fresh air.

When the Russians left, we were not confident that things would get better. All the Mujahideen were really interested in was advancing themselves, not the Afghan people.

When Zobida was two, we were still waiting for her to speak. First, we had a son. He still didn't speak when he was four. When our daughter didn't speak by the age of two, we were very unhappy. We took them both to India. The doctors there said they were deaf. Doctors in Kabul also examined them, and came to the same conclusion.

It is very lucky for Zobida that both of her parents are educated, because we were able to find services for her that people without education would not have known about.

We found a course in Kabul for deaf children and their parents, and we learned sign language. In this way, we can talk to each other, but she can only talk to people who know sign language.

We are not happy here in Pakistan. It is very difficult. My husband and I are not able to find suitable jobs. We are educated—how can we go sell vegetables? Our boy in Germany and our brother in Canada send us money.

My deaf son is with us in Peshawar. He works in the carpet industry. He doesn't get much money, but he's earning something, and it's better than sitting at home all day.

Future for Zobida? We don't know about our own future, how can we know about Zobida's? Wherever we are, she will be. Maybe she will find a good man to be her husband. Maybe she will go abroad. I don't know.

Here we live in one room, five people.

We saw war with our own eyes. We saw the blood, we didn't just read about it.

We were afraid of rockets. When they came, we ran downstairs and hid in the bathroom until they passed. When rockets came, there was lots of fire, lots of children crying. Everyone was crying, running, trying to find a safe place. We were very sad. We didn't know where the rockets would go next. We didn't know how many people died.

All the dead bodies were placed along the streets until they could be buried. If a body could be identified, it was given to the family for burial, if the family could be found. If not, it was just buried with the others in a big grave. Kabul at that time had only one or two ambulances, no fire trucks.

Zobida

My paintings are in the Persian tradition. They have designs of birds, deer, fruit, flowers, and vines, all arranged around a central picture. I do market scenes, people going into a mosque, a woman pouring a drink for a man on a settee.

I also embroider silk scarves. I know thirty-four kinds of embroidery. I sometimes do paintings for people from photographs they bring me.

I'm unhappy because I'm sitting in the room all the time. If you can take me to Canada, I'll have things to do. I like to know about the political situation in the world. My father and I read newspapers together.

When I was five years old, I always drew on Father's newspaper. He understood that I'd like to be an artist. My parents enrolled me in an art class, and I went everyday. I studied sculpture and drawing.

When I see something I like, I draw it. I don't work from images in my head, but from what I see. The design around the picture, that comes from my head.

In a corner of Nasir Bagh Camp, a small door in a high mud wall opens up into a compound full of women and children. Several mud houses line the inside of the walls. The women are washing clothes and sweeping away dead leaves from the yard. The children are playing with stones and chasing a few scrawny chickens. The families in this compound came here when the Russians were still in Afghanistan.

Shargul draws me aside from the others to a tiny, dark shed, with just

Shargul and her mother.

enough room in it for a single, narrow cot. She wants to introduce me to her mother.

Shargul

My husband was killed by the Russians, soon after we were married. He was with the Mujahideen. We had no children.

I have been here in Nasir Bagh camp for twelve or thirteen years. There are lots of families living in this house. Most of the children you see were born in this camp. This camp is all they know.

My mother is blind. I have to look after her. She is also ill. She stays wrapped up in a blanket, on her bed, all the time. She does nothing else, just lays or sits on her bed. I have to do everything for her, feed her, wash her, take her to the toilet.

She has been blind for ten years. Her other sons and daughters were killed in Afghanistan. After that happened, she cried a lot. Soon after that, she became blind.

Houzia sits on the floor of her house in Jalozai Camp with her young sons around her. She tells her story in a quiet voice, without emotion, as though all the emotion has been drained out of her.

Houzia (thirty-five years old)

I'm from Herat. I've been in this refugee camp for one year. When the Taliban came to Herat, the situation changed a lot. They don't allow women to go outside or go to school. That's why we came here.

Now I have three children. I used to have four. I had a fourteen-year-old daughter, but the Taliban abducted her, raped her, and brought me back her dead body.

Her name is Shauzia. All my photos of her are in Afghanistan, left behind.

She was a girl who liked to go to school. She was in the eighth grade, before Taliban. She especially liked studying English.

It was the daytime. They knocked on the door and they came into the house, searching for something to take. When they saw my daughter, they held everyone else in the family in one room, and they took the girl with them. The next day, they brought her back. They left her body on the doorstep.

I cannot say the sorrow that I had at that time, and now. My tears have all dried up.

Nine months after that, we left Afghanistan. These are my other children, all boys, ages twelve, ten, and seven. My husband is a shopkeeper in Peshawar.

There was no one to approach about my daughter, to find out who killed her and why, and bring them to justice. All the power was in the hands of the Taliban, and they, themselves, committed this crime.

The neighbors knew. They provided me with emotional support, but they couldn't do anymore than that.

I have a message for other women. My message is that women and girls should organize, and they should struggle against fundamentalism, and raise their voices for justice.

For my sons, in the future, I want them educated, to serve the people of Afghanistan, and to take revenge for their sister. I want them to struggle against the Taliban and the religious fundamentalists. And they will grow up to respect women.

PRINCESS

King Amanullah reigned from 1919 until 1929. During his ten-year reign, he secured independence for Afghanistan from the British, and he brought Afghanistan closer to the USSR. He liked the Soviets because Lenin said they were opposed to all forms of European imperialism. In exchange for Afghanistan's friendship, the Soviets began to provide aid to develop the country, including military aid, and a small airforce.

King Amanullah was highly reform-minded. Although he hated Western control of his country, he was eager to bring secular changes to an Afghanistan largely controlled by the conservative religious leaders. He began to send Afghans abroad for higher education, and brought in teachers from Egypt, India, and Europe. He opened schools to teach nursing and other vocations, and drew up plans for a national education program. The women in the Royal Family went about publicly without wearing the veil, and pressure was put on influential families to send their daughters to school.

Because of his disdain for Afghanistan's traditional tribal and religious leaders, he did not consult with them on the nature and implementation of his reforms. Alarmed at the threat to their power, the religious and tribal leaders led an armed revolt against him, eventually laying siege to Kabul. At this point, Amanullah abdicated and fled the country.[1]

Most of the royal family left with him, and over the years, successive royals who have been in power have also fled to Europe and North America.

Now, in Pakistan, one lone princess remains.

Bibijan.

Bibijan, as I have been asked to call her, is a sister to King Amanullah. She lives in an apartment in a large house in Hyatabad.

Bibijan *(eighty-two years old)*

Anytime there is a revolution in our country, it is bad luck for the women. Every bad thing belongs to the women in Afghanistan.

I have been in Pakistan for nearly five years. Our country was destroyed, and we didn't have anything to live in. Our houses, our material things, our furniture, all were destroyed. We like to have our honor, but if they treat us like animals, what can we do?

I waited to see if there would be peace in our country one day, but everything became destroyed, so I came here. I didn't go when I had the chance because I thought our country would be rebuilt, but I no longer think so. Now, I am suffering.

My grandfather was king, my father was king, my brother was king, and I am a princess. I try to be nice to everybody. If I can do something for someone, I do it.

After my brother stopped being king, we had a very simple life, but for a long time, we had, of course, a royal life. I know very good Persian. I can read and write. I taught myself privately. Most of the time, I didn't have a good life like a princess should have in her own country. I had a very simple life.

I have too many sisters. Five brothers and five sisters are still alive, but all of them are abroad, in Europe and the United States. I am here all by myself.

My father had three wives and many palaces. He took three wives because he wanted to be mixed with different provinces, to have people be happy with him and respect him, and to make relatives all over the country.

Sometimes my brothers and sisters telephone me. Sometimes they send letters. I miss having them close to me, but what can I do? My husband died a few years ago. Unfortunately, I have no child.

I adopted a young woman as my daughter. She is the daughter of one of the servants whose family has looked after my family for generations. I have adopted her brother also, and sent him to live in England to get an education there. The young woman takes care of me here in Peshawar. She is like my grandchild.

I have seen many revolutions in my country, many changes, from king to president and republic, to communism, to Mujahideen, to Taliban. I remember all of them, like a living history.

I volunteered my time for many years with the Afghan Women's Society. I was one of the women who started the society. I liked working with families, especially women.

We gathered together women who were just sitting at home, and we gave them jobs with a salary. We started sewing projects and clinics and kindergartens and literacy classes. The women who were involved in these projects were very happy because it was the beginning of a new life for them.

After we began the society, everyday things got better and better. We had a very large vocational high school for women in Kabul, and representatives in all the provinces. We traveled a lot in order to meet women, to see how we could help them better, to train leaders, and distribute materials and salaries.

At that time, many women wore the *burqa*, and we tried to get women to feel comfortable not wearing it. That was one of our major campaigns.

I never wore the *burqa*. It was very easy for me not to wear it, because I am a princess, and my family supported me not wearing it.

I was working also for family planning, especially with poor women. I was happiest when some of the poor women we worked with got some education, and when they got a better life because of our work. I was quite happy and proud about that. I remember those times best. I think about them, and my memories make me happy.

I remained in Kabul while the Russians were there. The Russians never threatened me or my family.

The Mujahideen destroyed my house. All of them were very bad, but especially Gulbuddin. That's why I eventually left Kabul. There were lots and lots of rockets and mines. I don't know the names of all these fighting things, but it was shocking.

The Afghan Royal Family are mostly all dead. King Zahir Shah is very old now. I don't think they will ever take power in Afghanistan again. The royal family has been in Europe so long, they are more like Europeans than Afghans.

Sometimes the women who used to be in the Afghan Women's Society come to visit me here. We talk for awhile, and they go away again. They like me a lot. The members of the group are now all living in different places. Those who could have gone abroad. If I hear that a friend of mine has got a good life, I feel very happy.

I don't go out anymore. I am old now. I have a few servants who take care of me. I sit and think and wait, and I hope. If a good person, a learned person comes, maybe Afghanistan can be built again. I cannot bear to see my country as it is now.

When somebody has fallen, maybe she will get up again, and stand up again. I will not live to see Afghanistan stand, because I am old, but the young generation may see it.

The world keeps moving. It changes everyday. One day, the Taliban will go. Things will get better. So, we wait.

NOTE

1. Nancy Peabody Newell, *The Struggle for Afghanistan* (Ithaca, N.Y.: Cornell University Press, 1981), 37–39.

PAVEMENT WOMEN

They are everywhere in Peshawar, Afghan women moving through the markets like ghosts in their enveloping *burqas*, one hand around the baby in their arms, the other stretched out toward anyone who might help them. Some sit on the sidewalks, babies in their laps, small bowls in front of them to receive people's coins and rupee notes. One woman who sits in the same spot almost everyday, beside the fountain in University Town, has a three-year-old boy who chases people up and down the street until they give him money. Other women spend their days knocking on doors, begging for bread or a few coins.

They are driven to this by their extreme poverty caused by the war. Here are some of their stories.

Nooria (twenty-four years old)

I am married with one daughter. Neither my husband nor I have jobs. We live with a few other families, all crowded together. My brother-in-law is in Germany, and sometimes he sends us money.

We are from a very famous area of Kabul. Once it was very beautiful, near Darulaman Palace and gardens. Now, it is all destroyed.

Our building was completely destroyed by a rocket attack. All the fighting factions, they are like wild animals, not human beings. I hate them all. Once I was a person. Now I am a beggar.

Bobogol and her granddaughter walk the streets each day, trying out different neighborhoods.

Bobogal and her granddaughter, Nabila.

Bobogol and Her Granddaughter Nabila

I am from a section of Kabul in the north of the city. I lost my young son. He was killed by the Taliban.

When the Russians were in my country, my husband was killed. Now the Taliban are there, and my son has been killed.

We have nothing now. My arm is twisted, my left one. I can't use it. My leg is bad from the war. My granddaughter, Nabila, and I walk the streets of Peshawar and beg for money, for bread.

My daughter has other children. They are small. So Nabila and I beg to feed everyone.

Nodwara begs in University Town, where many humanitarian organizations have their offices.

Nodwara

I live in the Nasir Bagh Camp. We came to Peshawar during the time of Taraki.

I have one son. He has one leg. My son has got a few children. There is nobody else to help them, so I beg.

Sultana (fifty years old)

I am a beggar. I've lost my son and my son-in-law. They were both police officers, killed in a rocket attack.

I came here six months ago, with my daughter, my daughter-in-law, and my grandchildren.

For all six months, I have been a beggar. In Kabul, I was a housewife and a tailor. Now I am a beggar. I am fifty years old.

From early morning until late in the day, I get thirty or forty rupees. I cry when I beg, under my *burqa*. I am a proud woman. We had a country, we had a small house, and now we have nothing.

Sometimes I go from house to house, sometimes I beg a piece of nan from the baker, sometimes I sit here on the sidewalk. It is all begging.

Two shabby tents are pitched in the mud of a vacant lot beside a newly built health clinic. Small piles of excrement mix with the mud all over the yard, as there is no proper toilet. Children of many ages with no toys stare at me as their mothers urge me to sit on the only dry spot in the yard. These women who have nothing offer me tea.

Simin, Sohila, Kokogal

We are from Parwan, north of Kabul. We have been here for five months. We left Afghanistan because of poverty. We had no food, no money. We sold everything we had to come here. We are lucky that the clinic gives us water, otherwise we would have nothing to drink.

Sometimes our husbands do construction work. Most of the time, we have to go from door to door, and beg for a little bread or a little money.

See all these children? What will happen to them?

Matob (thirty years old)

I came to Pakistan two years ago from Kabul. I am a widow. My husband was killed four years ago by a Mujahideen rocket.

Now, I go from house to house, asking if the people there will pay me to wash their clothes. If they have no clothes for me to wash, I ask them to give me some money anyway.

Two months ago, my eight-year-old son was hit by a Pakistani bus, and he died. The bus made a big cut in his head and threw him to the other side of the road. The driver gave some money to the police, and they let him go.

Now I have just two children left.

Bibi Shareen

I don't know how old I am. What does it matter? I am just old. I am weak. I have no teeth.

One year ago, I came to Peshawar from Kabul. There are eight people in my family, and we all came together.

We lost everything in the bombing. Our house was destroyed, and everything in it was destroyed or stolen.

We are just women and girls in the house. My sons and my husband were murdered by rockets. My husband had a wagon in Kabul, for carrying things and people from one place to another.

I've never been to school. I stayed in the house, looking after children, cooking, cleaning.

Now, we live in Nasir Bagh Camp. The girls are very young, eight, nine, and ten. They do not go to school.

Usually, I come to beg in this spot. Sometimes I go to other places. From early morning until late at night, I get ten, maybe twelve rupees.

Often, young boys will come and hit me. It would be better to die than to keep doing this.

Nozigul sits on the ground in a clearing by the railway tracks, on the edge of the Board neighborhood market. Nearby, several goats and long-hair sheep snuffle through a pile of garbage, looking for something to eat. Two children, dragging blue sacks behind them, are doing the same thing, right alongside the goats.

Nozigul (thirty years old)

Four years ago, my family and I came to Peshawar. Here, we are beggars. In Afghanistan, we were also beggars.

We left Afghanistan because of the war. We are from Mazar-e-Sharif, and there was lots of fighting, lots of rockets.

We live in a tent, not far from this market. I am not married, I have no children, just I live with my parents. My feet are not well. They hurt, and so do my knees. I can't walk very well. I was not wounded, just, I am sick.

Mogol.

Every day, I come to this spot. For nearly four years now, I have been coming here. I get maybe ten rupees a day.

Young boys are very mean to me. Sometimes many of them come by. If there is no one to stop them, they kick me or hurt me, and laugh at me.

I get maybe twenty rupees a day. This is a quiet area. People do not bother me as I sit here and beg.

Unlike many women, Mogol begs with her face uncovered.

Mogol (fifty years old)

I am from Jalalabad. Seven years ago, I came to Peshawar when the Mujahideen took control of Jalalabad. My son and son-in-law were both taken by the Mujahideen for the war. Both were killed after just a few days. The Mujahideen brought their dead bodies to me, and I buried them.

Before I knew they were dead, I walked many miles around the province, looking for them. The sun and the wind and the cold weather have put these marks on my face.

After I buried their bodies, I brought my daughter, with her five children under the age of six, to Peshawar.

I am a beggar. I beg money and bread from different places. Usually the men give me more money than the women. Some days, I make thirty or forty rupees.

We pay 150 rupees each month for rent of the land. We have no house, just a tent. We have lived this way for seven years.

Shafika is begging in Khyber Park.

Shafika (thirty-one years old)

Two years ago, I came here from Kabul. My husband died during a rocket attack on the middle of the city. He sold old things, nothing valuable, just old things no one wanted anymore.

We have always been poor people. I have four daughters and one son. My life in Pakistan? I am always working, or looking for work. I came here to the park, and I ask women if they need a servant. If I have to, I beg, but I don't like to.

Benazir sits in a shady spot on the sidewalk near one of the modern plazas on Jamrud Road. She breathes in fumes from the traffic, and endures the endless honking of horns from the cars and busses speeding by.

Benazir

I am from Kabul. I have been here since Daoud was in power.

I am a beggar. All day long, I sit and beg. All day.

Habiba

I have four children. They are all in school. It is a free school, so they are able to go, which makes me happy.

My husband was sick and died eight years ago. We are from Badakshan province. Now we live in Peshawar with family members. We left Badakshan during the time of the Mujahideen, because they were killing so many people. There was too much blood along the street.

To help support my children, I go from house to house, along the street, knocking on doors, and asking people for food and money.

Basbibi (seventy years old)

I am from Karabagh, in Parwan Province. I've been here since the Taliban came. We left because the poverty at home is so bad. There was no food, no bread, nothing. We were poor in Afghanistan, and we are poor in Pakistan.

My family is in Peshawar with me. I have a daughter, a sister, a daughter-in-law, and a son. My son sells things along the road to get a little money.

I miss Afghanistan, but we were obliged to leave. We think about our country, but what good does that do?

Obidah

I am a widow. My husband was sick and he died ten years ago.
I have five sons and one daughter, and I am always thinking of their future. Can you get me into Canada?

A WALK IN THE PARK

Khyber Park is a women's park in the Hyatabad section of Peshawar. A tall hedge blocks sight of it from the street, a hedge that continues around the whole of the park. Women and children enter through a narrow gate. A guard sitting just inside the entrance chases away any males past a certain age who wander in, unsuspectingly or on purpose.

The grounds are beautiful, and beautifully kept up by a handful of gardeners, all men, who cut the grass and till the flower beds with simple hand tools. There is a small pond, with fish that swim lazily through its murky waters. A little footpath goes from the front of the park to the back, where the trees and gardens give way to a large expanse of lawn. Park benches are placed here and there. A playground with swing-sets is in an area cooled by shade trees.

Benazir and I arrive at the park early one Friday afternoon. The park is still fairly quiet, Benazir says it will soon get busy.

A number of benches are placed in the shape of a square, under a group of big shade trees. "There is a woman who comes here and gives lessons in Holy Koran," Benazir says. "She is a very knowledgeable woman, and women come here each day to pray and learn."

We stand near the entrance for awhile and watch women arrive. They come in groups or on their own with their children. They come in cars, dropped off by their husbands. They get off busses which slow down not quite long enough for everyone to disembark with safety. Those who have not got three rupees for the bus come on foot.

It is not long before the park is full of women and children. Some are selling food they made at home. Some have set up small stacks of fruit on a blanket. One small boy carries around a bathroom scale, asking people if they would like to weigh themselves for just a few rupees each.

Boys not engaged in commerce try to get their kites in the air, a challenge on this windless day. A few small girls run with them, but most stay with their mothers or sisters. Many groups are sitting on blankets, talking and lunching on food they brought with them. Some women wander around the park, talking and greeting others. Some play on the swings.

Most of the women here are Afghan. Some are dressed up, with jewelry, making the most of a rare outing. Some are here to beg. Most are here to relax and get some fresh air and exercise away from the exhaust in the streets and the rude comments of men.

Every one of them has a story.

Homaira (forty-three years old)

In Kandahar, I was primary-school teacher. Then the Taliban closed the schools, and I was out of a job. We came to Peshawar, but I still have no job.

I am a widow, with two children—a son, twenty-two, and a daughter, nineteen. My husband was killed in a rocket attack in Kandahar, in the time of the Russians.

I had to wear the *chadori* all the time after the Taliban came, and I hated it.

My son sells small things from a box along the sidewalk, to get a little money. That's how we live.

Simeen (forty-three years old)

I applied to UNHCR for help, but so far, there has been no reply. I am an educated woman. My parents and brother and husband were all killed by rockets. I don't work now.

When my husband was alive, we both worked, and had two salaries coming in. We had a good life. Now, there's nothing left. I just stay at home, waiting for my son to earn some money.

I come to this park just to get out of the house.

Monica (twelve years old)

I came from the middle of Kabul. We came to Pakistan two years ago, when the Taliban came to my city.

My uncle worked with the Mujahideen, and the Taliban knew this, and they punish us. They kept coming to our house, demanding to know where our uncle was.

We left everything and came here. We didn't bring any of our things. Someone else is now living in our house, using our things.

We live in the Hyatabad section of Peshawar. I go to school here. I'd like to learn English and other languages, so that I can talk with everybody.

Maryam (eleven years old, sister to Monica)

There are twelve of us living together, all from one family. I don't like Pakistan. Afghanistan has better weather.

For fun, I like to read stories with my friends. Sometimes we talk about Afghanistan. Maybe one day I'll go back.

Hotara (twelve years old)

I am from Kabul. I've been in Pakistan for one year.

In Kabul, I was happy, until the Taliban came and closed down my school. I had to stay home all the time and do housework, just like my mother.

Here, I go to school, but my friends and I talk about Afghanistan all the time.

Asina (twelve years old)

I am from Herat. I've been in Peshawar for almost a year.

In Herat, things were very bad. There was no school, nothing to do. The Taliban were always hitting people. When the school closed, I had to stay home and help my mother around the house. It was very dull.

My best subject is math. I hope to be a doctor.

Rihlah (twenty-six years old)

I have two children, ages five and six. During the Mujahideen time, my husband was killed by a tank. We came here four years ago, and live here with my parents.

I am homesick for Afghanistan, even though I have no good memories from there, since that is where I lost my husband.

I make food at home and bring it to the park to sell to other ladies and their children. This way, I get a little money.

Shakila (thirty-five years old)

One of my sons was killed by a rocket when he was four years old. Another son was stolen by the Mujahideen when he was only six months old. I have three children left. We are from Kabul.

My husband was an educator at the Faculty of Economics. Now he sells fruit from a small wagon. We share one room in Hyatabad with another family.

Amanda (forty-six years old)

Eight years ago, we came to Peshawar from the rural area near Kabul. First, we lived in a tent in Nasir Bagh refugee camp. Now, we live in one room, seven people.

We came here during the time of the Mujahideen. Two of my sons, twenty-five and twenty-two, were killed in a bomb explosion.

My husband sells old materials here, things he finds that he thinks someone might pay a few rupees for. I have three other sons. They sell drinks of water to people in the market on hot days.

I come to this park because I get sick of staying at home, in that small, crowded room.

Amida (forty-seven years old)

Four years ago, we left Kabul and came here.

A rocket destroyed our whole house, and two of my sons were killed at the same time. My husband and one other son are still alive and here in Peshawar with me.

My son and I sew to earn money. He is a tailor, and I make dresses. He works at home, and does not go outside very much. People laugh at him because he lost his hair and eyebrows—we don't know why.

We live in a small, single room. It's made of mud, and it is always very damp. I come to this park almost everyday to get some sun, and to see people. I get sick if I stay home all the time, and my legs hurt from the damp.

Kareema

I have six children. My daughter, who is now thirteen, was injured in a bomb explosion. Now she is lame. My husband is sick with a bad heart.

We came to Pakistan during the time of the Taliban. Our house was destroyed in a rocket attack, then people came and stole what was left of our things.

My husband is no longer able to work. Our son earns some money, selling things.

We were very rich in Kabul, and now we have lost everything. I just pray that my husband will stay alive.

Safia

I sell fruit here in the park.

We came here two years ago from Kabul. My husband has been sick for three years with mental problems from hearing all the rockets and bombs. He gets up in the middle of the night and talks to himself.

We have three children, ages thirteen, eleven, and eight. None of us can sleep at night because of his talking. We live in one small room, and cannot get away from the noise that he makes.

Faheema (thirty years old)

I am from Kabul. We left Afghanistan when the Taliban came. It's difficult for us here. In Kabul, my husband was a shoemaker, but we don't have the money to start up here. Now, my husband sells things by the side of the road. We have lots of problems.

Sharifa (twenty-seven years old)

We came from Jalalabad nearly three years ago. My husband was a teacher there, but when the schools closed, he became out of a job.

Schools in Afghanistan used to be free, even university was free. Here, we have a hard time paying for the school fees for our four children. My husband works in a shop for a small salary.

I try to come to the park every Friday afternoon with the children. It is like a holiday for us. We live in the Board section of Peshawar, which is very dirty and noisy. The park here is clean and quiet, and there are flowers.

Rozdra (forty-nine years old)

We came here six years ago from Afghanistan. At that time, my son was seventeen, and he was killed there, by the war. We left soon after.

Two months ago, my husband returned to Afghanistan. He really wanted to see Kabul, to see what it looked like now. He was killed there in a rocket attack.

I had another son who was killed in Peshawar. Now, all I have left are three daughters, thirteen, eleven, and eight. We don't have anyone to look after us. To get money, I sew dresses for people.

We try to come to the park every Friday or Sunday, just for fresh air. It is good for the children.

Osona (nineteen years old)

I am from Kabul. I have been here for five years. I am a student. I like Pakistan a little, but I have good memories of Afghanistan. After all, that's my country.

There are four people in my family. I hope to one day be a journalist.

Faringas (nineteen years old)

We came from Kabul almost three years ago. At that time, my mother was ill with cancer, although she is better now.

We left Afghanistan because there was no school for girls. Now, the Pakistan government has shut down all the post-secondary schools for Afghans.

I would like to be a doctor, but that doesn't look possible.

Gullalai (forty-five years old)

I have nine children. We came from the middle of Kabul and have been here for five months. We were waiting for things to get better in Afghanistan, but they didn't, so we came here. My eldest son works along the road, selling things from a push cart.

Golbatic (twenty-five years old)

We came here two years ago from Kabul, when the Taliban took over. My husband was a teacher, and, of course, he lost his job when the schools were shut down.

People broke into our house in Kabul, and stole lots of things. We decided to leave.

Now my husband works in a fabric shop for thirty-five rupees a day. We have three children, and pay fifty rupees each month for them to go to school. In Afghanistan, education was free. I never went to school, but I think it's important that my children go.

I miss everything in Afghanistan—the country, our house, our relatives—everything.

Orfanow

We came here nine years ago from Mazar. Two years ago we all went back to Kabul, but a rocket attack killed my two brothers and one nephew, so we came back to Pakistan. My husband is sick. He is very old, and the room we live in is very small and wet. Other Afghan people live in the room with us, and they help to pay our rent.

I try to come to this park everyday, to get some fresh air and sun.

Roquia

My husband and I were both teachers in Mazar, but when the Taliban came and closed the schools, we both became unemployed, so we came here. We have two sons, but we are not able to send them to school because we can't afford the fees. We have a lot of problems.

Rodoss (forty-year-old Down's Syndrome Sufferer)

My parents have died, and I have a sickness. My father was a police officer in Afghanistan. One of my sisters is in America. I live in Peshawar with my other sister. Her children are always bothering me—hitting me and punishing me. My sister doesn't stop them.

Can you get me out of there? All the time, my nieces hit me and laugh at me.

Fareba (twenty-four years old)

We left Kabul seven years ago, because of all the fighting. We lived in the old city, which is completely destroyed now. All the time, we heard bombs and rockets and guns, so we left and came here.

I am not married, but all the time I sit at home. I cook, I clean, and sew, just like a housewife. Afghan girls cannot live alone, even if they are not married.

We don't know what will happen in our country, so we can't decide our own future. We don't know what to do or where to go.

We still have many relatives in Kabul, and we may go to visit them this summer, if the fighting has stopped. We will have to wear *chadori*, if we go. If we wear it we'll fall down, if we don't, we'll be hit. The first time I put one on and looked at myself in the mirror, I thought, "I am in a bag, I am in a prison."

Arzou (twenty-four years old)

[Arzou means "hope." She's the cousin of Fareba.]

Life in Pakistan is peaceful compared to Afghanistan, but we are unhappy about not being in our own country. But we had to leave. All the time we were there, we were just waiting to be killed.

Many Pakistanis think that Afghans are not cultured people. They think that all Afghans want to destroy things. Many Afghans get money from abroad and spend it in Pakistan, but the Pakistanis never remember that.

We live with other people in a very small room in a house. I come to this park to get fresh air and leisure. In Kabul, we had a big yard. Here, we have only one room, and it's always full of other people.

If we don't have peace in our country, if Pakistan kicks us out, where can we go? If no other country will take us, what can we do? The developed world must think of Afghans as human beings. Our country is now in the hands of wild people. The children who are there now will also grow up to be wild people, without education.

Fayeta (nineteen years old)

Five years ago, I came to Peshawar. I was living in Kabul, but now Kabul is like a cemetery. The houses are destroyed, everything is stolen. I had to stay home all the time and do housework—the school was closed.

I come to this park every two or three months, when I get sick of being at home. I come to get fresh air. Three families live in our house, and it is very crowded.

Our future looks hopeless. Things just get worse.

I don't want to marry. I want to get a high education and become a doctor or an engineer. It's very difficult not to study, to have no education.

Kobra (thirty-five years old)

I came here five months ago from Kabul. My life in Kabul was very bad— rockets, bombs, poverty. I have five children, and I want them to go to school. This is impossible in Afghanistan.

My husband is a shopkeeper here. I have friends still in Afghanistan. Most of my family is still there. They can't afford to come out. Pakistan is very expensive, but there is a much higher standard of life here.

I want my children to get a good education, as high an education as possible.

I come to the park when I get tired and homesick for Afghanistan. I come here with my children. There are two families in my small house. The rent is very difficult. There is only one room for all of us—seven people.

The Taliban don't allow kite flying. They don't allow TV, radio, cassettes, or cameras. If they find these things, they break them, and arrest the owner. They tear up photos, they tear up English books.

Atufa (twenty years old)

Everything you heard about the stadium is true. My brother saw someone's hand cut off. The Taliban then held up the hand, to show the people. My brother is a sportsman—he played football. Now, in the stadium, they cut people's hands off. People were not happy to see it. Many people were crying.

Miriam (fourteen years old)

We came here four months ago from Kabul. I didn't like it there. The Taliban were always hitting everyone and wouldn't let us go out and do what we wanted to do. I was in the fourth grade, before the schools shut down.

My family decided to come here because my brothers are tall, but they are young, and haven't started to grow beards yet. The Taliban would hit them whenever they went out of the house, "Why do you not have a beard?" So especially for them, we came here.

If I had gone outside without a *burqa*, the Taliban would have hit me, too. I either didn't go out, or I went out with the *burqa* on.

The *burqa* is difficult to use. It doesn't suit me at all. I had a hard time getting it on properly. The hat part would hang over my face, and the face part would hang over my shoulder.

There used to be foreign people in Kabul. They were kind, and they helped us. They gave us a card, and with that card we could get bread, fruit, rice, and soup. But the Taliban started punishing foreigners, so the foreigners left and didn't come back.

The neighbors were taken by the Taliban. The beautiful girls were sent to Kandahar. All the Taliban get married with two or three women. They steal women because they like to have them for free, they don't like to spend money to get them.

Here, also, it is difficult for people to live. Here, also, we have poverty.

I still have friends in Afghanistan: Meetra, Farzona. They're not coming here because they don't even have the bus fare to come here. They live with lots of problems in Kabul.

My father is a motor engineer. He fixes cars, but we are a very big family.

All of the women in our family go door-to-door. They are beggars. They say, "Give me a piece of bread or I will die." They are honorable women, here, and in Afghanistan. They are beggars because they have no other work.

Before Taliban, we studied and went to school. My uncle was killed by the Taliban. My cousin was a prisoner for one year. They hit him with an electric stick. They did the same to my uncle, until blood ran from his body. My cousin had iron bracelets around his feet.

I don't go to school here in Peshawar—there's not enough money. I'd need pens, books. If I ever get the money, I'd like to learn English, and talk to foreign people.

I come to this park twice a week. Ten people live in my room. I come here to get away from them.

MIGHTIER THAN THE SWORD

Walking up to a worried Dick York, Gene Kelly, munching an apple, tells him that the job of a reporter is to comfort the afflicted and afflict the comfortable. The movie is *Inherit the Wind*, about the Scopes Monkey Trial of 1925. John Scopes, a young high school teacher, was on trial for teaching the theory of evolution to his science class. The struggle between religious fundamentalism and rational thought that took place in that Tennessee courtroom would not be alien in present-day Afghanistan.

In this chapter, we meet four women who have risked their lives to afflict the comfortable, to learn the truth, write the truth, and present the truth to the women of Afghanistan.

Najiba Sara Biabani is a well-respected Afghan poet and journalist. A widow with four children, she has written for Peshawar newspapers. She was working for the BBC when she was shot at in the marketplace and had to go into hiding.

Before the attack, she had received threatening phone calls and letters. Some of the letters were written on the official letterhead of the Taliban, and carried their seal.[1] The threats forced her to change her home address three times, but she was always found again. Najiba is known as a vocal supporter of women's rights.

The project she created and worked on for the BBC, an on-going radio drama in Persian and Pashtu, is listened to by three-quarters of Afghanistan's population.[2] The show deals with issues such as land mines, narcotics, health, hygiene, women's rights, education, and domestic problems. There are three shows a week, and each show is repeated three times. All three episodes are played together on Fridays, to coincide with the time men are at the mosque. This way, women can listen without their husbands knowing, if this is a problem for them.[3]

Najiba Sara Biabani

I came to Peshawar nine years ago. I lived in Kabul. I was a radio newscaster there and a producer as well. I worked on different kinds of programs. I also did literary work, poetry and essays, in Dari and Pashtu.

Even before I could write, I could say poetry. My father and husband helped me a lot. My father was a writer. My husband was a scientist.

Each poem I write is different. I write about people, neighborhoods, the difficult lives of women.

Barbrak Karmal was the president when my husband was hanged. My husband was not politically involved, but they arrested him anyway, and put him in jail, and then they hanged him.

They said I was also doing political work, and were planning to imprison me too. I escaped with one of my sons to Peshawar, leaving the other ones behind in Kabul.

My children that time were four, three, two, and one. It was a difficult decision. I didn't have even one address of anybody in Peshawar. I didn't know where I would go, or where I would stay.

I didn't give up against these difficulties. Before I left Afghanistan, I wrote down everything, so I could let other women know. Because of what I'd been through, I had become a very strong woman.

I had a book of poetry ready to be published in Afghanistan, but then the Mujahideen burnt down the printing press, so that's what happened to my first book—up in flames. It made me quite ill. The poems were about what women do with their lives. I have no copies left of those poems.

I've written a lot. I've written two novels and a book of short stories about life under the Mujahideen. I have also written nearly nine hundred poems.

For awhile I worked as a nursery school teacher in Afghanistan. One of my novels is about that. The other one is about disappointment.

There are many women who are uneducated and uninformed. I write so they will learn there are all types of women in the world, women who work out in the world, women who work inside their homes, women who have their own businesses, women who work with men out in the fields, others who just waste all their time watching TV.

At first, when we came to Pakistan, the children had to stay out of school for a whole year, because I could not afford to send them. In the evening, I sewed clothes for people, and I wrote.

I started writing for Radio Pakistan and then did voice-overs on TV ads.

Then I wrote for a Peshawar daily. I did a women's page, the first page for women in the Pashtu language! All these jobs together gave me enough money to be able to send the children back to school.

The women's page had stories of women. I went to villages and did surveys, and to the Afghan camps, and wrote about their difficulties.

After this, I got a job with the BBC radio in Pakistan. I wanted to make a project for them to be employed.

What we came up with was a radio drama, "New Home, New Life." It's still going on! It's in Pashtu. I started off as a writer, and I also got other women writers on the project as well. I also became an actor in the dramas! I had never done that before! I wrote and I acted. Then I got too busy with acting, and I left the writing to others. The BBC gave me a certificate, saying I was one of their top actors in Pakistan! For this, I received a good salary, and I put my children in a good English school. I started doing this in 1993, and worked for five years there.

In August of 1998, there was Afghanistan Independence Day. The Afghan Elders at the Afghan Study Center on Abdara Road invited me to speak. It was a conference on unity, and a celebration.

I spoke about life in Afghanistan from Babrak until the Taliban. I told truthful things. When I got down from the stage and came home, I started receiving death threats over the telephone. The threatening phone calls came to my home and to the BBC. The men said, "If you don't stop writing and talking, we will shoot you." I paid no attention to the threats. I decided I would just keep working.

On October 5, I went to the bazaar after work to get some vegetables for dinner. From behind me, somebody shot at me, but he missed. I ran down a little side street, jumped into a rickshaw, and came home. Then I got back in a rickshaw, and went to a police station, and filed a report. I talked to my bosses on the phone, and they all told me to stay home.

Five times more I got threats. Some of them mentioned my daughters! Since then, I've been obliged to stay home. My daughters stay home too. My sons go to school nearby.

All this has kept me from sleeping. I can't rest during the day, either. Except for one time when I had to go out to the hospital when I was sick, and then I had to inform the police, I have not been out of this house. I don't go out to the markets, and I don't go out for walks.

The police did a good investigation. They found out that the threats and the shooting came from a terrorist group within the Taliban.

I have been accepted as an emergency case by the United Nations High Commission for Refugees. I don't know where I'll be sent to, or when. We have been told to be ready to leave at any time. For safety reasons, we won't know where we are going until we're handed our plane tickets.

Once I leave Peshawar, I'll finish writing my story, then women everywhere can know what it is like for Afghan women.

A few weeks after this interview, Najiba and her family were taken, quickly, out of Pakistan, and are now living in safety in a European country. She writes from her new home:

We are the only Afghan family in town. Three times a week, we attend language classes to learn the language of our new country. Our new town is beautiful and near to the ocean.

Although we are safe, it is hard being away from family and friends, and away from the work I loved to do. My thoughts are with those people who still suffer from the war, and those who are poor and uneducated. I feel myself to be dead because I can't do anything for them. . . . I am very homesick here, so please keep writing to me.

She ends the letter with a short poem:

May God bring us the day to meet again in a friendly way.

Maryam is now living in Toronto. We meet in the lobby of the Ontario Institute for Studies in Education building in downtown Toronto where we have gathered with other Afghan women to celebrate Mothers' Day.

Maryam

I am from Kabul. I left fifteen years ago. The Russians were occupying Afghanistan. They wanted writers, people who were working in TV and radio and newspapers to be involved with them. They asked me, too, but I didn't want that, so I escaped Afghanistan.

I was a writer and producer with Radio Afghanistan. I did my university education in Tehran. I was there for five years, studying Persian literature. I came back to Afghanistan, and after six months I had to escape.

It was very sad for me, because I wanted to work with our people, but I couldn't, because the Communists wanted me to write only good things about them, and I didn't want to do that.

My family was not with me when I left Afghanistan. I was with some of the other people from Radio Afghanistan. We were four women and two men. We paid someone to smuggle us out, and we escaped from Afghanistan by camel. It took five days and five nights. It was very, very dangerous, and very exciting also. I was very scared. It was a long trip, and eventually we arrived in Peshawar.

It felt like I was starting my life again from this point. This was in 1981. I spent one year in Pakistan, then three years in India, and after that I came to Canada.

I spent a few weeks in Peshawar, although mostly I was in Islamabad. At that time, the situation was different than now. There weren't as many Afghan people in Peshawar then as there are now, but the political situation was very, very bad. The people were fighting, especially the fundamentalist people.

The different Mujahideen groups were asking people to join them. They were asking us to come with them, to talk with them, to work with them. Especially, they wanted us to develop a radio station, but we didn't want to. That's why we had to go from Peshawar to Islamabad. I ran away from the Russians and then I ran away from the fundamentalists!

For two weeks, Gulbuddin's party put us in jail, in a place on the outskirts of Peshawar. They didn't torture us. They just locked us up.

They put us in jail because we didn't want to work with fundamentalist people, and this was very bad. They were thinking that we didn't want to work with them, we didn't want to work with the Russians, so who were we? This was a big question for them.

We continued our struggle in the jail with a hunger strike. For three days we didn't eat or drink. We wanted to show our jailers that we were human. We wanted to struggle, we wanted to be alive, that's why we escaped from the Russians. And now we were in jail? For what?

The conditions in the jail, after our hunger strike, were very good. They treated us very well. They cleared out the warden's office and made it comfortable for us to sleep in. We had three meals a day prepared for us. The four of us women got to stay together. One of the women had two small children, and the children stayed with us as well.

We were lucky because there were people in Peshawar who knew us, and who talked with Hezb-i-Islami, and helped get us out of jail. As soon as we were released, we went to Islamabad.

I decided to go to India to find a better situation. I am a writer, and I wanted to have a job to get money to survive. Things were much better in India. I found a job with the United Nations.

I was very glad to get a job so I could help my family back home. I also wanted to be able to rent a room and have time to write and read.

After three years in India, I applied to the Embassy of Canada, and after six months they prepared everything, my tickets, the forms, everything. I came here as a refugee.

Canada was not strange for me because I had been in Europe. Also, I knew I had to handle it, that I had to settle my life here. It was difficult at first, but I worked a lot and was too busy to think about how hard it was. I knew that eventually I would have a good life, and now I do. I have a very good life in this country.

I found my ideal job. This newspaper that I'm publishing, it is really my ideal job. I created this job. One day three or four years ago, I was sitting and thinking about what I could do for this community. So I started this newspaper, and I love it.

I have written a book of literary short stories, in Persian, about Afghan people, in Afghanistan and around the world. I love to write and I love to read. This is really my duty in life. I have a responsibility toward my people because I am educated. All of us Afghans have a responsibility to the people still in Afghanistan. We cannot be just thinking of ourselves.

Sajeda's office is up a steep stone staircase in the Tahkal section of Peshawar. Although it is near Jamrud Road, a main thoroughfare that is always full of traffic, the office is somehow sheltered from the noise. We sit on the couch and drink tea while she talks.

Sajeda Milad (twenty-six years old)

I am a journalist and a poet. I am responsible for *Khaharan Women's Journal.* It is the publication of the Relief Organization for Afghan Orphans and Widows, ROAOW. *Khaharan* means "sisters."

I graduated from Kabul University. I came to Pakistan one year ago. In Kabul, before Taliban, I wrote for a magazine, articles about women's issues, literature, culture, and social issues, often putting in twelve-hour days at work. I was very happy. Once the Taliban came, I had to stay home. I was going crazy at home with nothing to do but housework. So, I came here, to be useful again.

I put the magazine together by myself. It could use a staff of ten or twelve people, but I do it all myself. We sell some of them in Peshawar, but most go into Afghanistan, where they are given out free. We have to do this secretly, of course. People smuggle them in.

We hear sometimes from women inside Afghanistan. I know of many Afghan women who are wise, educated, and creative. Many have left Afghanistan. I feel sorry for the ones who are still there. They are not able to do anything, just stay in the house.

The Taliban do not like me, but this is Pakistan, not Afghanistan. They are not able to do anything to me here. They have given me warnings. "Stop your writing! Stop publishing your magazine!" But I refuse to worry.

Of course, if I go inside Afghanistan, they will get me, so I will stay here.

It is impossible to get books now in Afghanistan. A girl cannot get a pen in her hand, or a piece of paper. Women cannot get books, or magazines, or even a newspaper. Living under the Taliban for a year made me feel much older than my age. Afghan women are like the walking dead. They have nothing, they can do nothing.

Homa Zafar is one of those women who, when you meet them, they make you want to become a better person. Not only is she continuing to do her work in the face of numerous threats against her, but there is a calmness about her that seems to reach into the very core of her being.

We meet in the lobby of a guest house in the University Town section of Peshawar. She is there for a seminar with her organization, the Co-operation Center for Afghanistan, or CCA.

Homa Zafar

I am editor-in-chief of *Sadaf* magazine. It is a quarterly magazine for Afghan women, and my office is in the CCA office, which means Cooperation Center for Afghanistan.

I was born in Badakshan province, but I was raised in Kabul. It was in 1989 that we left the country, because of war, and also because of the Communist authority. Before we left, I was a journalist with an Afghan women's magazine. At the same time, I was studying at Kabul University.

The situation even then was much better than it is now, but there were still lots of things we could not do, particularly with women. So we fled the country and took refuge in Pakistan.

I was invited by the CCA to publish a magazine for women. It is much bigger than the other magazine I worked on. I have been here for two years.

Besides the magazine, I also work for women's rights. I look at cases of the abuse of women's rights in the camps, rape cases, things like this. I have contact with Human Rights Watch in America, and we cooperate in this area.

This magazine of mine is a magazine that I never want to make the authorities happy. I should tell you that I'm not afraid of terrorists, or people who would try to keep me silent, so I talk openly for women's rights in the magazine.

I've received many warning messages. There is a newspaper called *Sahar*, supported by the Pakistan government and put together by Pakistani and Afghan fundamentalists. They wrote two big articles against my magazine and against myself. They warned me that I would be kidnapped, but still, I am working.

I heard that three rape cases happened in the camps: a thirteen-year-old girl was raped by a commander, in Nasir Bagh camp; also, a sixteen-year-old girl was raped by a commander in Hekmatyr's party. They left the war and are now living in Nasir Bagh, and they have authority there. Everyone is afraid of them in the camp. Also, a woman with four children was raped in front of her husband. When I heard these things, at that time the Human Rights Watch people also came, and we went together to meet the people in the camps.

We discovered lots of bad things. For example, people said, "During the night the commanders are coming and taking our daughters and sons to dance for them. They put jewelry on the boys, like women, make them dance, then they rape the young girls and boys.

I wrote down all these things, and printed them in my magazine. I received warnings from these commanders who are living in Nasir Bagh that I shouldn't write these things. They were looking for me, trying to find my address. This was five months ago.

Working for Afghan women's rights is a very, very dangerous thing.

There is no security in Peshawar. Every week, there are terrorist actions. Every week, we lose good people. We are losing our good cultural people, our educated people. So that's why our educated people are afraid.

We have field workers inside Afghanistan, and we send our magazine in with them, and they distribute it. The magazine is smuggled into the country, hidden among their clothes. It is done with difficulty. Of course, we cannot send large numbers of the magazine, just small numbers. Also, I receive articles back from women through these same field workers.

On the back cover of the most recent issue of our magazine is a picture from Mazar-e-Sharif, from the last class of the Faculty of Medicine for women. The students are writing their last examination while wearing the *burqa*. One of these women came to our office and she said, "When we were in the examination, we were thinking that our eyes were giving out, because we could not see properly. We all got headaches."

Their teachers said, "How will we become sure that you are the exact person you are supposed to be under the *chador*? Lift your veils for one second so we can know that you are our student."

When the women flipped up their veils, a Talib came by, and beat the teacher in front of all these students, and called the girls very filthy names. After the Talib left the class, the students sat in stunned silence for fifteen minutes before they could start to write anything. This is the situation in Afghanistan. They say to everybody, "We give permission for the last students of the Faculty of Medicine to pass their examination," but this is how they give their permission!

Sometimes people are supporting very, very stupid things in the name of religion and culture, very stupid things, but I think most problems we have faced during our history is from the law. Religious law. If you study the Afghan history, whenever we find an opportunity for democracy or the movement of women, for having a democratic society, these movements have been stopped by Mullahs, through religious law. They are making Islam a cover for all the evil things they are doing.

NOTES

1. *CCA Newsletter* 5, no. 5 (October 1998): 9.
2. Edward Giradet and Jonathan Walter, editors, *Essential Field Guide to Afghanistan* (Geneva: Crosslines Communications, 1998), 175.
3. Ibid.

HELP

In this chapter four women whose lives have been entwined through their work in support of Afghan women talk about their lives and their work.

Fatana Gailani heads the Afghan Women's Council (AWC). I arrive at their headquarters in Hyatabad on inoculation day. Packed into the small courtyard and overflowing onto the street are mothers in many styles of tribal dress. They are carrying small children, many of whom are wailing as though they have premonitions of the injection to come.

I make my way through the crowd and am shown into Fatana Gailani's office, a large, bright room simply furnished. Photographs of the AWC's activities are tacked up on a long bulletin board.

Fatana Gailani, Afghan Women's Council

I have just returned from a trip to Spain.

I received a prize there from the United Nations Association of Spain. I received it for my work for peace. Four organizations invited me to Spain for International Women's Day, and I went to three cities. I met a large number of people in Madrid, including Queen Sofia. I discussed with her about our country's problems, and I asked her to help with peace and with the women's issues.

It is very nice for me and my colleagues and for women in Afghanistan when we receive such a prize. We are fighting for our future, and our duties are hard, and this prize gives us more hope for the future.

When the Mujahideen first returned to Afghanistan, after the Russians left, I did not think they were too bad. I thought, until now, they are not nice to each other, but when they go back to Afghanistan, they will take up their responsibilities for the people, and because these are big responsibilities, maybe they will not fight with each other.

When they went back to Afghanistan, from that moment, they started fighting each other, and kept fighting for five years. They made so many problems for the people of Afghanistan, especially for the women, and they destroyed all of Kabul, the capital city, and they stole all the things.

They did not think, "These are the treasures of Afghanistan, I have a duty to protect them." They just thought, "This is mine!" and they took it and sold it in Pakistan.

They did a lot of rape, a lot of thieving, and a lot of killing. More than fifty thousand people died in the five years after the Communists left.

Women started coming to my house, often more than one hundred women a day, from different places in Afghanistan. They said, "We had to leave our home," and "We've lost our house," and when they came to Pakistan, they came to me.

Ten years ago my clinic was a very big clinic, the largest in all of Peshawar. At that time, we had twenty-two doctors. Everyday we received more than two hundred patients. There was a German organization that was helping, giving us a lot of medicine, a good salary for the doctors. It was possible for us to help a lot of people.

At that time, I made a school for the children in one of the camps. There were ten thousand families in the camp, and I made a school for them. Every week I went to the camp, usually two times every week. It was two hours from Peshawar each way. I had no salary, nobody to support me, but I did it because it was important for the children to be educated.

Some Mullahs, some fundamentalists made publicity in this camp. They said, "She is working for Western countries, she has a Western idea, and this and that," but I didn't have a Western idea, I had an Afghan idea. I am a Moslem, and I am an Afghan, I love my customs, I love my religion, and I was not using them the wrong way.

One time, they kidnapped one of my nurses from my clinic. This was twelve years ago. She was fifty-three years old, a very nice woman. The day she was kidnapped, they sent three letters to my office. The letters said, "if you keep discussing about things, about women, then you will see."

When I received the news about my nurse, I was in shock, totally. We have never heard from her. Maybe they killed her. We still do not know.

For five full months, from April of 1992, I was in shock. I stayed at home, crouched up. All the time, I slept. I was very sad. I cried so much.

And then, my husband said to me, "You wake up! You fight! You wake up and you fight! This is not the solution, you being sad like this."

Women were still coming to my door, asking, "Help me!" My heart was full of pain, but I woke up, and I began to fight.

[She begins to cry.] I have worked so hard for twenty years. My best years, my nice time, my nice age, as a young woman, I could have led a good life. I could have spent my life abroad, going to movies, going to parks, doing things I enjoyed, having fun with the children, seeing the world, but, instead, all the time, I was fighting for my country, for our freedom.

We need support from some independent organizations. We need the support from the UN, and from Human Rights organizations. But nobody can use us. We are very strong women. We are not stupid.

The fanatic parties don't like me, but I don't like them, so it is! For me, it is the people of Afghanistan who are important, and they love me. They help me to be strong.

We also have a monthly newspaper, since 1993. It is eight pages, and we publish two thousand copies. We write about our country, political ideas, what we want, about the people's problems, about our rights.

We want the women of Afghanistan to have political ideas. We explain that politics does not only belong to men. It is also the women's duty. The women find it interesting, and a lot of women give money to support our newspaper.

The paper also goes into different parts of Afghanistan. We send it to Mazar, Kandahar, Kabul, Jalalabad. People who are going into Afghanistan carry a few copies with them, secretly, and that's how it gets in. We also have members of our Council inside Afghanistan, and they send articles out to us.

We also have courses in the refugee camps to help people become educated, to keep busy, because they are suffering from the war, they have lost hope, and we like to teach them. This way, their minds become busy, which is better for them than remembering all the time.

I have been to conferences all over the world—to Beijing, Germany, France, Spain, Africa, Thailand, Jordan, London—talking about Afghan women. We need two kinds of support from the women of the world: economic and political. They can put pressure on the UN to stop what is happening in Afghanistan, and they can put pressure on the Pakistan government to take care of the Afghan people who are fighting for human rights.

I have been threatened by the Taliban, not by just a letter, by more than a letter. A large group of Taliban have surrounded my car many times, making threats.

Security is now a very serious problem, but I don't want to leave Peshawar, not now. I'm fighting again. However much it is possible for me to fight, I fight.

Otherwise, life is in the hands of God. I worry a lot. I have three daughters. The oldest one turned twenty-two yesterday. She has finished her college, and she would like to go to university for her master's, but now she stays home.

The second daughter, I adopted from a camp. Now she is fifteen years old. She was in class five, but now she must stay home, too. The small one is five, and she stays home. For two of the girls, a teacher comes to our home. But for the older one, no, She is upset. She has grown up with the war. All the time, over the years, I told her, "The Mujahideen are fighting for our freedom." All the time, when she was small, I told her this. Now she says to me, "You lied to me. Those men were *not* fighting for our freedom."

And now, I have economic problems, because nobody supports me. I also have to pay salaries for four bodyguards to be with me. Life is hard.

The Pakistani government gave me five police to watch out for our safety, but I must pay for them as well. They stay in the back of my house.

This time is harder for me than the time of the Russians. I don't like body guards being with me all the time.

Now, the different parties are discussing something, but I don't trust them. They call it a "Peace Process." It is not a peace process. It is only peace for two groups, and I don't trust them. Neither side. Because both sides have killed so many people. They both make problems. They will never bring peace to Afghanistan.

At the moment, I have no hope for Afghanistan. If enough countries work together and put pressure on other countries to stop the weapons and the money going into Afghanistan, maybe that will give a chance for the Afghan people. Maybe at that time I will find hope for women's rights and the people's rights.

The Afghan Women's Resource Center (AWRC) is a compound of several buildings tucked away among narrow laneways in Peshawar. All the rooms are full of women working and learning. There is an office, a computer training room, several sewing rooms, and a craft shop where women can sell the handicrafts they learn to make at the AWRC courses.

Sonita, Program Consultant

My husband wanted to come to Pakistan. We had neighbors who were from Logar Province, and one of their brothers was in Pakistan, fighting with Mujahideen. My husband was from the same tribe as their commander.

Through the neighbors, we got in touch with this commander, and told them we wanted to go to Pakistan. In September of 1988, we left Kabul. We went to a Mujahideen stronghold in the north, a village full of Mujahideen. We stayed in the commander's house until transport could be arranged. We were there for twenty-two days. It was scary. Everyday there would be bombing. The bombs would come, and I would run downstairs, and then I would run upstairs again, because you can't do anything by running downstairs! It was just a reflex, to run somewhere.

The journey to Pakistan was very difficult and interesting—I mean interesting in retrospect, because at that time, it wasn't! It was difficult, but my husband said it was much easier than what many people had done, so we were lucky. Many people went by foot. We didn't go anywhere by foot. We traveled in a Mujahideen truck, which was used to smuggle arms and ammunition. It was a big truck, and we were able to get a seat just behind the driver. We shared that seat with another family, a woman who was bringing her daughter to Pakistan to get married.

It took us four days. We came by a very circuitous way, through areas that were not under the control of government forces. We stopped several nights along the way. We stopped in a Gypsy area somewhere, and stayed in Mujahideen homes. We crossed into Pakistan on the fourth night, through a small trading area, in the middle of nowhere.

Once we got into Pakistan, it was easier. The first night was hard, then we came to a town and found a small hotel and got clean. We found some reasonable human kind of transport, and we came to Peshawar.

We both managed to get jobs fairly soon, so things have worked out all right.

The Afghan Women's Resource Center started so that Afghan women could help other Afghan women to become self-reliant.

At that time, there was lots of Mujahideen influence in Peshawar. There was a lot of resistance to the free movement of women, for example. We had to pick women up and bring them to the Center. Most women were not allowed on public transport.

When the Mujahideen took power, the government of Pakistan asked us to wind up our operations here and go back to Afghanistan. They said, "Everything is OK there now, so go home." Before long, though, more refugees started coming, people from Kabul, so permission was granted for us to continue to work in Pakistan.

We keep our work low key. We feel we are doing important work, even if it is in a small way. We are trying to make a difference in the lives of many women, and we don't want to endanger that by being too revolutionary. Even the literacy we do, we include Koranic readings, and things like that. This program we have now is accepted by the community, even by the Mujahideen and the Taliban. For example, our landlord in the next building is a Talib, and we don't have any problems with him because we do our work quietly, we don't try to do anything which is objectionable.

One of our projects is in Accora Hattack camp, with new refugees from Kabul and surrounding areas. We assist women in the camp. We give them embroidery and tailoring instructions, provide them with materials, and then we sell their products for them, plus literacy instruction and day care.

Women who come to the Center live here in Peshawar, or in camps near the city.

We see changes in the women, especially women in the camps. When we start our programs in the camps, the women are at first very shy. At first they cannot even introduce themselves. After we give them some education, some information, they become braver.

The only hope I see eventually for Afghans in general is in the people themselves, that they're so resilient. If I were an outsider, and I heard an account of all that happened to them, I wouldn't think they could even live after all that, but they manage to survive, they manage to go on, they manage to continue struggling. That is the only hope that I see. People do manage to survive even after horrible things happen to them.

A few days later I go to Accora Hattack refugee camp with women from the AWRC, to visit the sewing classes they have there. We stop at the side of the Grand Trunk road along the way to pick up several more of their teachers, whose car has broken down. They leave the car with their male driver and pile into the van with us. We have a male driver, too, and there are curtains over the van windows.

As we weave in and around the insane traffic, there is speculation over whether any of the students will still be there. The vehicle problem has made the teachers two hours late.

There was no need to worry. When we get there, the compound is full of women, proceeding with their sewing, patiently awaiting their teacher.

The classes are held in two tents inside a mud-walled compound. A sheet of blue plastic has been stretched between the two tent roofs to provide shelter from the rain and sun for the program manager, who sits at a desk between the two tents. Outside the tents, a few flowers have been planted and show signs of recent, careful watering. A literacy class is held in a nearby mud room.

One of the women shows off her new daughter, just twenty-three days old. Toddlers wander in and out of the literacy class. The classrooms are all dark inside. "In the heat, they are ovens. In the rain, they are wet, muddy, and miserable," one of the teachers tells me.

Sandals are left in a pile outside, so that the mud and sand of the camp is not taken into the classrooms. On a low table, the tailoring instructor shows how to lay out cloth for measuring and cutting. She carefully sponges away yellow dust before beginning.

A small nook beside the literacy class holds a sort of a kitchen, with a one-burner gas stove on which to boil water for tea. Another corner holds a clay oven for baking nan. Water is from a communal tap, outside the compound.

Embroidery class is held nearby, in another tent. This tent is also full, and, like the others scrupulously clean. Women sit alongside the mud walls of the tent, working at their stitching.

Solia

I've been in this camp for two-and-a-half years. I came to Pakistan from a suburb of Kabul, soon after the Taliban took over. There was lots of fighting. My father was a butcher, and he was killed in the war.

I got married after I came here. In Kabul we had a house. Here we live in a tent, with two children. Sometimes we are given some wheat flour and some cooking oil.

Malalai

I've been in this camp for one year. We left Kabul and went to Jalalabad first. I was injured in the war. My wrist was hurt, and I have shrapnel wounds in my leg and elbow. I was hit by a rocket. Other members of my family were also hit.

I live with my husband and one son. There is no work for my husband. There is a village nearby where he sometimes gets work for one day and brings home twenty or thirty rupees, so we can get food. Other than that, we have nothing.

We want to learn something, so that maybe we can earn some money for ourselves. That's why we come to this course.

There is a tent used for a kindergarten class. A map of Afghanistan is tacked to the ceiling of the tent. Persian words and letters are written on scraps of paper, and the children sort through them.

Lena

I am the teacher of this kindergarten class. I've been working for AWRC for nine years. Before this, I was a knitting machine instructor. Funds for that project ended.

I usually have twenty-five children here. They are the children of the mothers in the program who don't have people at home to look after them.

We walk through the camp to another compound, where several women-headed families live in two tents. The tents are patched with sheets of plastic. We go inside on of them, and the parade of children we have picked up crowds in with us. A trunk against the far end of the tent holds embroidery that they have done. They are all graduates of the AWRC course. AWRC is arranging for markets so they can sell their work. Shawls, embroidered trousers, and handkerchiefs are spread out before us.

"See how close the stitching is?" the instructor points out to me. "Ultimately, it uses up their eyes. They have to count the threads of the cloth in order to make the precise geometric patterns. The trousers take six full days to embroider."

We walk over to the tented camp, where there are no mud houses and no mud walls. I am warned not to take pictures when there are men around. "You never know how they might react," as if they are jungle animals and we are on safari.

At the edge of the tented camp, full of tents made of shawls and plastic, a man comes out to ask us who we are. We obtain his permission to take photos of the tents. I snap as many as I can as quickly as I can. A crowd begins to gather. "OK, let's get out of here," the woman guiding me says.

We get back to the AWRC compound and have tea and candies in the now-empty literacy classroom. The classes have ended, and the women have stopped being students, and gone home to their tents to prepare the mid-day meal for their families.

"Most of the aid agencies concentrate their efforts in this camp," one of the AWRC staff tells me, "so the people here are luckier than in some other camps. There are some remote camps which are very, very poor."

One of the women gestures at a small boy in the doorway. We all laugh as the child tries to fit his tiny feet into the grown-up women's shoes on the doorstep.

We leave after tea, the AWRC women all covering their faces as we exit the walled compound and climb into the van and drive out of the camp.

While the Russians were in Afghanistan, a group of Canadian doctors and community people in Kingston, Ontario, took on the task of getting medical supplies to Afghan guerrillas and civilians. They also arranged for wounded Afghans to come to Canada for surgery and to be fitted with artificial limbs. Sheila Henriksen was part of this effort, and for several years, opened her home to Afghans recuperating from injuries received in rocket and land mine attacks.

Sheila Henriksen

We established a committee for Afghanistan in Kingston, and Alan, my husband, was elected president. There was a medical committee as well, for the selection of the candidates to come here for surgery, and Alan was part of that, also.

Mostafa, who is the grandson of the exiled king, was at a time and still is a friend of ours. He was attending Queen's University, and we established a relationship with him. He was very much a part of the organization as well.

Even before we went to Peshawar, we had a whole bunch of things going on in the Kingston area, such as fundraising and gathering medical supplies. We sent these supplies ahead of us.

There were lots of guns on the streets of Peshawar at that time. What was very disheartening was to see a lot of young boys, nine and ten years old, carrying Kalishikovs. We actually saw that. The day we handed over the medicine to the local doctors, one of the persons guarding the goods was a nine-year-old boy with a rifle. That was scary.

We visited some refugee camps. The atmosphere was deathly. It was very difficult to see the children and the older people living in the conditions in which they were living. They had just pieces of sticks and rags for tents, no running water of course, no toilets. It was extremely primitive. And this was at a time when there was foreign aid going into the camps.

We made a very quick trip into Afghanistan, but we didn't get in over the table. We went in to oversee the distribution of the medicine and the clothes that we had sent ahead of time. Also, we wanted to meet the first two patients we were bringing to Canada.

We were taken into Afghanistan secretly. I had to be disguised as a man. I had to wear a *pakul*, a woolen blanket that the tribal men wear, and take off any female identification, like my wedding rings. I wrapped myself up in the blanket and kept my head low at the check-points. I couldn't say anything. It was scary.

We had armed guards in the truck with us. They were sitting very close to me, with the guns going up and down as the truck drove over the bumpy dirt roads.

The depot where the medicine was delivered was just inside the border. It was a cave, carved out of a mountain. It was completely hidden. We stayed in Afghanistan for only one day, going and coming back on the same day. I was glad to get out of there!

Over the time of our involvement, we had fifteen Afghans staying at our house in Kingston, while they recuperated from their surgery. Three of them were female, two teenagers and an adult woman.

One of the patients was a twelve-year-old girl. She was badly wounded, both in her hands and feet. She was escorted by her brother, a very fundamentalist Moslem.

It was their first night in the house. Mostafa was there with us, some other Afghan patients, male, and Alan and I. I prepared Afghan food. We were still, at that time, sitting with them to eat on the floor, as is the Afghan custom.

This girl's name was Bibi. Supper was ready, and the men were already sitting on the floor, but Bibi was hanging back. I had served the food and was ready to sit down.

Mostafa got up and called me aside and told me he's sorry, but Bibi and I would have to eat elsewhere. I said, "What?" Mostafa was totally embarrassed, but Bibi's brother had insisted he tell me this. He said that it was the brother's custom that women can't eat with the men.

My blood pressure went way up! I can't begin to tell you how angry I was. But it was their first night, and if I made a fuss, the girl wouldn't get to eat. So she and I went downstairs, into the basement, away from them men, and had our supper down there.

That night, after the Afghans had gone to bed, Alan, Mostafa and I sat down at the kitchen table. I told Mostafa in no uncertain terms that this was *not* going to occur again! I would *not* be relegated to the basement in my own house! And it never happened again.

Both girls started their periods while they were here. That was kind of challenging to deal with, too. I tried to show them what a sanitary napkin looked like and what it should be used for, and how they should wear it. I had to give them basic body education, with a lot of sign language, showing and telling.

The Kingston community responded fantastically to the Afghans. We always got good press reports, and people were willing to donate time and money. Of course, as with all nonprofit organizations, it doesn't go on forever. People are gung-ho in the beginning, and after awhile, the pocketbook closes.

Another experience I had was when one of the young girls just did not want to take a shower. For the first few times, she took a shower with her clothes on, every piece of clothing. After awhile, I said, "This won't work out. She has to take a proper shower."

I showed her how to take off her clothes, but she kept pulling down her dress every time I tried to pull it up. So I took all my clothes off, too, as an example! Eventually, she did take all her clothes off, but I had to run out of the shower when she had her clothes off, because I wasn't supposed to see her in the nude. So I ran out of the shower and left her in there, and then when she was finished, I went back in, holding up this big towel in front of my face, and gave it to her. As time went by, she became more comfortable showering with her clothes off. The first time, it was like pulling tooth and nail.

Her brother was really upset when he found out we were both naked in the shower!

In Afghanistan, she had bathed in a river, fully dressed and washed herself and her clothes at the same time.

One of the females we took in is still living in Canada. She's now twenty-two years old. She graduated from high school, and is now studying tourism at Seneca College. She's done very well. Her father was her escort, and he decided not to go back to Afghanistan. After he had been here for two years, he got some assistance from church groups, and he was able to bring his wife and his five other children to Canada. They are all living in Toronto.

The girl who didn't want to take a shower lost her lower leg when she went back to Pakistan. When she was here, she had already lost one arm. We had her fitted with a prosthesis. She was really proud of that. She was using it to write and eat and so on. She had been with us for nine or ten months. Her brother is the one who insisted they go back even though because her wound had not healed properly. When she left, she was provided with a few months' worth of materials that she needed to get the wound healed. I don't know what happened, but she got infected again, and she lost her leg because of the infection.

The rooms inside the orphanage in Kabul are dark and cold, colder even than outside, where it is February 1999, the dead of Afghan winter. One small wood stove provides heat, as well as smoke that makes the children cough.

Long lines of children wait anxiously for their names to be called. Suraya Sadeed, founder of Help the Afghan Children, is handing out blankets, soap, notebooks, crayons, new clothes, things most of these children have never seen. They have smuggled a video camera into Afghanistan to give the world a window into what these children's lives are like.

Several men are in the room assisting with the distribution, so the women are all covered by *burqas*. We have to trust the caption on the video screen that says the woman talking to us is Suraya, since her face is hidden.

Seven hundred and fifty orphans live in this building. The girls are kept on the third floor. They are not allowed on the other floors, and they are not allowed outside. They are prisoners. Their journey downstairs today to receive their new belongings is a big adventure. It is difficult to imagine their future.

Suraya Sadeed

I am from Kabul, and attended college there. My father was the governor of Kabul for fourteen years, and his last job was head of the secret police, during the time of the king, before the coup.

My major was child psychology. I graduated in 1974 and got married. After a year, my husband and I went to Beirut on a scholarship. My husband studied for his master's. We were in Beirut for four years. After that, we were told by a relative not to go back to Afghanistan. Because of our scholarship, the government would have thought we were spies.

At that time, our passports had expired. There was no Afghan embassy in Lebanon to renew our passports, so we just stayed in Lebanon for awhile. Back then there was no visa required between Afghanistan and West Germany, so that's where we eventually went.

We stayed in Germany for two years, and applied to come to the U.S.

In June of 1993 I lost my husband in a massive heart attack. He was only forty-six. I lost him in seven minutes. He was a very healthy person, and we had no warning at all. It was very hard for me.

I began thinking about all the hundreds and thousands of women who had lost their husbands and brothers in Afghanistan. I kept wondering, "How do they cope? How do they do it? They have no future, no hope at all."

So I decided to go to the refugee camps and go inside Afghanistan, thinking I might learn something from the Afghan widows about how to cope with my own sadness. So I just went there.

I knew of some Afghan doctors who were working in Peshawar. I met up with them, then went with them inside Afghanistan. We went to internal refugee camps. I stayed in Afghanistan for a week, going from one camp to another, and I found out that I am a very ungrateful person.

I decided I could try to help the women I met, or I could feel sorry for myself for the rest of my life. I decided on the first direction. I came home and founded Help the Afghan Children, with very good support of Afghan Americans.

It has not been an easy road. It has been a lot more difficult than running my own business. The amount of hours I put into this organization, if I put it into my own business, I would be a very rich person. But this is a passion.

I go to Afghanistan two or three times a year. We have several primary health care clinics inside Afghanistan, and one near the border in Peshawar, and we treat hundreds of patients daily, mostly women and children. This is very valuable, because women are denied health care in most places in Afghanistan.

We run vocational training for orphans, where they learn skills to help them eventually earn a living. We have home-based schools for girls who are denied education, in Kabul and Herat. Taliban did not yet control that area, so we didn't face those restrictions, but it was still very difficult. The roads were rough. It took us eleven days on horseback to deliver blankets and things to different villages.

I was in Kabul in February of 1999. We distributed many items at the Kabul orphanage, which is under the rule of the Taliban. Seven hundred and fifty children are there, boys and girls. We made a videotape of the orphanage. We also opened another orphanage in Kabul, with 280 boys and girls, in separate buildings.

It was not easy to take the camera in. I don't want to give you details. We lost three video cameras. That was the hardest part of the trip.

When I cross the border, I just put on the *burqa* and go in. We buy all our supplies inside Afghanistan. Things are available there, but no one has any money.

On the last trip, we spent forty thousand in Kabul, and the local shopkeepers were so happy! So we help the economy, and we save the cost and the headache of transporting things. I speak both Pushtun and Dari, so we just sneak in and sneak out. We look like everybody else. We try to be invisible.

Kabul has changed a lot. I had seen some pictures of the destruction on television, but that's nothing like seeing it for myself. It was very hard for me. I couldn't find my house. Seventy percent of the city is just rubble, and people just poured land mines into the city. Children pick them up and lose their hands or their legs or their sight. Over thirty thousand children are on the streets of Kabul.

The Taliban is the product of the United States. It was not created overnight. The seed for it was planted in the early 1980s.

The U.S. State Department kept telling me that the Taliban is a part of Afghan culture, and I kept telling them that they should be reading their history and geography.

Individuals are not terrorists. Nations are terrorists.

Last year I spent four months in Afghanistan, from north to south, from Bamyan to Kabul, from Logar to Jalalabad, everywhere. I did not see any factories there making weapons. If Afghans had been fighting with their bare hands, they would have had broken hands by now, and the war would have been over.

Yes, Afghans are to be blamed for fighting with each other, but different countries are fueling the fires of war. If Afghans had oil in their veins instead of blood, they would be much more valuable to the rest of the world.

When I went to that orphanage, it was the saddest day of my life. These children, who are the product of that terrible war, some don't even talk. Their parents have been killed or maimed or burned alive in front of them. There are endless stories, but they don't talk to grown-ups. They don't trust them. The physical damage may go away, but the psychological damage is very deep.

People keep saying, "Afghanistan produces the world's most heroin," but they never ask, "What is the import of Afghanistan?" It is guns, bullets, and land mines. Garbage in garbage out.

I do believe there is hope for Afghanistan. If I don't have hope for that country, what else is there? We just have to have hope.

Winfrid Foster is a Canadian working in Kabul with her husband and infant daughter.

Winfrid

I teach physiotherapy at the Physiotherapy School of Kabul, run by the International Assistance Mission. I've been there since January of 1997. We started a two-year course this past May for women and men. We had the permission from the Ministry of Public Health for women to take the course, but the Ministry of Vice and Virtue said no, so the women are not allowed to go yet. I think the people who work at Public Health really are often thinking about the health of people, but Vice and Virtue is only concerned about keeping people to their code of behavior.

Before the Taliban came, there was lots of insecurity in the city, from rockets, theft, and looting. The Taliban brought security in terms of no more fighting in the streets, and also in terms of personal security. They came down really hard on people who steal. They chop their hands off. There is much less theft and looting than before.

The Hazara people, however, feel a lot less secure than before. The Pushtun Taliban really don't like them. Hazaras and Tajiks are still being taken and forced into the front lines of battles.

I have contact with Afghan women on a low-key basis. I don't drive my car to their homes. When I go to visit my neighbors, I first check my street to make sure there's not a lot of people around. It is still not the best thing, in terms of safety, to have a foreigner visit your home, if you're an Afghan.

The Taliban once took three of our female staff, ex-patriots, into custody for awhile at one of their posts because these women were in a taxi without a male escort. If a woman has a child, it's all right for her to take a taxi by herself, so, with a baby, I feel a lot more secure! I think they're afraid of what might happen between a single woman and a male taxi-driver, but with a child there as well, they figure there's nothing that's going to go on! So I take my daughter everywhere!

I don't like going into bigger markets by myself, because it's mostly all men, and I often get stared at, and I don't feel comfortable with that.

There's still a curfew in Kabul, nine o'clock in the winter, and ten o'clock in the summer. There are no women on the street at night, but in the daytime, you'll sometimes see women out with children. You'll almost never see a woman by herself. She must be accompanied by a man.

In Herat there were a lot of violent robberies targeted at NGO's [non-governmental organizations]. They don't know for certain who did the attacks, it was by armed gunmen, so you can probably guess who they are. There are not a lot of people who have access to weapons.

The Taliban are usually pretty thorough in disarming people once they've taken over an area. They'll grab somebody off the street and torture them until they admit they have guns, and then their victim will go and have to search for guns and hand them in, or risk further torture to themselves or their families.

We've heard that in Bamiyan there was a massacre of thousands of Hazaras. They massacred thousands of Hazaras in Mazar-e-Sharif, too. The Hazaras are Shi'a Muslims, and the Taliban don't like them at all. I don't think that gets around as much in the international press as the Taliban's attacks on women, but the Taliban are very, very harsh on Hazaras, kill them left, right, and center without any thought. We hear of the Taliban forcing Hazara men to walk through the mine fields, to de-mine it for them, of them taking Hazaras off the street and putting them in prison.

We see and hear of the Taliban beating people on the street breaking some rule. Some Talibs are just on a power trip. They have made so many rules, and they can always say somebody violated *some* rule! My neighbors in Kabul used to work, used to have a lot of freedom, and now they live in fear. I think the Taliban are here to stay for awhile.

Anyone who has a chance leaves the country. They know there's no future there for their children.

My husband and I would like to stay on in Afghanistan, doing what we're doing. Now that we have a child, we have to be more aware of what the safety limits are. A little bit of stress doesn't hurt anybody. As long as we feel we can leave when we need to, we are fine about staying.

The Afghan people really keep me in Afghanistan. They are very hospitable, very friendly, very hardworking. I think we give them a sign of hope, that we have not forgotten them. That's the one thing that really bugs me, hurts me, because when things get bad, we can always leave and not come back. But the Afghans have no way out. My neighbors, they have to stay.

For a lot of people, a foreign presence means hope, that they've not been left alone, especially for people who are educated and enlightened and who don't agree with what the Taliban are doing.

In Canada, there are not a lot of people who understand our desire to be in Afghanistan, even among our friends. Sometimes, we find it really hard to share heart-to-heart with people here. But in Afghanistan, our friends are there for the same reasons we are. They have the same vision, they enjoy being there, they want to be there.

FAR FROM HOME

Many Afghans have crossed the sea to begin new lives in North America. Here are some of their stories.

Jamilla (fifty-seven years old): Chicago

I was born in Kabul. I came to the United States in 1984. My husband left Afghanistan before me.

The week after my husband left, Afghan soldiers came to search my house. There were five of them, one woman and four men. They were all carrying Kalishmikovs. I was so surprised! This was around three in the morning. They wouldn't tell me what they were looking for. One of them showed me his ID card. They were from Khad, the secret police.

They found my typewriter, and they asked me what I was doing with a typewriter. I told them I used it for my work with the United Nations. I often brought work home with me. I also told them that there was no law against people owning typewriters. Only photocopiers were forbidden, because of the night letters, the *shabana*.

They couldn't find anything else. There was nothing to find.

Five months after my husband left Afghanistan, I also left, even though I had a good job. Even though I had many reasons to stay.

I didn't tell anyone I was leaving, only my best friend. I couldn't sell anything, because if the government heard about anybody selling their things, they knew that person would be leaving the country, and they didn't want that. I just left everything. The children and I came out with only what we were wearing.

I paid money to an old friend of my family's, a trustworthy person, and he took us across the border.

It was the longest journey of my life! Really, it was very hard. Nine days and nights on horseback! In all my life, I have never had such a journey. And the horse had no saddle! We took a very long route because my guide said it was safest. Eventually we arrived in Pakistan, the Lahore.

I had been to Pakistan before, for a vacation, so that was how I was looking at this, that we would stay with my sister in Lahore for a few months, then go home to Afghanistan.

However, while we were still in Afghanistan, my husband applied for visas for us to go to the U.S. Since he had worked for the American government, his application was processed quickly. Our interview took place ten days after we arrived! So our timing was very lucky.

I stayed in Lahore for five months while our application was being processed. Then we went to the U.S.

In Afghanistan, we had a good life. We had everything a middle class family could have, servants, a nice house, electricity, everything. I traveled a lot, to Egypt, Iran, Pakistan. There was not much change for me, living in the U.S. It was not a big transition.

My husband still talks about us going back to Afghanistan, but, for me, that hope is extinguished. There is nothing there for us. Everything is changed. If we go back there, we would feel like foreigners.

The Afghans Women's Organization holds an annual Mothers' Day celebration in Toronto with speakers, Afghan dancers, and Afghan food. It is a hugely popular event, attended by many women from the Afghan-Canadian community.

Aziza

I am a volunteer with the Afghan Women's Organization. Today is Mothers' Day, and we are celebrating Afghan mothers.

I left Kabul twelve years ago, during the Najib government. My husband was part of the Afghan army. He became tired of the war, so we left. We went to India.

I worked very hard when I came to Canada, and am now a Canadian citizen. My daughter is sixteen. She is in grade eleven, and I have two sons who were born in Canada.

I worked at the Afghan Women's Organization's day care center for nine years. Now I am working to improve my English skills so I can go to college. In Afghanistan, I taught physical education in high school.

I still have family in Afghanistan. I have not heard from them for over two years.

All the time when I eat dinner with my children, I remember that there are people in Afghanistan who have no food.

Maybe one day I will go back to Afghanistan, because they need me there. Our people need me there more than in Canada.

Maryam (twenty years old)

I came here in 1990. We left Kabul for India four years before that, then we came to Canada.

Everything was quite different from what I expected, because I was raised in a different environment and culture. Canada was completely different from what I had known.

My first days at school were crazy. I didn't know anybody. Everybody looked strange to me. I was embarrassed because I thought I was different, or looked different. I made friends quickly, though.

My parents would like to go back to Afghanistan, but they also like their life here. Since there's a war going on, they have to stay here.

If I were in Afghanistan now, I'd be living a very different kind of life. I was born there, but it seems like a foreign country, since I left such a long time ago.

I know things are bad in Afghanistan now, but I can't do anything about that.

Zargona

We left Afghanistan in 1990 because of the bad situation. The life was very hard. My father was a doctor. I was studying at the university, in the Institute of Language and Literature. I was in my third year when we went to Pakistan. We lived in Peshawar for two years, and finally came to Canada in 1992.

We were very sad when we left Afghanistan, but in Peshawar, we still felt very close to our country. It was hard to live in Peshawar because we couldn't find jobs.

Still, I am not really happy here in Canada. In our country, we are the kings. But still we miss something, because this is not our country. We hope that we will go back to our country one day and rebuild it.

Latsin

I left Kabul seven years ago, first to Peshawar, then to Canada.

I like everything in Canada, the law especially. The laws are very good, the people here are relaxed. I also like the many cultures that live in Toronto. It is good to see people from so many countries living together without trouble.

I love Canada, but still, I miss my country. I have many family members in

Afghanistan, in Kabul and Mazar. I hear from them sometimes. They are not doing well.

I was one of the first five women police officers in Kabul. I became a police officer because often women are too shy to talk to men. I came across a lot of women who had been raped.

My husband was an engineer with the army, but he also worked secretly with the Mujahideen. The Mujahideen helped us to escape Afghanistan.

Nadia (twenty-one years old)

I was born in Kabul, but originally my parents are from Parwan province. We came to Canada in September of 1991.

I will always remember a friend of mine who died, a boy I went to school with. He lived just in the next street. One day there was the sound of an explosion, and all the kids in the neighborhood went to look. It was his house. Everyone died. His parents were in a coma for awhile, but they died soon, too.

My friend was the same age as me, and he died. I'll never forget that.

There were a lot of explosions in Kabul. I got sick. After my friend's death, I kept asking my mother, "Are we going to die, too?" I kept asking these questions, until my parents decided, just because of me, to move to another country.

We stayed in Pakistan for two and a half years, then we came to Canada.

It is very hard to be a Moslem in a mainly Christian country. Recently, I started wearing a head scarf, and I have to answer lots of questions. People aren't being mean, they're just curious.

Sometimes, when I go shopping, I don't feel like buying anything, because I know my sisters, women in Afghanistan, are dying from hunger. Whatever I eat, whatever I wear, it's so hard on me, because I always remember those women.

I am studying chemical engineering at college. I hope to one day go back to Afghanistan. It's home.

Yalda (fourteen years old)

I left Afghanistan when I was eight. We lived with our grandmother and grandfather. We had a really big house.

From Afghanistan, we went to India, and we were there for four years. We lived in New Delhi. India is a good place for Afghans. There were a lot of Afghans there, and it felt like our country.

I'm in grade eight. I was very shy when we first came to Canada a year ago. I didn't know English very well. It was kind of hard.

My parents miss Afghanistan. They are always talking about Afghanistan, telling us stories about it.

In the future, I would like to help my people, and take my parents back to my country.

Palwasha

I am from Kabul. I have been in Canada for eleven years. We left Kabul because of the war.

Things were not that bad yet when we left. Kabul was still OK. Life was normal, except that once in awhile there would be a bomb blast somewhere, like in a bus, or in a shopping center, or a school.

Children were being kidnapped, and that was very scary. No one knew who was doing it. The government said it was the Mujahideen, and the Mujahideen said it was the government, so nobody knew who was taking the kids.

My parents were with the government. My father was in the army, and my mother was a police officer. We had to flee the country, because they didn't like what was going on in the government.

The journey out of Afghanistan was difficult. It took us two months to get to Peshawar, because if we were caught, it would have been very dangerous for us. Everybody knew my Mom and Dad. We had to flee through villages and Kandahar City, then to Chaman, then to Quetta, then to Peshawar.

The things we went through! Days without food! The way of life in the country was very different from the way we lived in Kabul. Sometimes we were in the deserts, with nothing. We couldn't find water for weeks to wash our faces, just barely enough to drink.

I was eleven at this time.

We lived in Peshawar for four years. That was a very different situation, too! I was fifteen when we came to Canada.

The first thing I remember about Canada is that it was very cold! Especially after being in Peshawar, which is a very hot city. We came to Canada in January, to Montreal, so imagine the difference! As soon as we stepped outside, my eyelashes became frozen and I thought I was blind! That was very new for me. Also, it had been a long time since I'd seen it snow.

But I liked it. It was freedom, freedom of whatever you wanted to do, whatever you wanted to wear, wherever you wanted to go. There was nobody to follow you, nobody wanted to stop you or say anything about anything you do. That's what I love about Canada. Nobody cares what you do!

Mobuba

I am from Kabul. I left in 1993. I am a doctor, and worked in Indira Gandhi Hospital. After high school, I went to Russia and was there for ten years. I did my medical education in Moscow, and then for my specialization, I worked for three years at a hospital in Moscow.

At the time, the government of Afghanistan had a good relationship with Russia, even during the time of the King in Afghanistan. A student who got very high marks would be sent by the government to study in Russia. There were two other women who studied with me. One is living in Germany, and the other has died of cancer.

I was very busy in Moscow, because medical school is very difficult, especially in a different language. The three of us lived in one small room. It was difficult. For seven years, I lived like that. I couldn't sleep well or study well.

The Russians were not inside Afghanistan yet.

My husband was with the diplomatic corps before the Russians invaded. That was a very tragic invasion in Afghanistan. A lot of people died. A lot of women lost their husbands. It was a very big mistake. When I worked in the hospital, I saw a lot of children who lost their hands or their legs from bombs and land mines.

I remember the day the Russians left. There were a few people celebrating on the street, but not many. My life didn't change when the Russians left. I continued with my work.

We left when it became clear that the Mujahideen was coming. I am a democratic woman. I couldn't work with them because I knew their history, what they had done. I could not live under their power, especially not with my two daughters. This was not a difficult decision to make, although it was difficult to leave. We left behind everything, and went to Mazar-e-Sharif, and we stayed there for nine months in the house of a friend. At that time, Mazar was quiet.

After Mazar, we went to Tashkent, then we went to Moscow. We had to pay smugglers, of course. A friend of mine made the arrangements. We spent two months in Moscow in a building with other Afghans who did not have much money.

All the people told us Canada is the best place in the world for immigrants, that it is a democratic country, and we could find work there. For these reasons, we decided to come to Canada.

We came to Canada secretly. We paid money for a guide from Russia who did up Russian passports for us, and that's how we came to Canada. I was scared when we came across the border into Canada, but there were no problems.

For one year, we had a very nice life. Everything was good, freedom, everything. We had been accepted into Canada as convention refugees. Then we got a deportation order from the Immigration Department.

It was terrible. I was in shock. I became very sick, with severe depression. I couldn't eat, couldn't work, couldn't sleep. It was very, very bad.

The deportation order was for the whole family. It came four years ago. They did not give us any reason, other than that my husband had been a diplomat under the Communist regime. But he had done nothing wrong.

Since we got that letter, our lives have been very difficult. My daughters and

I had to separate our case from my husband's, so that they can go to university and have a future. In order to get safety for my children, I had to sign a document that stated I realize this may result in permanent separation from my husband.

My daughters are very happy in Canada. They have many friends here and have become like Canadian. One of them is president of her school. The other one has volunteered at the nearby hospital almost since the day we arrived here. She wants to be a doctor. Both are straight A+ students.

I volunteer at the hospital also and with a settlement organization. At the settlement office I do translation, because I know Russian, Persian, and English. At the hospital I help the patients, give them water, make the beds, push them in wheelchairs. I am a full surgeon. Sometimes it is very hard for me to be able to do no more here than make beds in a hospital. Sometimes people command me, "Do this! Do that!" It is not important. At least I am helping people.

My husband works at a men's rehabilitation center. Many people have written to the Canadian government to say that my husband is a good man and should not be deported. Even former President Jimmy Carter has written such a letter. But the Canadian government still says he must go.

This uncertainty is very difficult for my whole family. It is destroying our life. We are all just sitting and thinking, not laughing and talking. My children come home from school, and they go straight to their rooms. All the time, my husband and I are very depressed. My husband has problems with his heart, and has had by-pass surgery. I'm taking a lot of medication because of the stress.

I would like to talk to the minister of immigration to have her explain right to me why she is doing this to us. My husband didn't do anything wrong.

Where will they deport my husband to? Surely not back to Afghanistan? If they deport my husband, we will go with him. We are a family, and we will stay a family.

Adeena Niazi is president of the Afghan Women's Organization based in Toronto. The organization supports Afghan women with language and literacy classes, culturally sensitive day care, counseling, assistance with getting settled in their new country, and other programs aimed at meeting the needs of Afghan women in Canada.

Adeena Niazi

My mother was an educated woman. She was the first Afghan woman to go overseas for a higher education, under King Amanullah. She first went to school in Kabul, then to Turkey. Due to the problem in the country, when the king was overthrown, she had to come back to Afghanistan without completing her education. She had been studying medicine.

Back in Afghanistan, my father worked with the government. My mother did a lot of volunteer work.

I got a scholarship, many years later, under the Afghan Cultural Exchange Program for Higher Education. At the time, I was teaching at Kabul University. I went to India, first to Lucknow, then to New Delhi. I have two BAs and two MAs. One master's degree is in Farsing language and literature, and the second one is in Dari language and literature. I was doing pre-Ph.D. work in New Delhi.

While I was in India, the Soviet army invaded Afghanistan. At the time, I was planning to continue with my teaching job at Kabul University. I loved that job. However, the coup took place, and a few months later the Russians occupied my country. That's when I lost hope of going back home.

It was a very difficult time for me. At that point, I felt I had lost everything. I felt I had lost my culture, my roots, my family members, my country, everything.

I knew I couldn't go back. If I had gone back, I would have been put in jail and probably tortured. My political views and my opposition to the regime would have put me at risk. The first few months of the Communists coming to power, they imprisoned twelve thousand intellectuals. Many women got tortured. My sister was one of them. She is now in Pakistan.

I did volunteer work with the UNHCR, helping Afghans, and eventually got a job with them. I also got involved with the liberation movement of Afghans. We were engaged in demonstrations and public education. India, politically, was a very important place, because of the Non-Aligned movement, and because of its relations with the Soviet Union. It was a very important place to do liberation activity.

At the beginning, when my country was first occupied and I became a refugee, I was very upset, and I was ashamed to be a refugee. Later, when I got involved with the liberation, my perception of refugees, including myself, changed. I wasn't ashamed any more. I was proud for standing up for my own ideology and for my rights and for the rights of my people. I realized I shouldn't be ashamed, that it was the big powers who should be ashamed. They created this refugee situation. I realized that my country had become a victim of the two superpowers, the USA and the Soviet Union. They were fighting against each other, and they used my country as a tool. I realized that my status as a refugee was not my fault and I shouldn't be ashamed.

I claimed refugee status at the Canadian High Commission in New Delhi, and I was granted permission to come to Canada.

I remember when I was in the airplane leaving India. The higher my plane climbed, the emptier I felt myself to be. I felt that all my roots had been cut.

As soon as I came here I started working with the other refugees and immigrants. Many people knew me from India, and they had some expectations of me. People kept calling me and asking for advice and help.

The Afghan Association of Ontario asked me to join their board, which I did.

From there, I organized women's groups and started some programs for women and also for the entire community.

I discovered, though, that women didn't really have a voice within the Association. Women were welcome at entertainment events because they were cooking, but they didn't have a part in decision making. There was a big gap in services for women, so I started the Afghan Women's Organization.

In the beginning, we didn't even have an office. We were not funded. All our work was done by volunteers. We didn't even have a regular space for counseling. I would often counsel women in my car or in a restaurant.

It grew fast in terms of the variety of services we are able to offer, and now I am very happy with the organization. I'm very glad we have it, because through this organization I can reach back to Pakistan and provide assistance to the refugees in the camps, and also inside Afghanistan.

The politics in Afghanistan always have some influence on what is happening among the community in Canada, whether it was the Communist regime or the war lord who came after them, or the Taliban. The difference is that when the country was occupied, there was a unity among the community, because they all had a single, target enemy to fight. After that, the politics affected things more. People were divided into groups inside Afghanistan, and that had an influence on people here in Canada also.

With the Taliban regime, we are very happy because the media is paying attention again to Afghanistan. Although not much constructive work is being done to improve things, at least there is growing awareness about what is happening in Afghanistan, and to Afghan women. Before that, nobody knew what was happening. It makes things easier for us, because now people know what we are talking about.

This spring I went back to Pakistan, and into Afghanistan, after twenty years of being away.

When I went to Kabul, I felt like a stranger in my own city. Some areas of the city were completely destroyed. I was with my cousin, and we went to my old street, where I used to live. She asked me, "Do you know where you are?" I didn't know. It was not because of the changes of new construction, which you would expect after twenty years. It was all because the area was destroyed. It was flat.

The culture had changed completely. I felt Afghanistan had gone backwards for centuries.

Of course, in Kabul, I was completely covered. I had never used a *burqa* in my life. It was the first time I had to cover completely. I bought the *burqa* in Pakistan, and used it from the time I crossed the border.

One thing that really bothers me, in terms of people who are not aware, is that the culture and the religion is blamed for what's happening in Afghanistan. In fact, that's not the culture.

I left Afghanistan twenty years ago. Before I left, I was teaching at Kabul

University. The majority of my students were men. I had a class of eighty students. I never felt a barrier or an obstacle because I was a women. I dressed then the same way as I now dress in Canada. My skirts were actually a little shorter then! The students were so nice and respectful, my colleagues, the whole community was respectful.

In those days, women enjoyed good status. Women in Afghanistan were elected to Parliament. We had women in Cabinet. We had women who were diplomats, we had women physicians, doctors, engineers. Having women as members of Parliament means a lot, because in the countryside, not just in the city, men voted for women, elected them to sit in the Parliament. This is of great value.

There was a good deal of respect for women in the Afghan culture in those days, but now everything has changed, and they're treated as third class citizens.

I was surprised at the way women were treated after the Russians left Afghanistan. Women had been very involved in the struggle for freedom during the occupation. Many women were killed on the streets, just for the sake of freedom. When they were peacefully demonstrating on the streets, many were shot to death. They struggled side by side with the men, and provided a lot of support, but that was not acknowledged and respected.

I don't know why, when the war lord groups came to power, they were all fighting against women. The whole culture of war was all against women.

I was surprised, throughout, whether it was by the war lords, or by the Taliban. They all treated women very badly.

I always have hope for Afghanistan, but how practical my hope is, I don't know.

FIGHTING BACK

I'll Never Go Back

> I'm the woman who has awoken
> I've arisen and become a tempest through the ashes of my burnt
>   children
> I've arisen from the rivulets of my brother's blood
> My nation's wrath has empowered me
> My ruined and burnt villages replete me with hatred against the
>   enemy
> O' Compatriot, no longer regard me weak and incapable.
> My voice has mingled with thousands of arisen women
> My fists are clenched with fists of thousands of compatriots
> To break together all these sufferings, all these fetters of slavery.
> I'm the woman who has awoken,
> I've found my path and will never go back.

Written by Mena Keshwar Kamal, founder of the Revolutionary Association of the Women of Afghanistan, assassinated in 1987 by people opposed to justice for women.

There's something different about the RAWA women. They look you straight in the eye when they talk to you, and their handshakes are firm.

Since 1977, the Revolutionary Association of Women of Afghanistan has been working for the liberation of Afghan women inside Afghanistan and in exile in Pakistan. They have held noisy demonstrations in the streets, been outspoken in press conferences, and developed programs to make Afghan women feel proud and strong. They run employment projects, a hospital, and a school in Quetta. Many of the young women who are organizing with RAWA today are products of that excellent school.

The outspoken honesty of the group has made them a regular target of fundamentalists. However, RAWA does not let security concerns interfere with their work. With the help of modern technology, including a cell phone, e-mail, and a website, they are in regular touch with women all over the world.

"People write about Afghan women being oppressed," says Sajida, one of the young organizers, "but because you are here you can see that Afghan women also fight back."

Sajida comes to my two-dollar-a-night hotel room in the Saddar Bazaar. The power is off of course, and the only light in the cement-block, windowless cell that is my temporary home comes from the small candles we have lit. We sit on the bed and talk while the flames flicker.

Sajida

Our organization was established in 1977 in Kabul. In the beginning, the purpose was to fight for women's rights, but when our country was occupied by Russian troops, our goal became to struggle against those troops. Women's rights would not have any meaning while our country was occupied. RAWA took part in the resistance work also. At that time, the organization moved to Pakistan.

We had a clinic, and we had a school. Both of these were based Quetta. Unfortunately, we had to close the clinic recently because of lack of funds. The school still functions.

We also held literacy classes for adult women, and we staged demonstrations against the Russian troops. At that time, Russia was the main enemy of our people, the government, not all the people of Russia.

I am twenty years old. I'm a member of RAWA, and attended the RAWA school to the twelfth grade. Now I'm involved with RAWA in different activities.

I left Afghanistan ten years ago. I am living with my family. They are in Quetta, Peshawar, and Islamabad, and where I live depends on where I am needed with RAWA. If it is in Peshawar, I am in Peshawar. If it is in Islamabad, I am in Islamabad. I stay with my family and friends in these places.

When I left Afghanistan, there was not much fighting, not like is going on now in Afghanistan.

I had heard very bad things about the Afghans in Pakistan. In Kabul, we heard from TV and radio that people were suffering miserable lives. I thought it would be difficult, but we found some members of RAWA that we had known in Afghanistan. We went to Quetta, and I attended the RAWA school there. It was a very high-level school, with very high standards.

In many ways, RAWA was a lifeline for women coming out of Afghanistan. My mother became a teacher in that school. Many illiterate women came to Pakistan, and RAWA taught them to read.

When we first got to Quetta, we were in a refugee camp. I began going to school right away, and studying was my main activity. We made a life for ourselves, even in the camps.

We work in Pakistan and Afghanistan. Inside Afghanistan, we have activities in Kabul, in Herat, in Mazar, in the northern areas, but all of them are completely underground. We cannot have obvious activities inside Afghanistan. We have literacy courses and political courses about women's rights. We also take our publication to different parts of Afghanistan. As much as we can do inside Afghanistan, we do. We are in need of funds, which limits us. We would like to do much more.

In Pakistan we have open activities, such as selling our magazine in the market. We celebrate International Women's Day, and we stage demonstrations. Last year in Peshawar we staged a demonstration on April 28 to condemn the Taliban and Jihadist activities in Afghanistan. This is the anniversary of the day the Jihadis first took the power in Afghanistan.

We wanted to stage a demonstration on December 27 last year. We had it all planned. We had already been to some of the camps and had gathered some people to go to the demonstration. But we got threatening phone calls and letters from the Taliban. They said that this time, if we held our demonstration, we would be hurt.

We went to the government of Pakistan, to the police of Pakistan, to tell them they should take the responsibility for our security problem. They said the Taliban had also called them and said this time they would do anything that they wanted. So our demonstration was postponed.

Most Afghan women are illiterate women. They just know about their own house, their own relatives. They don't know about the outside world. They don't have education. That's why, now, our main activity is concentrated on women's knowledge. We want to at least raise their awareness of their own rights, because most Afghan women don't know about this. They think women *should* be the slaves of men. Our political courses are about women's rights, about the criminal activities of the Taliban, to disclose the real nature of the Taliban, so they know that what the Taliban is doing is *not* part of the Koran.

Many NGOs will not fund us because we have the word "Revolutionary" in our name. But the things we are doing with Afghan women, such as publishing a magazine, teaching women to read, letting women know about their rights, and fighting back against the fundamentalists, these are all revolutionary things for Afghan women. Why not call it that?

There is a weekend market in Hyatabad, near the construction sight of a huge new mosque. People in stalls sell everything from food to clothing to household goods. Vendors who cannot afford a stall display their goods on blankets spread over the ground.

Sahar and her ten-year-old daughter Chansoursa walk slowly through the stalls, holding the RAWA magazine out in front of them. Women and men come up to them and buy a copy and chat awhile. Sahar is careful not to stand for long in one place. It is safer if they keep moving.

Sahar, Magazine Seller (thirty-five years old)

I have been a member of RAWA for eight years. I am originally from Herat, but have been in Pakistan for fifteen years. We left Afghanistan because of the war and the bad situation.

I have participated in RAWA demonstrations and other functions, I have sold magazines, and things like that. When I participate in RAWA demonstrations, it makes me very happy, because I know we are working for women's rights and for the betterment of the whole country.

The women of Afghanistan should struggle for their rights, and for the rights of other women in the world. Women who are not Afghans must help us to do this. They must help us to achieve social justice in Afghanistan.

I come to this market every few weeks to sell magazines, sometimes with my daughter only, sometimes with other members of RAWA. When our magazine first comes out, a lot of people crowd around to buy it.

We have men here who are guarding us, providing us with security. You cannot tell who they are. They blend with the crowd. There are lots of Taliban and other fundamentalists in Peshawar, so we must be careful.

Often when people read our magazine, they cry. I have seen them, both men and women. They cry, because the stories inside are sad, because they miss Afghanistan, because they miss family members and friends who have been killed or lost there.

Chansoursa (ten years old)

I like coming to the market to sell magazines with my mother, to help work for women's rights. I am in school, and hope to be a doctor.

Fahima and I talk in the taxi after a trip to visit women in Nasir Bagh refugee camp. We were not able to stay long at the camp, as RAWA activists have been followed and threatened on previous visits there.

Fahima

I am from Jalalabad. I have been in Pakistan for fifteen years and a member of RAWA for fourteen of those years.

Sahar and Chansoursa, selling magazines.

I lost my sister in the fighting. My brother was injured by a mine, and now he's blind and has no legs. My two brothers-in-law were also killed.

I was illiterate when I left Afghanistan. RAWA taught me to read. If I had not become a member of RAWA, I would still be illiterate, and would suffer a very bad condition of life, like others do who are illiterate. Now I am an educated woman.

I think that the ultimate victory is with us, because we struggle. We struggle for women's rights. That's why one day the women will have their rights in Afghanistan.

INTERNATIONAL WOMEN'S DAY

In the early 1920s groups of women from the Soviet Union went to Soviet Central Asia, into the area along Afghanistan's northern border, to provide revolutionary ideas to the women there. In the Islamic city of Bukhara, a couple of hundred miles from the Afghan border, poor women ecstatically threw off their *burqas*.

They went even further, snatching the *burqas* off wealthy women, throwing some into bonfires, and setting up community sewing rooms to remake the others into clothing women could more easily and comfortably wear.

At an International Women's Day Celebration on March 8, 1927, tens of thousands of burqa-wearing women gathered in the main square in Bukhara, around a huge statue of Lenin. A small procession of women, unveiled, their faces to the sun, walked among them. They got to the base of the statue and began to speak, calling for the liberation of women from oppressive customs and practices. The band played "The Internationale," and thousands upon thousands of women threw off their *burqas*. A huge bonfire was built, and women watched the flames with eyes unscreened for the first time in their lives.

The unveiling didn't last. Most women were harassed by relatives who considered the family shamed by the woman's behavior. Many were raped by men who used as their excuse the notion that women without the *burqa* were eager for sex. An estimated four hundred women were murdered. Mullahs, outraged at the threat to their authority, spread the rumor that unveiled women's children would be stolen by the Communists and made into soap. They said that natural disasters would befall their country because of the women's sin. An earthquake in 1927 was blamed on women who had removed their *burqas*.

When women, worn down by the repression, put their *burqas* back on, the men had a festival and celebrated. Women were back under cover, and all was right with the world.[1]

Since the turn of the century, women have been marking International Women's Day, March 8, with demonstrations, rallies, and other events to call for justice.

In 1998, women's groups around the world joined Emma Bonino, the European Commissioner for Humanitarian Affairs, in giving Women's Day the theme "A Rose for the Women of Kabul," to help raise international awareness of the situation for Afghan women.

The Taliban have threatened to cut the legs off women celebrating International Women's Day. The heavy Taliban and fundamentalist presence in Peshawar made organizing and attending the celebrations in the city an exercise in courage.

The first celebration was sponsored by the Afghan Women's Network and the Afghan Women's Resource Center. Attendance was by invitation only, as it was not safe to openly advertise such events. The Afghan Women's Resource Center walks a fine line with its programs, keeping them effective and yet not of a nature that will upset the fundamentalists and put the women in their programs at the risk of an attack.

Held in a meeting room in Hyatabad, I get there early to watch women arrive. On the table at the front of the room is a stack of brightly wrapped gifts. Celebration banners hang from the walls. It is obvious that the organizers have put a lot of work and thought into creating an event that is comfortable for women to attend. The atmosphere is friendly and intimate.

There are speeches, and a group of small children, in colorful national dress, sing a song about mothers. There are competitions. Two teams of women sit facing each other in a poetry recitation competition. The winners receive prizes from the pile of gifts.

A stack of small blocks is brought out and piled on the table. A woman is blindfolded, and she tries to build a house with the blocks. She has to ask for advice from others. The message of the game is that nothing can be built in isolation and ignorance.

Awards are given out for completion of the AWRC programs. One award is given to a woman who lost her leg in the war and who has managed to support herself and her children by making carpets. Another is given to a woman whose husband evicted her and her children from their home eight years ago, and who supports herself by being a servant at an organization that serves Afghan women. She hopes her daughter will be able to earn her own living one day.

Maryam has been in AWRC literacy courses for two years, and she reads a statement she's written about how difficult her life has been, and what it's meant to her to be able to learn how to read. Both she and her teacher get a prize. She is obviously very proud.

Maryam (forty-three years old)

I am from Kabul. I have been in Pakistan for five years. I am here with my family. We left Afghanistan because of the war. For two years, I have taken literacy classes with the Afghan Women's Resource Center.

I am not married. I live with my brother's family. I felt very helpless because I could not read anything and I could not write anything. I could not read letters and I could not write letters, so I felt that if I were literate, I could help my nieces and nephews, and be a little more active with my brother's family.

At first it was difficult, learning to read, but gradually, it became easier.

My father died twenty-two years ago, and my mother died twenty-three years ago, and I lived in Kabul with my brother's family. My brother was killed by the regime of Hezb-e-Islami, and at that time, I started living with his wife and children.

When I was a marriageable age, my father was sick, so I had to look after him. Later on, my brother was taken away. His family was left, so I decided I didn't want to marry.

The RAWA function is a little bit different. RAWA is not afraid of aggravating the fundamentalists. In fact, they seem to enjoy it. The banner over the stage sets the tone:

> Neither the Fundamentalists Nor the Taliban!
> Power to the People of Afghanistan!

Because of on-going security threats against RAWA members from Taliban and other fundamentalist supporters, RAWA sought and received the help of Amnesty International. Amnesty called on the government of Pakistan to protect those women attending the Women's Day events. In spite of the risk, eight hundred people are packed into the hall. Most are women, and most are Afghan.

RAWA has gone into the refugee camps, where many of its members live, to tell women of this event. International donations have helped to pay for the hiring of busses to gather women together from all across the city. Women have also come from Quetta and Islamabad.

Through their secret networks inside Afghanistan, news of this event has spread to women in Kabul, Heart, Jalalabad, and elsewhere. Some of the women here today have come out of Afghanistan at great expense and risk, just so they can do what they have been forbidden to do in their own country: celebrate Women's Day.

A group of children come on stage and sing in loud, proud voices.

> While Taliban are destroying women's lives inside Afghanistan,
> Still we celebrate the Eighth of March.
> Even though Afghan women lead hard lives,
> Still we celebrate the Eighth of March.

Their next song is about Kabul. While they sing, they hold up large pictures showing the destruction of the city.

Some of the women speak with their faces covered. One woman, her face uncovered, reads a poem in a loud, powerful voice. Her poem talks about how the Taliban are afraid, even of children, so afraid that they will not even allow children to hold a pen.

One of the speakers dedicates this day to oppressed women around the world. She talks about how Afghan women have been burdened and oppressed by two decades of war, that women are valued less than animals in Afghanistan. She says that the Taliban cut off the hands of people who steal, but that Gulbuddin should be strung up because his rockets killed hundreds and thousands of people. She calls for people around the world to feel the pain that Afghan women are in, that democracy is not just for the West and that Afghanistan also needs democracy.

A man selling bottles of soft drinks goes up and down the aisle, like in a baseball game. Children pass out cups of tea and plates of cookies. The children's choir comes on stage and sings another song:

> The Taliban hit us, they burn our books,
> They close the schools, they kill those we love.
> They force us to leave our country.
> Join us as we rise up against our enemy!

Noora

I'm from Kabul. I have been in Peshawar for six months. I was a student in the faculty of medicine, but unfortunately, we couldn't continue our lessons when the Taliban came. My family sent me to Peshawar to live with my uncle so that I could continue my education, but here, also, the university is closed. It is a big disappointment. Now I'm studying computers and English instead of medicine.

After Taliban, our life was very bad. The situation was very poor for girls. Everyday, along the street, the Taliban punishes women. It was very difficult. I saw women being hit by the Taliban. I, myself was punished by them.

One day I was crossing the street and a group of Taliban saw me. They ran after me, and they said, "Why are your trousers so tight?" and for this reason, they punished me and my friend who was with me. It was very bad. We were both wearing the *burqa*, but the pants, around our ankles, were too tight. They started hitting us. I ran away, but they kept hitting my friend.

When the school was closed, I had to just stay at home, and try to study by myself, nothing else. Sometimes I got very tired of just staying at home, and I would cry. There wasn't anything else for us.

The Taliban have said, on BBC radio, that they will cut women's legs off if they celebrate Women's Day in Afghanistan.

Asho Shaheen

I am a Pakistani journalist, working with the Peshawar Bureau of *The News*. Afghan women is not my usual beat. I usually cover human rights issues that come up in the North West Frontier Province. I got assigned to cover Women's Day.

The Pakistani people have so many economic problems, they want these people, these Afghans, to go back to their home. They think this might be a way they can find solutions to their own problems. They find it difficult to cope with the refugees. The government is being pressured to force these people to go back home.

I have no Afghan women friends. There is no restriction between Afghans and Pakistanis mingling, but many Pakistanis don't consider it good to mix with these Afghan People. There is a biased attitude. The Pushtuns don't want to mingle with us, either.

Some people want a Taliban-style government in Pakistan. Corruption is the root cause of all the problems prevailing in Pakistan, and the people who want to create a fundamentalist sort of government, they think if the Taliban can remove corruption from Afghanistan, then why not try it here?

I am asked to deliver a short message of solidarity on behalf of West-ern women, which I am honored to do. My words are supportive, not inflammatory, yet the risk these women take everyday is brought home to me a few days later. A threatening letter is delivered to the place in Peshawar where I'm staying:

In the name of almighty Allah
   WARNING!
   Foreigner woman,
   Open your eyes and ears and read what we have written!
   We have found that you are in contact with a group of prostitutes called RAWA. These whores fight Islam and great Taliban because they have been stopped to sell their bodies and do prostitution business. They rise bass-less [*sic*] propaganda against Islamic teachings because they are not allowed to be naked in front of people freely and they have to cover their bodies. There [*sic*] function was just to prepare a facility to touch their bodies with the bodies of hundreds of men there wearing un-Islamic cloth to shape their legs and tits more attractive to sell.
   You better cut your relations with these besoms and don't try to hurt the soldiers of Islam by your anti-Islamic actions. <u>YOU ARE BEING FOLLOWED BY US STEP BY STEP</u> and this is the first and last WARNING to you. The punishment for RAWA women is clear and Inshallah soon their courtesans will be shut down and they will face the result for what they have done against Islam and Taliban. You better save your life and leave this city and let RAWA call girls continue to sell their bodies but they will be stoned to death by our brothers and you will be informed about it soon.
   This was clearly and timely conveyed to you and now its up to you for perception otherwise we better know what to do.
   A soldier of Islam

The letter ends with a drawing of a knife dripping with blood.
   The eighth of March event ends with a play that makes fun of the Taliban. People laugh and cry and applaud, then Women's Day is over for another year.
   Women file out of the hall, hoping that, at the next International Women's Day, they will have much more to celebrate.
   The next day, several women who have come out of Afghanistan for Women's Day agree to talk with me. We meet in the lobby of the Green's Hotel in Saddar Bazaar, an open, airy place with flowers, foun-tains, skylights, and round stone tables.

Zargona (thirty-two years old)

I live in Kabul. I joined RAWA five years ago.

I experienced the time of the Russians and the Jihadis, and the Taliban, and their brutalities against women. At the time of the Russian occupation, at least women had the right to go to school, to have a job, and to go outside of their house without any worries, but when Jihadis and Taliban captured the power, they committed such criminal activities against women.

I have two children. My husband is a shopkeeper in Kabul. I was a teacher. I used to teach grade six and seven. Because of the Taliban, I cannot teach anymore.

At first when the Taliban captured Kabul, we didn't know their attitudes towards women were like this, but gradually, when they stopped everything, especially for women, and they stopped music and things like this, we understood more about Taliban.

In my life, it was the first time that I was jobless. I couldn't go outside, and I had to stay at home. This was a big change in my life when the Taliban took over. Whenever I go outside of the house, all the time I am in constant fear of the Taliban's beatings and other things.

My sister was walking on the street, and my three-year-old daughter was with her. My daughter was wearing an outfit with short sleeves. When the Taliban saw, they beat my sister because my daughter had short sleeves.

Working with RAWA, especially under the Taliban regime, is very difficult, especially from a security point of view. If the Taliban know there are women working for women's rights inside Afghanistan, then of course they will follow us and punish us. We know this, and so do other members of RAWA, but still we work inside of Afghanistan for women's rights and for human rights. We are proud of our work.

Inside Afghanistan, we do cultural work, economic work, and political work about women.

The cultural work involves the publishing of our magazine for women, and distributing it among women, and of course this is done in a very secret way. We carry the magazines under our *burqas*, and take them to the houses of women who want the magazine.

In our economic work, we have some carpet-making machines for women, especially for widows, for those women who have no other breadwinner inside their families.

The political work among women is the courses we put on, some literacy courses, and also some political courses. These are done in underground schools.

Both the courses and the schools are done in a very secret way, because of the Taliban. They have, in the courses, three, four, or five people. Because of the Taliban, there cannot be a lot of girls or women in one course. For example, if ten women at the same time everyday go to a particular house, then the

Taliban will know about it. That's why there are just three or four women in a course. They also meet at different times, not always at the same time, so they don't draw attention to themselves.

My request for Western women is that they should learn about the real situation of women in Afghanistan. It is my request that they should truly understand the condition of women under Taliban, and tell others about it, as much as possible.

I will go back to Kabul in a few days. I came to Peshawar especially for the Women's Day celebration. The eighth of March is a very important day for all women, but especially for Afghan women.

I am proud that we are celebrating the eighth of March in a city like Peshawar.

Rozia (thirty-eight years old)

I come originally from the northern part of Afghanistan. I have lived in Kabul for eighteen years.

During the time of the Russians, life was better than now. It was also difficult, but at least it was better than now. My husband had a job. But now, it has been two years that my husband has also been in the house—he doesn't have any job.

Everything is very expensive in Kabul. It is difficult for us to afford what we need. The United Nations distributed some cards among the people, and those people who have cards can get bread less expensively than other people. So we get bread that way.

My son was a shopkeeper. He was selling things like sugar, tea, things like this. He had a very small shop. Six months ago, my son was injured by a rocket, and now, there is no one who can work outside and earn money for the family. We have sold everything out of our house. Now, we just have the United Nations card for our bread, and we spend our lives with only water and bread.

People in Afghanistan call their guests, "rockets." Because when a guest comes, of course it will not destroy the house, but because they are very poor, they cannot afford for themselves, and it is difficult to afford a guest. Both the rocket and the guest can ruin a family.

I go back to Afghanistan in a few days.

The stories about the Taliban are endless. This is a story about my brother, who was a shopkeeper. A woman had come to his shop to buy something. The Taliban doesn't allow women to go inside the shops. They say that women should stand outside and call to the shopkeeper, "I need this thing or that thing."

While the woman was in my brother's shop, the Taliban came, and they took my brother. He was put in prison for fifteen days. They tortured him, and now one of his eyes is blind. They beat him very badly, and some of the parts of his body, like his arms, they are also not right. They tortured him a lot.

One of my relatives spent time in Iran before going back to Afghanistan. The

Taliban thought that because he came from Iran, he may have a lot of money. One day, they came to my cousin's house, and they searched, and they said, "We are searching for weapons. We think you have weapons in your house," and they kept searching. They had a knife, also, with them.

They told my relative, my cousin, "You should bring us the weapons! Where are the weapons? If you don't bring them out, we will kill you with this knife!"

My relative's wife, she wanted to prevent the Taliban from killing her husband. The Taliban then killed her with their knife. They just cut her throat.

Now, the poor husband and children, they are left without her, and they don't know what to do. Her name was Farzona. She had two children.

There is no law to prevent the Taliban from doing these things.

Tahar (forty-one years old)

I am from Kunduz Province originally. When the situation got bad there, we came to Pakistan. We returned to Afghanistan about one year ago but couldn't go back to our home province, so we went to Kabul.

If the situation gets worse, then we will come back to Pakistan. At least my husband has a job right now, in a shop. The men are also under the rule of the Taliban—they have to wear a long beard, and a hat.

When the Russians were in the country, many of the Jihadis were in Peshawar. I predicted that under the Jihadis the situation would get worse. For eighteen years, I was in Pakistan. We left during the first years of the Russian occupation. Just last year, I went back to Kabul.

I was living in Nasir Bagh Refugee Camp for all those years. We got some aid from some aid agencies. My husband was a teacher in that camp. Then the aid agencies didn't help us anymore, and my husband also lost his teaching job. That's why we left Pakistan and went back to Afghanistan.

I have four children. Life is very difficult under the Taliban, especially because of what they have done to women. During the past year, I have been out of my house only three times, always accompanied by a male family member, or my husband.

Once, I went to the baker's. There I saw another woman. She was picking up some bread, and her sleeves moved up her arms a bit, and a Talib came and beat her. I became very afraid, and I ran away.

My house in Afghanistan is not very big. It has two rooms, one bathroom, and a kitchen. All the day, I am inside the house, doing housework—cooking, washing, cleaning, things like this. My husband is a shopkeeper.

We have a courtyard, so sometimes I can go outside and feel the sun on my face. It is surrounded by a high wall, so no one can see in.

I do not see my women friends. If the women have the time to go outside, the male members of the family don't have time to escort them, or don't want to. So we all stay in our houses.

Women's Day is a very important day for women, because it's a solidarity day of all the women around the world. Especially when I heard that the women of RAWA were planning to celebrate this day, I was very interested to come and meet the members of RAWA. I see their magazine in Afghanistan. A friend gives it to me. I read it in fear, because of the Taliban. When I finish reading it, I hide it very carefully, where the Taliban will not find it. They go into houses and search for things sometimes, and if they come into my house and find the magazine, of course they will punish me. I hide the magazines inside a pillow, and in other secret places.

I find it very interesting to read their magazine. Although I am not well educated, still I am interested, especially when I read about the criminal activities of the Taliban, which are happening every day.

Kobra (fifty-five years old)

I am from Logar Province, near Kabul. Now I live in Kabul. I was invited by the members of RAWA to come to the Women's Day function. It is a problem to come to Pakistan, only to participate in the function, because it cost a lot of money. But even though we don't have money, it is important to come. I sold some of my belongings to pay for the bus fare. It was important to come here, because we cannot celebrate Women's Day in Afghanistan.

When Jihadis first took the power, I thought that, they are under the name of Islam, they might be good government for the people. But when gradually I saw their attitudes towards people, especially women, I realized that they were greater traitors than the Russian troops and their stooges.

I am married. I have three children. I have not gone to school. I was twenty-five when I got married.

My husband used to be a teacher. Now, he works with one of the aid agencies. He gets paid in a daily ration of wheat.

The Taliban has increased our economic problems. Now there is no money, no jobs, women cannot go out, we have to stay as a slave in our homes. Just my husband works for wheat, nothing else.

The Taliban do not commit as many criminal acts in Logar as they do in Kabul, but, of course, they are still Taliban. They go to the houses of people and demand bread or money, or something else, and they take these things by force.

Mostly, I stay at home. It is very rare that I go out of my home and go walking.

Once, I had gone to a baker, to cook my bread. Some of the women who had come from Mazar-e-Sharif, especially the Hazara women, become bakers. They build ovens, and other women can bring their dough to them for baking.

When I was there, the baker-woman said the Taliban had come to her house and searched for weapons. When they couldn't find any weapons, they beat her husband until he died.

Beating women and insulting women by the Taliban is an everyday experience of the women of Afghanistan.

Ahjira, daughter of Kobra (fifteen years old)

I was in grade eight before the Taliban, but when the Taliban came, I couldn't continue my education. Now I am at home. I was going to a secret home-school for awhile, learning different things, but the Taliban found out about the course.

One day, the Taliban realized that ten girls everyday were going to this one house. That made them think that maybe there was a school or a course for girls in that house, which is against Taliban law. Sometimes they get reports of schools in people's homes—some people pass information on such things to the Taliban.

I was there when the Taliban came to the class. They beat the teachers and some of the students also. They warned that, "If another time you open the course again, we will come and we will punish your men, and also yourselves."

I was one of the students who was beaten, but I ran away quickly, so they didn't beat me too much.

It is very difficult and very boring to wear the *burqa*. It is like a hell under the *burqa*. It is almost impossible to see through it.

Now that the Taliban are in Afghanistan, I do not hope to have the opportunity to continue my studies. When peace and prosperity come to my country, then I will continue my education.

Now, all I do is work inside the house and help my mother, because my mother is not well. All I do is washing and cleaning and cooking—nothing for fun.

I have two sisters. One of my sisters dresses like a boy. She cut her hair. Outside of our house, everyone considers her to be a boy. She sells cigarettes and things along the street. She is just like a boy. She is ten years old. When she's a boy, her name is Javed. When she's a girl, her name is Shufa. It was the whole family's idea, because someone needed to work outside the home. We need more to live on than just the wheat my father gets from the aid agency. Shufa is the only one who can work outside the home, because she can look like a boy. A girl cannot work. My sister is very happy to do this, and very brave.

We don't talk about what will happen when my sister is no longer able to look like a boy and has to stay inside with the rest of the women. I hope that, by that time, the Taliban will have left the country.

My sister did not come with us to Peshawar—she stayed in Afghanistan.

I want to say to girls my age in the world that they should realize that the situation of children in Afghanistan is very bad, and they should help in whatever way they can, and they should get as much education as they can.

I know of another girl who dresses like a boy to go out to work. When she is a boy, her name is Ali. She is sixteen.

I don't think I will marry, not as long as Afghanistan is in such bad shape.

All the time, the people of Afghanistan are very brave, but now, the people of Afghanistan have empty hands. They don't have anything to fight with, but still they are brave.

NOTE

1. Pam McAllister, *This River of Courage* (Philadelphia: New Society Publishers, 1991), 154–156.

AFTERWORD

Zohra Rasekh, Physicians for Human Rights

It will soon be too late to rehabilitate women in Afghanistan. Right now, it is not too late to mentally and psychologically reverse some of their problems. They would have difficulties, but they would be able to function again. After a few more years, though, it will be impossible. These women will be lost forever.

Doctors, teachers, journalists, lawyers, all these women who have gone to school for many, many years are now staying at home, losing their skills, living under tremendous pressure. Young women who were studying to become something, they are now all hopeless, suicidal. They won't be able to go back and simply pick up their studies where they left off. After so many years of living under such oppression, their memory, concentration, and ability to focus is going to be damaged. Their ability to learn again is probably going to be gone.

The young generation, those who are now children, they're going to all be illiterate. They will need to start learning the alphabet when they are all grown up.

The Taliban has basically killed all these women, if not physically, then emotionally and mentally.

The Taliban are not going to change in how they think about women, about women going to school or to work.

The only way to save Afghan women from a dark future, from a very difficult future, is to get rid of the Taliban, and replace it with a different government, a just government, one that will allow women to choose their own lives and do what they need to do.

An Afghan Woman's Speech at International Women's Day

It is hard for people in other countries to believe that we women in Afghanistan are beaten everyday by the Taliban. The sadness in our story is endless.

I know that they beat us, lash us, and lock us in our homes all because they want to destroy the dignity of women. But all these crimes against us will not stop our struggle.

Will other women in the world join with us?

ORGANIZATIONS THAT WORK WITH AND FOR AFGHAN WOMEN

Cooperation Center for Afghanistan
P.O. Box 1378
GPO, Peshawar
Pakistan

Afghan Women's Organization
2333 Dundas St. W.
Toronto, Ontario, Canada
M6R 3A6

Afghan Women's Council
P.O. Box 1215
GPO, Peshawar
Pakistan

Physicians for Human Rights
100 Boylston Street
Suite 702
Boston, MA USA
02116

Revolutionary Association of the Women of Afghanistan
P.O. Box 374
Quetta, Pakistan
e-mail rawa@rawa.org
website http://www.rawa.org

Help the Afghan Children, Inc.
4105 N. Fairfax Dr.

Suite 204
Arlington, VA USA
22203

Rehabilitation Organization for Afghan Orphans and Widows (ROAOW)
Jamal Road
Shaheen Town
Peshawar, Pakistan

Center for Women's Global Leadership
160 Ryders Lane
New Brunswick, NJ USA
08901–8555

Afghan Women's Resource Center
2 Canal Bank Road
Peshawar, Pakistan

Women's Alliance for Peace and Human Rights in Afghanistan
P.O. Box 77057
Washington, DC USA
20012–7057

International Center for Human Rights and Democratic Development
63 Rue de Bresoles
Montreal, Quebec, Canada
H2Y 1V7

Women for Women in Afghanistan
P.O. Box 32014, Bankview Post Office
Calgary, Alberta, Canada
T2T 5X6

Feminist Majority Afghanistan Campaign
1600 Wilson Blvd., Suite 801
Arlington, VA USA
22209

SUGGESTIONS FOR FURTHER READING

Adamec, Ludwig W., *Historical Dictionary of Afghanistan* (London: Scarecrow Press, 1991).

Dupree, Louis, *Afghanistan* (Princeton, NJ: Princeton University Press, 1973).

Giradet, Edward and Jonathan Walter, editors, *Essential Field Guide to Afghanistan* (Geneva: Crosslines Communications, 1998).

Hyman, Anthony, *Afghanistan Under Soviet Domination* (New York: St. Martin's Press, 1984).

Maley, William, editor, *Fundamentalism Reborn? Afghanistan and the Taliban* (London: Hurst and Company, 1998).

Overby, Paul, *Holy Blood: An Inside View of Afghanistan* (Westport, CT: Praeger, 1993).

Rogers, Tom, *Soviet Withdrawal From Afghanistan* (Westport, CT: Greenwood Press, 1992).

Sarin, Oleg, *The Afghan Syndrome* (Presidio Press, 1993).

Urban, Mark, *War in Afghanistan* (New York: St. Martin's Press, 1988).

INDEX

About the Author

DEBORAH ELLIS is an anti-war and women's rights activist who works as a mental health counsellor at Margaret Frazer House in Toronto.